THE
ITALIAN ARMY
IN
NORTH AFRICA

THE
ITALIAN ARMY
IN
NORTH AFRICA

A POOR FIGHTING FORCE OR
DOOMED BY CIRCUMSTANCE

WALTER S. ZAPOTOCZNY JR.

FONTHILL

Fonthill Media Language Policy

Fonthill Media publishes in the international English language market. One language edition is published worldwide. As there are minor differences in spelling and presentation, especially with regard to American English and British English, a policy is necessary to define which form of English to use. The Fonthill Policy is to use the form of English native to the author. Walter S. Zapotoczny Jr. was born and educated in the US; therefore American English has been adopted in this publication.

Fonthill Media Limited
Fonthill Media LLC
www.fonthillmedia.com
office@fonthillmedia.com

First published in the United Kingdom and the United States of America 2018

British Library Cataloguing in Publication Data:
A catalogue record for this book is available from the British Library

Typeset in 10.5pt on 13pt Minion Pro
Printed and bound in England

Preface

When most people think of the Italian Army in North Africa during World War II, they are inclined to believe that the average Italian soldier offered little resistance to the Allies before surrendering. Many believe the Italian Army, as a whole, performed in a cowardly manner in North Africa. The reality is not so simple. The question remains as to whether the Italians were a poor fighting force or actually doomed by circumstance. While the Italian soldiers' commitment to the war was not as great as that of the German soldiers, many Italians fought bravely. The Italian Littorio and Ariete Divisions earned Allied admiration at Tobruk, Gazala, and El Alamein. The Italian Army played a significant role as part of the German *Afrika Korps* and made up a large portion of the Axis combat power in North Africa during 1941 and 1942. In the interest of determining whether the Italian Army deserved its reputation, it is necessary to analyze their organization for combat and how the Italians fought. We will review the major battles that took place in North Africa and the Italian Army units stationed there. This book provides an analysis of how the Italians fought by examining the Italians' performance in the major battles in North Africa, the organization of the Italian Army in North Africa, and the comments of Allied and Axis commanders.

CONTENTS

Timeline of the Italian Army in North Africa

The Abyssinia Crisis (1934–1935):
The Italians gain a foothold in Ethiopia, undermining the authority of the League of Nations. This would lead to Italy allying itself with Nazi Germany.

Italy Conquers and Annexes Ethiopia (October 1935–May 1936):
Italy conquers and annexes Ethiopia and turns it into Italian East Africa. This is known as the Second Italo–Ethiopian War.

British Commonwealth Forces Counterattack (December 1940):
British Commonwealth forces attack Italian troops in Egypt and Italian East Africa.

Germans Arrive in Africa (February 1941):
Hitler sends forces to Libya to aid his failing Italian allies and pushes British and Australian troops back into Egypt and the port city of Tobruk.

Operation Crusader (November 18–December 30, 1941):
The British Army relieves the Siege of Tobruk in North Africa and reclaims gains made by the Germans and Italians.

The First Battle of El Alamein (May 26–July 27, 1942):
The German "Desert Fox" Colonial General Erwin Rommel goes on the offensive in North Africa and pushes the Allies back into Egypt. The Germans are stopped at El Alamein, only 106 kilometers from Alexandria.

The Second Battle of El Alamein (October 23–November 11, 1942):
An Allied offensive, under the command of Lieutenant General Bernard

Montgomery, pushes the Germans back across Egypt and Libya. Some historians say the battle marked the turning point of the war.

Operation Torch (November 8–16, 1942):
British and American forces invade French North Africa. Vichy French troops there nominally on the side of the Axis defect and join the Allies. Germany and Italy occupy Vichy France in response.

Montgomery Takes Tripoli (January 23, 1943):
Axis forces are forced to retreat as the Allies take Libya. Rommel links up with a Panzer army in Tunisia and the Axis are facing a war on two fronts—from Montgomery's Eighth Army in the west and the multi-national force from Operation Torch.

Tunisian Campaign (November 17, 1942–May 13, 1943):
Allied forces push the remaining Axis troops into a corner and they are forced to surrender on May 13, effectively ending the war in North Africa.

Introduction

When people think of World War II in North Africa, they usually think of the German, British, and American armies, with the Italian Army only having a minor role. The Italian Army actually played a significant role in North Africa and made up a large portion of the *Deutsches Afrika Korps* (German Africa Corps). During the entire African campaign, Italian troops fought resolutely and with extraordinary bravery. They contributed to the success enjoyed by the *Afrika Korps* between 1941 and 1942. The Italian Littorio and Ariete divisions earned Allied admiration at Tobruk, Gazala, and El Alamein.[1]

In his book *Iron Hulls, Iron Hearts: Mussolini's Elite Armored Divisions in North Africa*, Ian Walker describes how Field Marshal Erwin Rommel spoke admirably of the Italian soldiers. Rommel said:

> The Italian soldier is disciplined, sober, an excellent worker and an example to the Germans in preparing dug-in positions. If attacked he reacts well. He lacks, however, a spirit of attack, and above all, proper training. Many operations did not succeed solely because of a lack of coordination between artillery and heavy arms fire and the advance of the infantry. In spite of poor leadership, the Italian soldiers performed well in North Africa.[2]

Italian dictator Benito Mussolini ordered attacks on British positions in East Africa and Egypt. In 1940, it appeared that German successes in Poland, France, and Norway would bring the war to a rapid close. Mussolini had intended for Hitler to keep his forces in the north while he maintained control of the Mediterranean. Concerned that Italy might lose her share of the spoils, Rome declared war on Britain and France.[3] On September 13, 1940, Marshal Rodolfo Graziani, commander of the Italian Army, began his advance into Egypt with seven Italian and Libyan divisions. They met little resistance from British General

Archibald Wavell's forces and eventually pushed forward to Sidi Barrani, which was approximately 97 kilometers inside the Egyptian border. Once Graziani's forces reached Sidi Barrani, he set up defenses facing east and south and waited for supplies from Italy. By mid-February 1941, having not received the support he requested, Graziani's Italian forces were overrun and 115,000 men surrendered.[4]

Hitler was already planning to invade Russia and knew that for that campaign to be successful, his southern flank had to be secure. He believed that the free use of the Mediterranean by the British would seriously impact his chances of victory. Therefore, he sent Colonial General Erwin Rommel to North Africa under control of the Italian Supreme Command. Rommel was subordinated to Italian Commander-in-Chief Libya General d'Army Italo Gariboldi, who replaced Marshal Rodolfo Graziani in February 1941. This proved to be a contentious relationship throughout the campaign. Rommel and his commanders did not have faith in the Italian army commanders and often disagreed with orders from the Italian Supreme Command.[5]

When Rommel arrived with a Panzer and Motorized Infantry Division in February 1941, the Italian Ariete and Armored Division Trento arrived as well from Italy. The formidable Ariete Division was composed of 6,949 men, 163 tanks, thirty-six field guns, and sixty-one anti-tank guns. Motorized infantry consisted of the 101st Motorized Division Trieste and the 102nd Motorized Division Trento. The semi-motorized infantry contingent consisted of the 17th Infantry Division Pavia, 25th Infantry Division Bologna, and the 27th Infantry Division Brescia. These units were semi-motorized rather than true motorized formations, which made them equivalent to a typical German infantry division in terms of mobility. Like the motorized formations, these units had two regiments of infantry. Italian infantry divisions consisted of the 55th Infantry Division Savona and the 60th Infantry Division Sabratha.[6]

Immediately after his arrival at Tripoli on February 12, 1941, Rommel began organizing the defense of Tripolitania, in Western Libya, and making plans for offensive actions. He integrated many of the Italian forces with the German units under the command of German officers, while other Italian units were left under control of Italian commanders. In March 1941, Rommel launched his offensive, which decimated the British forces defending Cyrenaica. During this battle, the Italians were the first to use self-propelled guns in close support and in anti-tank attacks. The German–Italian forces occupied El Agheila on March 24, and on April 1, they took Mersa Brega. Benghazi Libya fell on April 3, and Mechili was taken the next day. By April 11, the Axis forces had reached Bardia and Sollum. In the face of the threat to the Suez Canal, British General Wavell decided to reconstitute his Western Desert Force, consisting of all the troops he could make available, and to hold the port of Tobruk at all costs.[7] By June 12, the British had abandoned the Gazala–Bir Hakeim line. On June 21, the British garrison of

Tobruk was forced to surrender. By this time, the combat power of the *Afrika Korps* was comprised of 66 percent Italian personnel, 57 percent Italian tanks, 57 percent Italian artillery, and 55 percent Italian aircraft.

On August 31, Rommel, impatient to break through the El Alamein–El Qattara line and move on the Suez Canal, launched an attack against the Alam el Halfa Ridge, committing his armored 15th and 21st Panzer Division, the Italian Ariete, Littorio, and the Italian Paratroopers Division Folgore.

The Italian infantry advanced through the British minefields throughout the entire day as a sandstorm raged, making life miserable for the men. During the nights of August 31 and September 1, the Italians were the targets of heavy British bomber and fighter aircraft attacks. With the help of countless parachute flares, every movement was subject to an immediate strafing attack. Soon, a great number of the Italian vehicles were in flames and burned out. The Italian infantry suffered heavy losses but held the line. The attacks south from the New Zealand forces met with fierce and stubborn resistance from the German–Italian troops, and the Italian infantry, supported by the German armor, made heavy and repeated counterattacks. Fighting continued throughout that day and the next, but on September 2, the British pushed the Axis forces back. By September 6, due to fuel shortages, Rommel decided to withdraw his forces. During this time, the German–Italian armored forces were beginning to suffer severe supply shortages. Allied air and naval attacks in the Mediterranean were sinking the Axis convoys.[8] The British Navy had succeeded in significantly cutting the German–Italian supplies from Italy. The German and Italian troops fought bravely, but were outmatched by the number of British weapons and the lack of air superiority.[9]

On October 23, 1942, the Second Battle of El Alamein began. The attack on the German–Italian lines started with over 800 artillery guns firing at the German and Italian positions. The infantry attacked as the shells pounded Rommel's lines. The Allied engineers set about clearing mines. The plan to get the tanks through in one night failed. The infantry was not able to get as far as Montgomery had planned due to the fierce resistance of the Italian forces. The second night of the attack was also unsuccessful. The rate of attrition of the Allied forces was taking its toll. The attack was called off and Montgomery withdrew his tanks. Rommel's *Afrika Korps* had also been suffering: he only had 300 tanks left to the Allies 900-plus. Rommel became convinced that the main thrust of Montgomery's attack would be near the Mediterranean and he moved a large amount of his *Afrika Korps* there. The British and New Zealander infantry attacked south and Rommel was taken by surprise. Across from the 25th New Zealand Infantry Battalion and the South Africans of the Cape Town Highlanders, the Italian 3rd Battalion, 61st Regiment, continued to hold its ground along Miteirya Ridge even after experiencing heavy losses. Rommel put tank against tank, but his men were hopelessly outnumbered. The overwhelming number of Allied tanks tipped the balance. The Allies were resupplying, while the *Afrika Korps* was not. On November 4, 1942, Rommel started his retreat. The German and Italian troops of the *Afrika Korps* never recovered from this defeat, eventually losing all of North Africa to the Allies.[10]

The initial success of Rommel's *Afrika Korps* is well known and publicized. Rommel was promoted to field marshal in June 1942. However, the reason why is usually attributed to Rommel's genius and tactical ability. History has crowned Rommel as a tactical genius. There is certainly no doubt as to his ability when his battles are analyzed. However, contributing to Rommel's and the *Afrika Korps'* success in North Africa between 1941 and 1942 was the Italian Army; they provided the majority of the soldiers and equipment that made up the *Afrika Korps*. While their leaders may not have been up to the same standard as the Germans, the Italian soldier fought bravely alongside his German counterpart, and in the end, Rommel and the *Afrika Korps* suffered the same problems as Marshal Graziani did earlier: lack of transport, supplies, and an enemy who had air superiority and almost limitless supplies. It was not for a lack of resolve or determination by the Italian soldiers. We begin our analysis by examining how Italy got involved in Africa.

The Abyssinia Crisis

Many in Italy dreamed of recreating the Roman Empire. Mussolini wanted those former possessions under the control of Italy once again. Italy had not become unified as a state until 1860 and did not have a large navy; therefore, it was not able to talk part in the nineteenth-century colonization of Africa by the countries of Europe. As they partitioned the continent of Africa, Italy was left with Eritrea and some small and very poor colonies in East Africa.

The ongoing conflict between Ethiopia (known in Europe as Abyssinia) and Italy escalated into what became known as the Abyssinia Crisis. As a result of the incident, the League of Nations voted for economic sanctions ruling against Italy; however, the sanctions were never fully implemented. Italy rejected the sanctions and withdrew from the League of Nations, and then made separate deals with France and Britain that gave Italy control of Ethiopia. The League of Nations' reputation was damaged and Italy moved closer to joining in an alliance with Nazi Germany. As Italy grew ready to invade Ethiopia, both countries engaged in a policy of provocation against each other. The League of Nations described the situation as follows:

> At places where there is not a single Italian national, a consul establishes himself in an area known as consular territory with a guard of about ninety men, for whom he claims jurisdictional immunity. This is an obvious abuse of consular privileges. The abuse is all the greater that the consul's duties, apart from the supplying of information of a military character, take the form of assembling stocks of arms, which constitute a threat to the peace of the country, whether from the internal or the international point of view.[1]

The border between Ethiopia and Italian Somaliland was defined in the Italo–Ethiopian Treaty of 1928. It established the border of approximately 118 kilometers to be parallel to the Benadir coast, which covers most of the country's central and southern seaboard opposite the Indian Ocean. In defiance of the treaty, Italy built a fort at the Walwal Oasis that was well within the Ethiopian border. Ethiopia and Italy issued a joint statement rejecting any hostility against each other on September 29, 1934. A force of 1,000 Ethiopian militia arrived on November 22 near the Italian Walwal fort and requested that the Italians leave.[2] The Italian commander refused and then informed the commander of the Uarder garrison, approximately 20 kilometers away, what had occurred.[3] Members of the British–Ethiopian boundary commission arrived at the Walwal Oasis to survey the border between British Somaliland and Ethiopia on November 23, and Italian troops confronted the group. The British commission members left while the Ethiopian members remained.[4] A scuffle occurred between the Ethiopians and the Somali members of the Italian contingent: the Italian account states that the Somalis were attacked by rifle and machine-gun fire and the Ethiopian account states that the Italians were the ones who attacked with two tanks and aircraft.[5, 6] Approximately fifty Italians and Somalis and 107 Ethiopians and were killed in the skirmish.[7]

Neither the Italians nor the Ethiopians did anything to avoid disagreement. The Italian fort was frequently menaced by the Ethiopians, and the Italians sent two planes over the Ethiopian base. One of the Italian airplanes fired a machine-gun burst at the camp.[8, 9]

Ethiopian Emperor Haile Selassie formally protested aggression at Walwal on December 6. Italy demanded an apology from Ethiopia for aggression at the Walwal Oasis on December 8, and on December 11, Italy demanded financial compensation from Ethiopia. While Ethiopia appealed to the League of Nations on January 3, 1935 for help with the crisis, the League's analysis did not assign responsibility to either country.[10] Foreign Secretary Samuel Hoare of the United Kingdom and Minister of Foreign Affairs Pierre Laval of France met with Italian dictator Benito Mussolini in Rome shortly after Ethiopia appealed to the League of Nations. A subsequent meeting with Mussolini and Laval on January 7 produced the Franco–Italian Treaty, which gave parts of French Somaliland to Italy and a free hand in dealing with Ethiopia. In exchange, France wished for Italian support against Germany. Five Italian East African soldiers were killed by Ethiopian forces near Walwal on January 25.[11]

Two army divisions were mobilized by Mussolini on February 10, and on February 23, Italy started sending troops to the Italian colonies of Somaliland and Eritrea that bordered Ethiopia to the south-east and north-east respectively. There was only modest international objection in reply to this build-up. Ethiopia appealed to the League of Nations again on March 8, citing the Italian build-up of forces, and on March 11, Ethiopia and Italy agreed on a neutral zone in the Ogaden territory, comprising the eastern portion of Ethiopia. Ethiopia appealed to the League of Nations again March 17. Italy submitted to arbitration by the League on March 22, but continued to mobilize troops in the area, which resulted in Ethiopia submitting a formal protest about Italy's mobilizations to the League of Nations on May 11.[12]

The League of Nations held a special meeting to talk about the crisis in Ethiopia between May 20 and 21. Ethiopia requested neutral observers on June 19, and British Under-Secretary of State for Foreign Affairs Anthony Eden tried to negotiate a peace deal from June 23 to 24. When his attempt failed, it became obvious that Italy's intention was conquest, resulting in Britain imposing an embargo on arms sales to both Italy and Ethiopia on July 25 and moving its warships from the Mediterranean. This allowed Italy unimpeded movement of men and supplies to Eastern Africa.

The United Kingdom and France offered Italy large concessions in Ethiopia on August 16 in an effort to avert war, but Italy rejected the proposal. Once again, the League absolved Ethiopia and Italy of any responsibility in the Walwal Oasis incident.[13]

The British Parliament supported the imposition of sanctions against Italy on September 27, should it continue its policy towards Ethiopia. Ethiopia began to mobilize its large, but poorly equipped army on September 28. Italian forces from Eritrea invaded Ethiopia, prompting Ethiopia to declare war on Italy on October 3, 1935. On October 7, the League of Nations declared Italy to be the aggressor, and commenced the process of imposing limited sanctions on Italy; these sanctions did not prohibit the exports of vital materials, such as oil, and were not adhered to by all members of the League.

In late December 1935, Samuel Hoare and Pierre Laval proposed the secret Hoare–Laval Pact, which would have ended the war, but allowed Italy to control large areas of Ethiopia. Mussolini approved the plan, but it caused a protest in the United Kingdom and France when the plan was disclosed to the news media. Hoare and Laval resigned when they were blamed of betraying the Abyssinians. After the Hoare–Laval Pact was dropped, the perception spread that France and the United Kingdom were not serious about the values of the League of Nations. The war with Ethiopia continued, and Italy turned to Adolf Hitler for association.

After German troops marched into the Rhineland in March 1936, France was desperate to gain Italy's support against Germany and was ready to give Abyssinia to Italy.[14, 15]

Italy Conquers and Annexes Ethiopia

Estimates place the size of the Ethiopian Army at 760,000 men as the hostilities with Italy began. However, the men were poorly trained and armed with all sorts of rifles, in various conditions.[1]

In *Rape of Ethiopia*, Arthur J. Barker writes:

> They [Ethiopian Army] had about 200 antiquated pieces of artillery mounted on rigid gun carriages. There were also about 50 light and heavy anti-aircraft guns. The Ethiopians even had some Ford truck-based armored cars and a small number of Fiat 3000 World War I-era tanks. The serviceable portion of the Ethiopian air force included three outmoded biplanes.[2]

Haile Selassie's Imperial Guard were well-trained and better-equipped than the rest of the Ethiopian Army; however, they wore a distinctive greenish-khaki uniform of the Belgian Army, which stood out from the white cotton cloak worn by the majority of the Ethiopian fighters, and proved to be an excellent target.[3]

By around July 1935, eight Italian regular army divisions arrived in Eritrea, with twelve divisions arriving in Italian Somaliland—amounting to around 480,000 soldiers. There were already 200,000 Italian troops in Italian Somaliland, which brought the total Italian force to over 680,000 men. Arriving with the Italian troops was an impressive array of equipment, which included 2,000 pieces of artillery, 595 tanks, 150 aircraft, and 6,000 machine guns. The Italians already had 275 artillery pieces, 200 tanks, 205 aircraft, and 3,000 machine guns, with tons of food, ammunition, and other supplies. The Italian Army had motorized vehicles to move troops and supplies, while the Ethiopians hauled supplies in horse-drawn carts.[4]

Marshal Emilio De Bono moved his force of 25,000 Eritrean and 100,000 Italian soldiers from Eritrea into Ethiopia on October 3. At the same time,

General Rodolfo Graziani advanced with a smaller force consisting of Somalis, Libyans, and Italian soldiers from Italian Somaliland into Ethiopia. Adwa was captured on October 6 by De Bono's troops, and on October 15, they captured the holy city of Axum. Marshal De Bono was replaced by General Pietro Badoglio because the Italian High Command felt his advance was too slow and cautious.

The Italian force continued their offensive at the First Battle of Tembien on January 20, 1936, but the fighting was inconclusive. After the Italians captured Amba Aradam on February 15, the Italians began the Second Battle of Tembien on February 27. This time, the Italians were victorious and Worq Amba was captured. On March 31, the Italian force defeated an effort by the Ethiopian Army at the Battle of Maychew. The Italian forces also advanced from Somalia through the Ogaden Desert in the final months of 1935. The Italian Army defeated the southernmost Ethiopian Army in the Battle of Genale Wenz during the early part of January 1936, and on March 29, they began a push towards the city of Harar. Graziani's forces captured the city on March 29. On May 7, Ethiopia was annexed by Italy and was merged with Eritrea and Somaliland to form Italian East Africa and the Ethiopian Emperor Haile Selassie was forced into exile. All the sanctions that had been put in place by the League were dropped after the Italian capture of the Ethiopian capital of Addis Ababa on May 5, 1936.

In addition to conventional weapons, the Italian forces also made considerable use of mustard gas in both aerial bombardments and artillery. This substance was also sprayed directly from above like an insecticide onto enemy combatants and villages.[5]

Ethiopian Emperor Haile Selassie gave a rousing speech before the League of Nations, condemning Italy's actions and criticizing the world community for doing nothing to stop it.

He said, "It is us today. It will be you tomorrow." The League of Nations condemned Italy's actions, which resulted in Italy withdrawing from the League. On November 18, 1936, the Empire of Japan officially recognized the Italian Empire.[6]

In June 1936, Italy created a constitution that merged Italian Somaliland, Eritrea, and Ethiopia into Italian East Africa. Marshal Rodolfo Graziani replaced Marshal Pietro Badoglio on June 11, 1936. In December, Italy declared the whole country to be under their effective control.[7]

The Italian Army Before World War II

Before World War II, Mussolini and Hitler were bragging to each other about the size of their military. According to Gerhard Schreiber, writing in *Germany and the Second World War, vol. 3*, "Mussolini announced in 1934 that he can mobilize 6 Million soldiers; in 1936 he increased the number to 8 million and in 1939 to 12 million."[1] These numbers seem high when we look at the German Operation Barbarossa, which was the largest military invasion in history. The German force was approximately 4 million men. Italy did, however, manage to mobilize about 3 million men. In contrast to the Japanese and the German soldiers, the Italians were worse equipped than the Italian troops during World War I. Schreiber writes, "Italian forces were not ready for a war against any major force."[2]

As we examine Italian Armed Forces before World War II, several reasons stand out for their ill-preparedness: Italy was not properly prepared for the production of armaments; Italy had a lack of essential resources and did not allocate what they did have sufficiently; and, additionally, the wars in Ethiopia and Spain continued longer than anticipated and drained their limited resources. Mussolini realized that Italy needed time to build up resources and insisted on a period of peace after he signed an agreement with Germany. As a result, Italy did not join the war effort until June 1940.[3]

While Italy had learned lessons from its experiences in Ethiopia and in Spain, the Italian Army was still reorganizing when World War II started. Italian industry was not organized to meet the basic requirements of the military. As part of its reorganization, the Italian Army restructured its division to a bipartite system from a tripartite one, with each division consisting of two infantry regiments instead of three. The intention of the bipartite system was to make the army units more mobile, more capable, and easier to command. The thinking was that Italy's lack of manpower could be made up by modern equipment. However, this did not materialize since Italian industry could not keep up with the demand. The bipartite system created more divisions but did little to increase the capabilities of the Italian Army.[4]

The Italian Army had the following divisions in September 1939, not counting the units deployed in Ethiopia: forty-three infantry, three tank, two motorized, three fast divisions, five alpine, and eleven other divisions for special purposes. Only sixteen of these divisions were completely restructured. There was a lack of tanks, artillery, transport vehicles, and anti-aircraft and anti-tank guns, and even basic supplies like quality food was lacking. Basically, the army had a severe shortage of almost every commodity.[5]

After Italy declared war in June 1940, the material situation was slightly better. Gerhard Schreiber writes:

> First the Army, in June 1940 Italy entered the war with a bit less than 1.7 million soldiers and a total of 73 divisions. Whereas in 1915 the Italian army joined the war with more men, it was also an army that had similar quality weapons and equipment like other major [participants], but in 1940 this was clearly not the case.[6]

Of the seventy-three divisions the army had mobilized, only nineteen had the necessary number of men, weapons, equipment, and transport capacity. Another thirty-four divisions were operational, but lacked personnel and transport capacity. The last twenty divisions lacked more than 50 percent of the required men, 50 percent of transport capacity, and a significant amount of equipment.[7]

The infantry division formed the foundation of the Italian Army, but the firepower of an Italian infantry division was, according to Gerhard Schreiber, only about 25 percent of a French Infantry division or around 10 percent of a German infantry division.[8]

Comparison between a Typical Italian and German Infantry Division in 1940

Italian	German
449 officers	518 officers
614 NCOs	2,573 NCOs
11,916 men	13,667 men
None	18 × 150-mm Howitzers
12 × 100-mm Howitzer	36 ×100-mm Howitzers
None	24 × 75-mm guns
20 light infantry support guns	8 × 65-mm mountain guns
8 × 47-mm anti-tank gun	75 × 37-mm anti-tank guns
30 × 81-mm mortar	54 × 81-mm mortar

126 × 45-mm mortars	84 × 50-mm mortar
80 heavy machine guns	110 heavy machine gun
270 light machine gun	425 light machine guns[9]

An important comparison between the typical Italian and the German division is the number of non-commissioned officers. This low number of leaders caused problems with the overall effectiveness of the Italian division. Additionally, the largest artillery piece the Italians had was 100 mm, while the Germans had 150-mm guns. The Italian's smaller caliber guns offered a reduced firepower effect due to the smaller shell weight. The Italian Army had a variety of calibers, but this caused logistical and resupply problems.[10] Italy also had a severe lack of modern anti-aircraft guns and anti-tank guns. Artillery and ammunition was always in short supply due to production shortcomings.[11]

In 1940, the Italian armaments industry offered some dire predictions of their ability to meet some of the military's requirements: artillery (all types), 6 percent; ammunition, small caliber, 25 percent; ammunition, medium caliber, 7 percent; ammunition, heavy caliber, 10 percent; rifles (Model 1891), 35 percent; machine guns, 10 percent; mortars, 81 mm, 70 percent; mortar ammunition, 8 mm, 10 percent; airplanes, 42 percent; engines, 40 percent; and bombs under 1,000 kilograms, 40 percent.[12]

Italian Units in North Africa

17th Infantry Division Pavia

The Pavia Brigade originated during the nineteenth-century movement for Italian unification on March 1, 1860, and was formed of the 27th and 28th Infantry Regiments. The 17th Infantry Division Pavia was formed in August 1939, reinforced with the 26th Artillery Regiment, and was transformed into a division. The 17th Infantry Brigade Pavia was sent to Libya in October 1939. The division was never entirely motorized, and as a result, the members of the division could not be transported all together by cars or trucks.[1]

The division headquarters was in Ravenna until 1939, while the 27th Regiment's barracks was in Cesena.[2] Originally deployed June 10, 1940 on the Tunisian–Libyan border, the 17th Infantry Brigade Pavia remained at the exact same positions until June 25, 1940, when it had been ordered to perform coastal defense in the Sabratha–Surman sector of Tripoli Libya.[3]

By March 1941, it had been transferred nearer to Benghazi to be involved in the Axis counterattack of March–April 1941. Under Major General Pietro Zaglio, it attacked via the Balbia coast road from Ajdabiya on March 31, 1941, driving the Australian rearguards back once again to Mechili. In the aftermath counterattack, the remainder of the Infantry Division Pavia was put in the Sirte area to protect an airfield close to Wādī Thāmit. The Fabris and Montemurro Bersaglieri Motorized Battalions were in support, combined with the advance components of the German 5th Light Division.[4]

The majority of forces continued an advance to Derna, Libya, and Martuba on May 22, 1941. In June 1941, it was involved in the Siege of Tobruk, and was involved with often intense action from highly aggressive Australian probing attacks.

On November 19, 1941, a British column of tanks tried to move westwards towards the track that ran up from Bi'r al Ghabī to Al Adm, but encountered infantry of the 17th Infantry Brigade Pavia and were forced to turn back.[5] However, on the 27th, the 19th Battalion spearheading the 6th New Zealand Brigade finally linked up with part of the British 70th Division at El Duda, weakening the position of the 17th Infantry Brigade Pavia, but who still contained the enemy breakthrough.[6] On December 4, Rommel ordered a withdrawal to the Gazala Line, which entailed giving up Tobruk. During the withdrawal, the 17th Infantry Brigade Pavia served as a rearguard at El Adem, managing a brief, but competent defense. Further British attacks were launched on the positions of the 17th Infantry Brigade Pavia on December 3–4, 1941.[7] The heavy rearguard action continued from December 7, 1941 until December 16, 1941.[8] According to Barton Maughan:

> On 15 December, the bulk of the Pavia on the Gazala Line fought against the attacking 2nd New Zealand Division and Independent Polish Brigade, managing to hold their lines after a poor initial beginning, losing hundreds who surrendered, allowing a strong German Armored force to counterattack and overrun the 1st Battalion, Royal East Kent Regiment.[9]

The 17th Infantry Brigade Pavia rearguard was annihilated on December 14, 1941, when the New Zealand 22nd Battalion encountered weak resistance from them. Under the cover of darkness, the New Zealanders took the rearguard position and 382 Italian prisoners at a cost of three killed and twenty-seven wounded.

On December 17, 1941, the division fought at Timimi, 70 kilometers west of Tobruk, then on the Mechili–Derna line. From this point, the retreat of the 17th Infantry Brigade Pavia became faster. The British advance was halted due to logistics problems following a rapid advance, giving the division a brief quiet time.[10]

Throughout May 28–29, 1942, the division encircled the British formations at Tobruk and ʿAyn al Ghazālah. The division had begun to improve steadily from late January 1942, attaining the original positions west of Tobruk on May 26, 1942. Throughout the Struggle of Gazala, the 17th Infantry Brigade Pavia were found in a mopping up position, capturing 6,000 Allied prisoners on August 16, 1942.[11]

Throughout the first stage of the action, the 17th Infantry Brigade Pavia functioned as a rearguard for the Ariete Division, where it had defensive success.[12] A couple of units of the division set up a persistent defense on Ruweisat Ridge, combined with Brescia Division on the night of September 14–15, letting a German armored force to arrive in time the following day to supply a counterattack against the approaching British armor and New Zealand infantry.[13,14] One battalion of the 17th Infantry Brigade Pavia struggled along with the Paratroopers Division Folgore throughout the Second Battle of El Alamein.

On December 3, 1942, the 17th Infantry Brigade Pavia was ordered to retreat to the Qattara Depression in order to escape the increased British attacks. At the conclusion of the struggle, the division, combined with other sections of the Italian X Corps (see Appendix I), was abandoned. Without transport, they retreated from El Alamein to Fukah and Mersa Matruh on December 4, 1942. The 17th Infantry Brigade Pavia was formally dissolved on December 25, 1942.[15]

25th Infantry Division Bologna

From 1926 to 1934, the 25th Infantry Division Bologna was called the 25th Territorial Division of Naples. It had been stationed in Tripolitania and was providing support in Libya for the Italian invasion of Egypt. In 1934, the division was renamed the 25th Infantry Division Volurno and again renamed in 1939 to 25th Infantry Division Bologna.

The 25th Infantry Division Bologna was an auto-transportable division, indicating soldiers and gear might be sent on vehicles and trucks, but not simultaneously. Garrisoned in Naples, it was created completely of citizens of the city.[16] At the start of the Italian intrusion of France on July 10, 1940, the 25th Infantry Division Bologna was garrisoned at the Libya–Tunisia border. Following the final outcome of hostilities in Europe in July 1940, the division was assigned to occupation responsibilities in the Bir al-Ghanam community south of Tripoli.

Initially, in 1941, most of the infantry was quartered in Gharyan, while artillery regiments with some support soldiers was provided for the front line between Derna, Libya, and Mechili. Following the overcoming of Allied opposition on January 23–25, 1941, the division was ferried, landing on the beach in western Libya, and proceeded quickly along the Marj–Benghazi–Qaminis route, achieving its location on March 5, 1941.[17]

The sector manned by the 25th Infantry Division Bologna consisted of several strong points manned by infantry and artillery units, all surrounded by minefields.[18] The Australians launched a counterattack on May 3, employing the 18th Brigade, but by May 4, they were only able to recapture one bunker from defending Italian troops.[19] It was reported that thirty Australian soldiers shot themselves during that week in order to be evacuated as their morale took a dive.[20] A total of 207 soldiers were admitted for treatment to a British underground "war neurosis clinic" that was built in Tobruk.[21]

On November 21, 1941, elements of the British 70th Infantry Division attacked, overrunning a number of positions held by the 25th Infantry Division Bologna, but other attacks were defeated. The 25th Infantry Division Bologna repulsed a British attempt to approach their positions as part of Operation Crusader.[22] In summing up the experience of the 2nd Battalion in the attack, Murphy Fairbrother wrote in the *Official History of New Zealand in the Second World War*: "The superlative élan of the Black Watch in the attack had been equaled by the remarkable persistence of the defense in the face of formidable tank-and-infantry pressure."[23] A German report recorded that the 25th Infantry Division Bologna withstood an attack from Tobruk on November 23, allowing the 17th Infantry Division Pavia to organize a counterattack and stop the British assault:

> After a sudden artillery concentration the garrison of Fortress Tobruk, supported by sixty tanks, made an attack on the direction of Bel Hamid at noon, intending at long last unite with the main offence group. The Italian siege front around the fortress tried to offer a defense in the confusion but was forced to relinquish numerous strong points in the encirclement front about Bir Bu Assaten to superior enemy forces. The Italian Division Pavia was committed for a counterattack and managed to seal off the enemy breakthrough.[24]

The British advance was finally halted by the timely arrival of reinforcements from the Bersaglieri Battalion of the Trieste Division. The 25th Infantry Division Bologna front now extended some 8 miles, and on November 25, the thinly spread-out division was assaulted by fifty British tanks and forced to withdraw some distance.[25]

Meanwhile, the divisional command on November 27, 1941 started a retreat with some breakthroughs of units from the east of Tobruk. The division's defenders were gradually pushed back again, covering their retreat with mines and machine-gun nests, but by the end of the month, the Tobruk breakout was judged successful among British commanders.[26] By December 5, 1941, the consolidation of forces was nearly complete and Italians had retreated further to 'Ayn al Ghazālah and then to Derna, Libya. In spite of the German 90th Light Division pulling out from the Tobruk sector, the 25th Infantry Division Bologna rearguard held out through the nights December 8–9, when trucks were finally assigned to offer them some support.[27] By December 11, 1941, almost all 25th Infantry Division Bologna forces were between Ajdabiya and El Agheila, over 400 kilometers from Tobruk. An Australian historian, when talking about the Italian role during Operation Crusader, stated "… the Axis units fought well, such as the Italian Division, Ariete and Bologna-semi-motorized formations."[28]

On July 15, 1942, the 25th Infantry Division Bologna was transferred from Qārat al Ghazālah to bolster the El Alamein front; lacking vehicles, the division was forced to march some 400 miles, being reviewed by Mussolini on the way. Nevertheless, the 25th Infantry Division Bologna arrived near Alam al Ḥalfā on August 30, 1942. The attacking Zealanders later reported that there had been 100 Italian dead, wounded, or captured throughout the attack. The division and German 433rd Infantry Regiment attacked several Indian, South African, and New Zealand units on Ruweisat Ridge throughout the Battle of Alam el Halfa, and managed to fully capture Point 211 with the Italians reported to possess seventy captured British soldiers; however, the attackers were later driven back by counterattack.[29] A noted military historian later wrote an article about the Italo–German counterattack:

In the first attack on Ruweisat Ridge, during the Second Battle of Alamein, the Bologna Division supported by two battalions of the Ramcke Parachute Brigade achieved some success, taking 40 prisoners. In the center of the British front a good Italian division, the Bologna, delivered a strong attack on the Ruweisat Ridge, and a considerable counter-attack was required to expel it from the footing it gained.[29]

On December 4, 1942, the 25th Infantry Division Bologna was in fast retreat, yet the escape was unsuccessful as disparate units were found by the British and annihilated one by one. Remnants of the division struggled on December 5, 1942 in Ra's al Ḥikmah and on December 6 in Fukah and then in Mersa Matruh. The units were overcome by December 21, 1942. Some escaped detachments went to Tunisia, but all were merged to different units by February 1943. Private Sid Martindale, 1st Battalion Argyll and Sutherland Highlanders, wrote about 25th Infantry Division Bologna, which had taken the full weight of the British armored attack:

> The more we advanced the more we realized that the Italians did not have much fight on them after putting up a strong resistance to our overwhelming advance and they started surrendering to our lead troops in droves. There was not much action to see but we came across lots of burnt out Italian tanks that had been destroyed by our tanks. I had never seen a battlefield before and the site of so many dead was sickening.[30]

The remainder of the Trento and the Bologna had tried to battle their way out of El Alamein and marched in the desert without water, food, or transport before surrendering tired and desperate from dehydration.[31] It was noted that Colonel Dall'Olio, commanding the 25th Infantry Division Bologna, surrendered, saying, "We've halted firing not because we have not the need but because we have spent every round." No one in the division raised their hands in a symbolic act of ultimate defiance. The division was formally dissolved on December 25, 1942. Harry Zinder of *Time* magazine noted that the Italians fought better than had been expected:

> It was a terrific letdown by their German allies. They had fought a good fight. In the south, the famed Paratroopers Division Folgore fought to the last round of ammunition. Two armored divisions and a motorized division, which had been interspersed among the German formations, thought they would be allowed to retire gracefully with Rommel's 21st, 15th and 19th light. But even that was denied them. When it became obvious to Rommel that there would be little chance to hold anything between El Daba and the frontier, his Panzers dissolved, disintegrated and turned tail, leaving the Italians to fight a rear-guard action.[32]

27th Infantry Division Brescia

Composed of draftees from Calabria, in south-west Italy, the 27th Infantry Division Brescia was formed on January 1, 1935 as the 27th Infantry Division Sila and was reorganized to the 27th Infantry Division Brescia on May 24, 1939. Already in Ethiopia in October 1935, the Sila had participated in the capture of Mek'ele. From November 4, 1935, the Sila was stationed in the Adigrat, and in March 1936, it was deployed to the Finarwa-Sek'ot', a region where it stayed until the end of the Ethiopian war. The Brescia was labeled as an auto-transportable division.

The division was in the area of the French XXI Infantry Corps in North Africa alongside the 17th Infantry Division Pavia and the 25th Infantry Division Bologna. Together they participated in the Siege of Tobruk, the Fight of Gazala, the Fight of Mersa Matruh, the First Battle of El Alamein, and the Second Battle of El Alamein.

By June 1940, the 27th Infantry Division Brescia was located around Zawiya, Libya, and fought French-supported Tunisian irregulars from June 1, 1940 until June 25, 1940. In early March 1941, the division had consolidated at El Agheila and started a counter offence on March 24, 1941, together with German forces defeating British troops at Brega by March 31, 1941. On April 12, 1941, as Italian and German forces commenced their Siege of Tobruk, the division along with the German 3rd Reconnaissance Battalion captured the port of Bardia, taking several hundred prisoners and a large quantity of plunder.[33]

From January 1942, the 27th Infantry Division Brescia was defending a front around Qabr al Fārigh, south-west Derna, Libya. It had moved to forward positions at Qabr al Fārigh south of Derna, Libya, in April 1942. During the Battle of Gazala, the division played an important role in the capture of 6,000 prisoners on June 16, 1942, after the Trieste Division and 15th Panzer Division had destroyed the British 2nd and 4th Armored Brigades operating at the Ghawṭ al 'Abīdī depression. On June 20, 1942, the 27th Infantry Division Brescia passed to the south of Tobruk, and then rapidly moved through Bardia.

From the beginning of July, the Allied resistance had mounted up. During the First Battle of El Alamein in July 1942, the division, deployed on El Mreir, repelled a strong force of the 5th New Zealand Infantry Brigade in the initial fighting, and during the defense of Ruweisat Ridge, the 19th Regiment of the 27th Infantry Division Brescia put up a tenacious defense, losing a battalion and three company commanders in the night action.

After the Second Battle of El Alamein, started on October 24, 1942, the 27th Infantry Division Brescia was able to hold the positions against British armored units until November 4, 1942. The lack of transport resulted in Allied units catching up and annihilating the division remnants on November 7, 1942, within the sight of the Fukah, where other shattered Axis units has already gathered. The division was officially dissolved November 25, 1942. Australian military historian Level Johnston said that there clearly was an unwillingness to acknowledge successes of the Italians in Australian standard Allied accounts.[34]

55th Infantry Division Savona

The 55th Infantry Division Savona was created in May 1939 in Salerno. Their soldiers were drafted from Naples, Salerno, and their surroundings. The 55th Infantry Division Savona was categorized as an auto-transportable division.[35]

The division occupied prepared villages of Sollum, Bardia, and Naqb al Ḥalfāya at the start of September 1941. By November 1941, the division was at the defensive roles at Bardia-Sīdī ʿUmar.

All through November 22–23, in the defense of Operation Crusader, almost 1,500 prisoners from the 55th Infantry Division Savona were taken following intense fighting.[36] The division counterattacked and regained their previous positions, and on December 4, 1941, while the *Afrika Korps* was preparing to escape to the Gazala Point, the Infantry Division Savona was handed directions to protect the Axis withdrawal. Of the divisional leader, Rommel noted: "Outstanding management was revealed by Giorgis [General Fedele de Giorgis], who commanded that Italian–German power in their eight weeks' struggle." The remnants of the 55th Infantry Division Savona in Naqb al Ḥalfāya were permitted by German order to surrender on January 17, 1942 because of insufficient food and water.[37]

64th Infantry Division Catanzaro

The 64th Infantry Division Catanzaro was created on June 3, 1940. The division was labelled an auto-transportable division. Originally, the division was used at Acroma to shield the approach to Tobruk. Until September 16, 1940, the division transferred slowly to Sidi Barrani to safeguard the coastal railroad.[38]

On the evenings of December 7 and 8, 1940, the Western Desert Force, comprising British 7th Armored Division and Indian 4th Infantry Division strengthened by British 16th Infantry Brigade, advanced a total of 110 kilometers for the attack.[39] The 64th Infantry Division Catanzaro was guarding the Buqbuq segment, north of the 63rd Infantry at Cirene at Ābār Abū Safāfī, south of the first Libyan Section Sibelle at Al Maktīlah, and second Libyan Pescatori at ʿAlam aṭ Ṭummār.

The major bombardment and British armored strikes at ʿAlam Rimth on December 9, 1940 penetrated the 64th Infantry Division Catanzaro defenses. Struggling to avoid disaster, the division linked-up with combined Italian units at Buqbuq and escaped over the coastal railroad on December 10, 1940, with the 4th Blackshirt Division and the Headquarters for the Libyan Corps from Sidi Barrani. By December 11, Buqbuq have been removed of most resistance and several Italian soldiers and weapons have been captured. On December 13–14, 1940, the 64th Infantry Division Catanzaro retreated to Sollum, and on December 15, 1940, it dropped back again to the defensive edge of Bardia. The division was destroyed in the Battle of Bardia on January 5, 1941.[40]

132nd Armored Division Ariete

The 132nd Armored Division Ariete was created in Milan in February 1939. It was at first made up of the 8th Bersaglieri Motorized Infantry Regiment, the 32nd Armored Regiment, equipped with L3/35 light tanks and a few M11/39 medium tanks, the 132nd Artillery Regiment, and additional divisional support units.

In Libya, the 1st and 2nd M11/39 Medium Tank Battalions arrived and were included in the Maletti Group. The 132nd Armored Division Ariete was attached with the Italian Tenth Army. From December 1940 to February 1941, during Operation Compass, the British Western Desert Force overran the Tenth Army and occupied the whole of Cyrenaica.

After this setback, it was decided to employ the whole 132nd Armored Division Ariete in North Africa. From February 1941 to November 1942, the division fought alongside the German *Afrika Korps* in the North Africa campaign. The division was attached to the Italian Mobile Corps. This unit was later to become Italian XX Motorized Corps (see Appendix II).[41]

On May 1, 1941, the Germans and Italians attacked Tobruk in significant strength. During Operation Crusader, the division very successfully defended Bir el Gubi from the British 22nd Armored Brigade, inflicting heavy losses on the inexperienced British forces. During November 29–30, the 132nd Armored Division Ariete and supporting Italian infantry and motorcycle units were in charge of capturing a substantial amount of New Zealand, Indian, and British troops throughout the Italo–German counterattacks. Recalling the loss of the 21st Battalion, Lieutenant Colonel Howard Kippenberger, who later rose to command the 2nd New Zealand Division, wrote, "About 1730 damned Italian Motorized Division [Ariete] turned up. They passed with five tanks leading, twenty following, and a huge column of transport and guns, and rolled straight over our infantry on Point 175."[42]

During the Second Battle of El Alamein, the 132nd Armored Division Ariete sacrificed its obsolete tanks in the attempt to counter the Allied offensive and cover the withdrawal of the army. On November 4, at about 3.30 p.m., the few surviving tanks, surrounded by an overwhelmingly superior enemy, broadcast their last message:

Enemy tanks broke through South of Ariete Division. Ariete thus surrounded, located five kilometers north east of Bir-el-Abd. Ariete tanks keep on fighting! Rommel mourned the loss of the division, writing that its final action had been conducted with exemplary courage and that in the Ariete we lost our oldest Italian comrades, from whom we had probably always demanded more than they, with their poor armament, had been capable of performing.[43]

The division was disbanded on November 21, 1942. Its name was kept by a task force gathering up its remnants, which kept fighting throughout the retreat and subsequent campaign in Tunisia. It was forced to surrender along with the rest of the Axis army in North Africa.[44]

101st Motorized Division Trieste

Formed in 1939, from the 8th Infantry Division Po (named after the Po Valley in northern Italy), the 101st Motorized Division Trieste was mobilized for war in 1940. The 101st Motorized Division Trieste was sent to Libyan North Africa in August 1941 as part of the Italian XX Motorized Corps under General Gastone Gambara with the 132nd Armored Division Ariete. During Operation Crusader, the division took advantage of the British 4th Armored Brigade's withdrawal from the Tobruk sector, and achieved a notable success on December 1, when its armored columns moved forward and cut the tenuous link the 6th New Zealand Brigade had established with Tobruk on November 27.[45]

On December 13, the 1st Battalion, Royal East Kent Regiment, captured a critical point on the Alam Hamza Ridge, but the 101st Motorized Division Trieste successfully defended another. During the Battle of Gazala, the division played an important part in the destruction of the British 2nd and 4th Armored Brigades south of Knightsbridge on June 12. During the First Battle of El Alamein, the 101st Motorized Division Trieste on Ruweisat Ridge put up a tenacious defense and lost two regimental commanders before being partly overcome, delaying the Allied advance for several hours and allowing German armored forces to launch a devastating counterattack. The division fought against the British Eighth Army in Tunisia, first on the Mareth Line, then at Wadi Akarit, and eventually on the Enfidaville Line.[46]

The division formally surrendered to the Allies on May 13, 1943. The division participated in all the major Western Desert battles from then on: Operation Crusader; the January 1942 Axis counteroffensive; the Battle of Gazala in 1942; the Battle of Bir Hakeim; the First Battle of El Alamein; and the Second Battle of El Alamein, where it was virtually destroyed.[47]

102nd Motorized Division Trento

The 102nd Motorized Division Trento was formed in 1939 and kept in reserve in Italy until it was moved to North Africa in February 1941. The division was then reformed and took part in all of the major battles of the Western Desert Campaign.

It took part in Axis attacks across North Africa, following the Allied Operation Compass, and suffered heavy losses at Tobruk. The offensive resulted in the destruction of the Italian Tenth Army and the Allied occupation of the Italian province of Cyrenaica.[48]

The 102nd Motorized Division Trento took part in the Axis counterattack of March 1941 that forced the British and Commonwealth forces into retreat. While the Australian 9th Infantry Division fell back to the fortified port of Tobruk, the remaining British and Commonwealth forces withdrew a further 160 kilometers east to Sollum, on the Libyan–Egyptian border. These moves initiated the 240-day Siege of Tobruk, in which the 102nd Motorized Division Trento was involved.

After the failure of the Axis attack on El Adem, Erwin Rommel, the German officer commanding the counterattack, decided to attack the western sector of the Tobruk perimeter, around Ras el Medauar, on April 15, using the 132nd Armored Division Ariete along with the 62nd Infantry Regiment Sicilia of the Trento.[49] A British *communiqué* on April 17, 1941 described the actions:

> One of our patrols successfully penetrated an enemy position outside the defenses of Tobruk capturing 7 Italian officers and 139 men. A further attack on the defenses of Tobruk was repulsed by artillery fire. The enemy again suffered heavy casualties. During yesterday's operations a total of 25 officers and 767 of other ranks were captured. In addition over 200 enemy dead were left on the field.[50]

Italian casualties turned out to be twenty-four dead, 112 wounded, and 436 prisoners, including their colonel. The extra firepower finally stopped the Italians, and all firing ceased. The 2/43rd Battalion war diary reported, "The Italians attacked our 48th Battalion and while withdrawing they [the Italians] were fired upon by German tanks believed to be supporting the attack." The Australians sent out Bren-gun carriers specifically to find the Italian battalions' flank. An intelligence assessment by the 2/43rd Battalion concluded:

> Reports from PW indicate that a large-scale attack was to have been launched on the Tobruk defenses on or about 16 April 41. There appears to have been no co-ordination between enemy tanks and infantry units. The Italians appear to have been somewhat in the dark as to their actual objectives and the method of co-ordination by means of German liaison officers working with Italian units

has not been successful. PW also state that the spasmodic attacks in different sectors between 14 and 16 April, sometimes infantry alone, sometimes tanks alone sometimes both, were all intended to be a simultaneous assault which apparently went badly astray in its timing.[51]

On the night of April 30, a strong Italo–German force attacked the Tobruk defenses, and the Motorized Division Ariete, Infantry Division Brescia, 8th Bersaglieri Regiment, and combat engineers captured seven strong points. On the night of May 3, the Australians counterattacked, but the Trento and Pavia repelled the attack and the attackers were only able to recapture one strongpoint from the defending Italian troops. On the night of May 16, the Brescia retaliated with the help of two platoons of the 32nd Combat Engineer Battalion and breached the defensive perimeter of the 2/9th and 2/10th Battalions. Although the Australian Official History admits losing three positions, it claims the attackers were Germans. With the obstacles removed, the Brescia troops, who brought flamethrower parties and tanks, captured the three strong points.[52] The Australians fought back and the CO of the combat engineers, Colonel Emilio Caizzo, was killed in a satchel attack and won a posthumous Gold Medal for valor. An Italian narrative recorded:

> With great skill and speed the *Guastatori* [combat engineers] open three lanes in the mines and obstacles to let the Brescia Fucilieri through. Side by side with the Brescia assault troops they inflict heavy losses on the enemy and take out further strong points with explosives and flamethrowers.[53]

The division next saw action during the Allied attack codenamed Operation Battleaxe in mid-June 1941. The rest of the division was located at Bardia. Operation Crusader was launched by the British Eighth Army between November 18 and December 30 1941, with the objective of relieving the Siege of Tobruk. The plan was for the armored and motorized divisions to perform right flanking attacks while the Italian XXI (see Appendix III) and the Italian X Corps, which included the 102nd Motorized Division Trento, would advance parallel to the coast road. The division played an important role in the capture of 6,000 prisoners at Gazala on June 16. During the Battle of Mersa Matruh on June 26–30, 1942, Trento, with the 46th Artillery and 7th Bersaglieri Regiments attached, played an important part in the capture of 6,000 defenders of the X British Corps, along with large quantities of supplies.[54]

During the First Battle of El Alamein, elements of the 102nd Motorized Division Trento put up a tenacious defense on Miteiriya Ridge, delaying the Allied advance for several hours and allowing an Italian armored reconnaissance force to launch a devastating counterattack. Before the start of the Second Battle of El Alamein, the 102nd Motorized Division Trento was positioned along the

Miteirya Ridge. On August 2, the Australian 2/43rd and 2/28th Battalions, in a final attempt to recover the lost strong points, carried out a determined attack but were repulsed with heavy loss of life. After much fierce fighting, the Bersaglieri troops were finally ordered to move back to Gazala to rest and refit.[55]

On October 24, they came under attack from the 2nd New Zealand Division supported by 10th Armored Division.[56]

The 102nd Motorized Division Trento in the form of its 7th Bersaglieri Regiment soon arrived to replace the weary Italian forces defending the captured strong points, and the Australians continued to fight hard to recover them. By October 25, the Allies had broken through the minefields and were positioned on top of the Miteiriya Ridge.[57] The division was destroyed during the Second Battle of El Alamein.

136th Armored Division Giovani Fascisti

The 136th Armored Division Giovani Fascisti was formed from volunteers from the Young Fascist University. The division was sent to Libya in July 1941, but the 3rd Battalion remained in Italy for training and was later used as a source for replacements. The officers of the division claimed they could unhinge the Allied positions on the coast from Siwa if only they had the fuel.

The division made its mark during Operation Crusader. Tasked to defend the small hill known as Bir el Gubi, they fought off repeated attacks by the 11th Indian Brigade and British 7th Armored Division during the first week of December 1941. The 1st and 2nd Battalions of the 136th Armored Division Giovani Fascisti held a hilltop position successfully and fought off repeated attacks by the British armor and Indian infantry units. During the course of the battle, the remaining battalions went forward to assist the 102nd Motorized Division Trento's penetration of the Allied minefield zone.

The division began the Gazala battle in May 1942 as part of the army reserve, with four infantry battalions—the two original battalions, plus the 9th Independent Infantry Battalion and the 3rd Battalion of the San Marco Marine Regiment (which was later detached to join the Hecker amphibious group).[58]

The division occupied the Oasis of Siwa in Egypt in summer 1942, in order to prevent possible military actions from the British Army to the south of the Axis Army attacking El Alamein.

In July 1942, German Ju 52 transport planes transported one battalion of the 136th Armored Division Giovani Fascisti to seize the strategic Oasis of Siwa, the largest air-transportable assault conducted by the Axis forces in Africa. While they waited, the Italians set up an Egyptian government-in-exile, complete with postage stamps, and flew the Egyptian flag alongside the Italian tricolor flag.[59]

Field Marshal Erwin Rommel visited on September 1942 and reviewed the unit.[60] Some units of the 136th Armored Division Giovani Fascisti fought in the Second Battle of El Alamein with the 185th Paratroopers Division Folgore. Despite overwhelming odds, they inflicted massive casualties on the Allies and held their ground despite severe hunger and thirst.

In mid-November, after Montgomery's victory, the division withdrew from Siwa to Agedaiba and later to Tunisia. In the Mareth Line, the division fought the Allies bravely with the remaining Axis troops. The volunteers were subject to a power struggle between the army and the Fascist Blackshirts, and of the original twenty-five battalions, only two battalions survived to see action. It was in action during Operation Crusader when the 11th Indian Infantry Brigade was heavily engaged against a strong point near Bir el Gubi, 25 miles south of Ed Duda.[61] The division was nearly totally destroyed in 1943, during the fighting in Tunisia. Almost decimated, the 136th Armored Division Giovani Fascisti was the last Axis military unit to surrender to the Allies in North Africa on May 13, 1943.

80th Infantry Division La Spezia

The 80th Infantry Division La Spezia was an air-transportable division formed in 1941, for the planned Invasion of Malta. An Italian infantry division normally consisted of two infantry regiments (three battalions each), an artillery regiment, a mortar battalion with two companies, an anti-tank company, and a Blackshirt Legion (regiment of two battalions). Each division was authorized 7,000 men. The infantry and artillery regiments contained 1,650 men, the Blackshirt Legion 1,200, and each company 150 men.[62]

The division was transferred to Libya in October 1942. In December, it was reinforced by a battalion of the San Marco Marines and additional artillery. It suffered heavy losses during the Battle of the Mareth Line in Tunisia in March 1943 and the surviving elements surrendered in May 1943.[63]

185th Paratroopers Division Folgore

In 1938, Marshal of the Air Force Italo Balbo established the School for Paratrooper of the Libyan Troops under the command of Lieutenant Colonial Goffredo Tonini; it was stationed at the airport of Castel Benito near Tripoli.[64]

By 1939, there were two Libyan paratroopers battalions. However, it left the 1st Paratroopers Infantry Regiment with one battalion in Italy as foundation for the 184th Paratroopers Division Nembo. After the cancellation of the invasion of Malta, the division was sent to the North African theatre. In July 1940, first paratroopers units were established: 1st Paratroopers Carabinieri

Battalion and 2nd and 3rd Paratroopers Battalions. In the spring of 1941, the 4th Battalion, the Anti-tank Cannons Company, and the 1st Paratroopers Regiment were established.[65]

During the Battle of Alam El Halfa (August 30 and September 5, 1942) the 185th Paratroopers Division Folgore had been positioned to guard the left flank of the German 90th Light Division and the Ramcke Brigade, and was successful in driving off an attack by New Zealand Infantry during a fierce encounter between September 3 and 4. The performance by the Italians in this clash was greatly respected by their German allies, so much so that Wehrmacht leaders awarded eleven Iron Crosses to Folgore soldiers for their heroics on the battlefield.

By the end of September, the 185th Paratroopers Division Folgore was opposed by the British 131st Infantry Brigade, which boasted heavy artillery and a contingent of tanks, supplied by the Scots Greys, which had been attached to them in order to provide support against the division. In a preview of what would come to pass at the Second Battle of El Alamein, the soldiers of the 185th Paratroopers Division Folgore, in particular members of the 9th Battalion, delivered an impressive defensive victory, mauling the British in this encounter. Inflicting approximately 400 casualties upon the British forces, the 185th Paratroopers Division Folgore suffered less than fifty casualties of its own while repulsing the attack.[66] Through two hard fought encounters over the span of approximately one month, the soldiers of the 185th Paratroopers Division Folgore were quickly establishing a reputation as a formidable opponent.[67]

During the Second Battle of El Alamein, the 185th Paratroopers Division Folgore was under attack from three British divisions, the 44th Infantry Division, 50th Infantry Division, and 7th Armored Division, and the 1st Free French Brigade. Operation Lightfoot, launched on October 24, 1942, was designed to break through the weak Italian-held southern sector of the Alamein line where the Bologna, Brescia, Pavia, and Folgore divisions anchored the right flank. Each Paratroopers Artillery Group fielded one headquarters and two paratroopers' artillery batteries armed with 47/32 M35 cannons. The 7th Armored Division had been ordered to spare their tanks, so their attacks were called off after the bloody fighting during the night of October 24. Thirty-one British tanks were destroyed or disabled during that night alone.[68]

At the end of the Second Battle of El Alamein, Harry Zinder of *Time* magazine noted that the Italians paratroopers fought better than had been expected, and commented: "In the south, the famed Paratroopers Division Folgore fought to the last round of ammunition."[69] With a few survivors and some replacement, the 285th Parachute Folgore, a battalion-sized unit commandeered by Captain Lombardini, was formed and participated in the defense of the Mareth Line in Tunisia in mid-1943; it also participated at the Battle of Takrouna, where it was destroyed.

For its conduct during the Second Battle of El Alamein, the division was awarded a Gold Medal of Military Valor. The 185th Paratroopers Division Folgore used everything at its disposal, including letting the enemy advance into a cul-de-sac and then launching a counterattack from all sides. It also used its 47-mm anti-tank guns from enfilade positions and Molotov cocktails to knock out the advancing tanks. In the initial British assault alone, the 185th Paratroopers Division Folgore had destroyed over 120 armored vehicles and inflicted over 600 casualties. On November 6, after having exhausted all its ammunition, the remainder of the division surrendered.[70]

Blackshirt Division 23 March

The Blackshirt Division 23 March was an Italian Blackshirt militia unit formed for the Second Italo–Abyssinian War. It was encircled at Bardia and surrendered to the British forces in January 1941. It was named 23 March in honor of the founding of the Fascist Party on March 23, 1919.[71]

2nd Blackshirt Division 28 October

The 2nd Blackshirt Division 28 October was an Italian *Camicie Nere* (Blackshirt) militia unit formed for the Second Italo–Abyssinian War. It was named 28 October in honor of the Fascist March on Rome on October 28, 1922.[72] The division took part in the invasion of Egypt and was destroyed at Bardia, Libya, in January 1941.

4th Blackshirt Division 3 January

The 4th Blackshirt Division 3 January was one of seven Blackshirt Divisions that were organized and fought in the Second Italo–Abyssinian War. Its commander was General of the Division Alessandro Traditi. The name "3 January" was given in honor of the date of assumption of dictatorial powers by Benito Mussolini on January 3, 1925.[73] The division took part in the invasion of Egypt and was destroyed at Sidi Barrani while protecting the retreat of the other Italian units.

1st Libyan Division Sibelle

The 1st Libyan Division Sibelle was a formation of colonial troops raised by the Italians in their colony in Libya. By 1913, these comprised seven battalions of infantry, three squadrons of regular Libyan cavalry, one squadron of camel troops, a mountain artillery battery, and a section of camel artillery. Libyans also served in the military police, desert troops, and irregular cavalry units. By the 1930s, the

Libyan units had been brought together into the Royal Corps of Libyan Troops comprising infantry, cavalry, artillery, motorized troops, and support services.

The division participated in the invasion of Ethiopia in the Second Italo–Abyssinian War. The formation was reorganized into the 1st Libyan Division Sibelle by the beginning of Italy's entry into World War II.

In September 1940, the 1st Libyan Division Sibelle participated in the Italian invasion of Egypt. From the beginning, the Italian Army made use of the former Turkish-organized Arab gendarmerie as auxiliaries, augmenting them with regular colonial units recruited among the indigenous peoples of Libya. By December, the division was dug in at Maktila and was forced to surrender during Operation Compass.[74]

2nd Libyan Division Pescatori

In December 1940, the 2nd Libyan Division Pescatori was in Libya as part of the Italian XXII Corps (see Appendix IV) and together with the 1st Blackshirt Division 23 March and 2nd Blackshirt Division 28 October took part in the Italian invasion of Egypt.[75]

Operation Compass was originally planned as a five-day raid. On December 9, the 2nd Libyan Division Pescatori was located at Tummar. The attack commenced on Tummar at 1.50 p.m., after the British 7th Royal Tank Regiment had refueled and rearmed and artillery had softened the defenses up for an hour. Following the Italian advance, the British planned a limited operation to push the Italians back; however, the defenders put up stronger opposition at Nibeiwa, and by 4 p.m., Tummar West was overrun, except for the extreme north-east corner. The tanks shifted their point of attack to Tummar East, the greater part of which was captured by nightfall.

On December 10, the 16th Infantry Brigade was brought forward from the 4th Indian Division reserve and, with elements of 11th Indian Brigade under command, was sent forward in trucks to attack Sidi Barrani. The town was captured by nightfall and the remains of the two Libyan Divisions and the 4th Blackshirt Division were trapped between the 16th Infantry Brigade and the Selby Force. By December 15, Sollum and Halfaya had been captured, as well as Fort Capuzzo, while all Italian forces had been cleared from Egypt. The 2nd Libyan Division Pescatori lost twenty-six officers and 1,327 men killed and thirty-two officers and 804 men wounded, with the survivors being taken prisoner.[76]

40th Infantry Division *Cacciatori d'Africa* (Hunters of Africa)

The 40th Infantry Division *Cacciatori d'Africa* was formed July 27, 1940. The division and the 65th Infantry Division Granatieri di Savoia with other colonial troops in Italian East Africa were out of the normal chain-of-command, being subordinated directly to Prince Amedeo, Duke of Aosta.[77]

After the East African Campaign had started, the supply and reinforcements for Italian East Africa were sporadic to non-existent, resulting in the 40th Infantry Division *Cacciatori d'Africa* being severely under strength. On March 31, 1941, the 211th Infantry Regiment Pescara was placed under direct command of Italian East Africa High Command and sent to Amba Alagi mountain massif. On the same day, the divisional headquarters moved to Dessie, and the remnant units of the 40th Infantry Division *Cacciatori d'Africa* were sent in multiple locations to come under command of the various other units. On April 25, 1941, Kombolcha airbase defenses failed, and Dessie was overrun on April 26, 1941, forcing the divisional command to transfer to Bati and then immediately to Tendaho in the desert to the east. Increased shelling by British artillery forced a full abandonment of the first line of defenses near Bati on April 22, 1941.[78]

After the disastrous Battle of Keren on March 23, 1941, the 40th Infantry Division *Cacciatori d'Africa* transferred its 210th Infantry Regiment (Bisagno) and 65-mm artillery to 65th Infantry Division Granatieri di Savoia.[79] The defenses came under attack on April 17, 1941, by the 1st Infantry Brigade (South Africa) and Campbell's Scouts.

Units of the 40th Infantry Division *Cacciatori d'Africa* were tasked with the defense of the line Danakil Depression–Amba Alagi–Addis Ababa. After Addis Ababa fell to British forces on April 6, 1941, the 40th Infantry Division *Cacciatori d'Africa* erected a defensive position at Kombolcha airbase and at Bati. By April 19, 1941, the Italian defensive lines were in disarray due to airstrikes, allowing multiple sections to be overrun by British armored forces between April 19 and 21, 1941.[80]

By May 6, 1941, the survivors of the 40th Infantry Division *Cacciatori d'Africa* retreated to Danakil, where the division made its last stand. It continued to fight until been destroyed on May 22, 1941, in the area of Sodo.

60th Infantry Division Sabratha

The 60th Infantry Division Sabratha was created in May 1937, in Gharyan, Libya. While standing on the Tunisia–Libya border from 10 June 1940 to 25 June 1940, the division soon returned to the garrison duties in Tripoli. In December 1940, the division had moved to defensive positions south of Derna. During late January 1941, it fought a series of desperate delaying battles against superior British forces advancing according to Operation Compass in Derna–Al Qubbah region.

By September 1941, the 60th Infantry Division Sabratha was transferred to the reserve east of Tobruk. The reformed division met with mixed fortune during the balance of the Western Desert Campaign. At this point, contact with the British forces was lost and the remnants of the division retreated in order through the Ajdabiya–Sirte route. There it was assigned for coastal defense at Al Khums region. Under fierce pressure, the Australian troops were forced to withdraw from their forward positions, but their main defenses remained largely intact. The defeat of the 60th Infantry Division Sabratha marked the turning point of the First Battle of El Alamein.[81]

After the Fall of Tobruk on June 21, 1942, the division accelerated its movement, passing in quick succession through Bardia, Sollum, and Sidi Barrani, and reaching a locale of El Alamein on July 1, 1942.[82]

The 60th Infantry Division Sabratha was thoroughly routed under heavy artillery barrage on July 10, 1942, with over 1,500 Italians taken prisoner—of these, 835 (largely part of an infantry battalion and artillery group) were taken prisoner by the Australian 2/48th Battalion. On January 23, 1942, the 60th Infantry Division Sabratha started to advance again, partially enveloping Ajdabiya from the north-east. Finally, on December 23, 1941, it made a stand at coastal road at Brega, blocking Allied advance through coastal road.[83]

The survivors of the division were incorporated into the 61st Infantry Regiment of the 102nd Motorized Division Trento, and the 60th Infantry Division Sabratha was officially dissolved on July 25, 1942.

61st Infantry Division Sirte

The 61st Infantry Division Sirte was formed on May 9, 1937 in Misrata, located in northern Italian Libya. The 61st Infantry Division Sirte was classified as an auto-transportable division. The division was mobilized for action in October 1939, and by 10 June 1940, it was deployed on the Tunisia–Libya border.

In September 1940, it was part of the Italian XXII Corps that took part in the Italian invasion of Egypt, performing supply line defense roles behind Kambut and the airfields of RAF Gambut. At the start of Operation Compass on December 9, 1940, the division was stretched from 'Ayn al Ghazālah to hills south of Saqīfat az Za'farānah.

On January 8, 1941, parts of the division were encircled and subjected to heavy bombardment while still on the initial positions. At this point, the rest of the 61st Infantry Division Sirte started to retreat, but by January 20, 1941, the situation became desperate as British forces managed to make several breakthroughs, capturing large swaths of the poorly manned second line of defense of the 61st Infantry Division Sirte. It was completely overrun by January 23, 1941.[84]

62nd Infantry Division Marmarica

The 62nd Infantry Division Marmarica was formed on May 9, 1937 in Derna, Libya. The 62nd Infantry Division Marmarica was classified as an auto-transportable division. The 62nd Infantry Division Marmarica was mobilized in October 1939. By June 10, 1940, it was relocated to Bardia, and from June 14, 1940 to July 23, 1940, it was used to attack Fort Capuzzo on the hills south of Saqīfat az Za'farānah. After some hard fighting, one position after another surrendered. On September 9, 1940, the 62nd Infantry Division Marmarica arrived in Egypt to participate in the Italian invasion. The division's intended role was to protect the right (inland) flank of the advance to Sidi Barrani. On September 13, 1940, the division passed the Halfaya Pass, and soon the orders were received to stop and prepare for the defense.

Operation Compass, started November 18, 1940, cut the division from the bulk of the Axis forces. On the first day of fighting, it became obvious that the 62nd Infantry Division Marmarica's positions were untenable; therefore, a retreat was made to the stronghold of Bardia–Abyār ar Rujm–Zawiyat al Manestir–Bi'r al Ghirrīdīyah. At the Battle of Marmarica, which began on December 11, 1940, the division was located at Sidi Omarto, to the south of Sollum. The 62nd Infantry Division Marmarica settled on the new defensive positions on December 16, 1940. On January 3, 1941, the British resumed the offensive, resulting in Battle of Bardia. As the Allied forces advanced, several large Italian units were surrounded, cut off from supply, and defeated. The division was destroyed on January 5, 1941 in Bardia.[85]

63rd Infantry Division Cirene

The 63rd Infantry Division Cirene was formed on October 1, 1937 in Marj, Libya. The 63rd Infantry Division Cirene was classified as an auto-transportable division. By June 10, 1940, the Cirene was stationed at Al Adam, and assigned rear area protection duty. As the Allied forces advanced, the Italian units were surrounded, cut off from supply, and defeated.

In August 1940, the division was transferred to the Sollum–Bardia front area. The Italian divisions defending the perimeter of Sollum to Bardia included remnants of the 63rd Infantry Division Cirene, the 62nd Infantry Division Marmarica, the 1st Blackshirt Division 23 March, and the 2nd Blackshirt Division 28 October.

The Australians captured Bardia on January 5, taking 45,000 prisoners and 462 guns for a loss of 130 dead and 326 wounded of their own. Whenever the Italians chose to fight, the fighting was fierce. An Australian historian later wrote: "… in parts their defense was most efficient and often extremely brave."

Yet the majority of Italian units surrendered without fight, their morale having been sapped by hunger, thirst, lice, and dysentery.[86]

On September 13, 1940, the 63rd Infantry Division Cirene started to participate, entering Egyptian territory and reaching Sidi Barrani on September 16, 1940, but situation deteriorated rapidly due to heavy aerial bombardment and further Allied attacks. On January 3, 1941, the British forces resumed their offensive, starting the Battle of Bardia. However, enemy bombardment on the front line increased to an intolerable level, necessitating the bulk of 63rd Infantry Division Cirene personnel to retreat to Bardia city.

On December 11, 1940, a patrol from the British 7th Support Group entered Rabia to find it empty. The division was destroyed on January 5, 1941 in Bardia.[87]

65th Infantry Division *Granatieri di Savoia* (Grenadiers of Savoy)

The 65th Infantry Division *Granatieri di Savoia* was created on October 12, 1936 in Latina, Italy. In November 1936, the division was transferred to Addis Ababa, the capital of Italian East Africa. The 11th Blackshirt Legion, 65th Heavy Machine Gun Battalion, and 5th Artillery Battalion were permanently posted at the border with British Somaliland. Also, they provided protection to the Djibouti–Addis Ababa railroad. After three days of fighting with the British rearguard, the soldiers of 65th Infantry Division *Granatieri di Savoia* entered already abandoned Berbera on August 19, 1940.

After Emperor Selassie returned to Ethiopia January 18, 1941, the last units of 65th Infantry Division *Granatieri di Savoia* left Addis Ababa to cover as many threats by insurgents and foreign powers as possible. By that time, the British have already decided to leave the colony. The training battalion (comprising two machine gun companies, infantry company, and mortar company armed with 81mm mortars) was located north-west of Lake Tana, and 2nd Battalion of the 11th Blackshirt Legion was at Gondar.[88]

As the Battle of Kerenhave started February 5, 1941, the 65th Infantry Division *Granatieri di Savoia* mostly held positions and counterattacked, resulting in British attack failure by February 13, 1941. The Machine Gun Company and 2nd and 3rd Close Support Battalions, armed with 65-mm cannon, took positions at Amba Alagi. In the aftermath of the less-than-successful capture of Kassala, the elements of 10th Indian Infantry Brigade have captured the border fort Qallābāt near Metemma, but retreated after facing superior Italian ground and air forces.[89]

Renewed British attack from March 15, 1941 have not penetrated initially, but by March 27, 1941 the British armor had penetrated Italian defenses and were rampant on the Keren plain, forcing Italians to fall back.[90]

British forces destroyed or forced to surrender the Italian garrisons at Adi Tekelezan on April 1, 1941. On April 20, the surviving elements of divisional command and machine gunners were blended with the remnants of the 25th Colonial Infantry Division.

The units of 65th Infantry Division *Granatieri di Savoia*, entrenched at Togora Pass, Kalaga, and Cerarsi around Amba Alagi have participated in the Battle of Amba Alagi from April 21, 1941 to May 17, 1941. Massawa fell on April 8, 1941.[91] The last elements of the division surrendered on May 19, 1941 after their drinking water supply was destroyed in Soddu, Ethiopia.

16th Infantry Division Pistoia

The 16th Infantry Division Pistoia was created by dividing the Infantry Division Fossalta in 1939.[92] The 16th Infantry Division Pistoia was classified as an auto-transportable division. The division was mobilized in June 1940 as an infantry division and was sent to the French border and held in reserve for the Italian 1st Army. Original deployment was in the Varaita Valley. In June 1940, the 16th Infantry Division Pistoia was transferred to the Maddalena Pass, with only an artillery regiment ending up at occupied French territory by July 1940. After a few days, despite some successful counterattacks at the west of the Takrunah road junction, the Allies had effectively put the division under siege.

On October 10, 1941, the 16th Infantry Division Pistoia was partially motorized and sent to Athens, Greece in the end of July 1942.

In September 1942, it began transferring to the positions in North Africa at the border with Egypt, finally taking responsibility for the Bardia–Sollum–Naqb al Halfaya defensive line. On March 6, 1943, the 16th Infantry Division Pistoia attacked the British positions *en masse* with the goal of disrupting British offensive preparations and trigger a premature counteroffensive, as part of the Battle of Medenine. After the attack failure, the division fell back to the Mareth Line, leaving previous positions without a fight. It failed to hold the positions after the severe British attack, starting November 11, 1942.[94]

The 16th Infantry Division Pistoia was targeted again by British forces on April 5, 1943, and again started to retreat 7 April 1943. By the time it reached Enfidha on April 13, 1943, the division was severely decimated. When the British started the heavy attack March 19, 1943, it held the positions until March 25, 1943, but then retreated to El Hamma under the threat of being outflanked.[95] The last of its positions were overrun by May 13, 1943.

British Commonwealth Forces Attack the Italians

The Western Desert Force with about 30,000 men, advanced from Mersa Matruh in Egypt on a five-day raid against the Italian Tenth Army, which had about 150,000 men in fortified posts around Sidi Barrani and in Cyrenaica.

The Tenth Army was swiftly defeated and the British prolonged the operation, to pursue the remnants of the Tenth Army to Beda Fommand El Agheila on the Gulf of Sirte. When Governor-General of Libya Italo Balbo was killed by friendly fire, Marshal Graziani took his place. After being reinforced by the Fifth Army, the Tenth Army controlled the equivalent of four corps with 150,000 infantry men, 1,600 guns, 600 tankettes and tanks, and 331 aircraft.[1] The Italian XX Corps had the 60th Infantry Division Sabratha and the Italian XXI Corps had the 1st Blackshirt Division 23 March, the 2nd Blackshirt Division 28 October and the 63 Infantry Division Cirene. Once the French in Tunisia no longer posed a threat to Tripolitania, units of the Fifth Army were used to reinforce the Tenth Army. Marshal Graziani expressed doubts about the capabilities of the large non-mechanized force to defeat the British, who though smaller in numbers were motorized. The British took 138,000 Italian and Libyan prisoners, hundreds of tanks, and over 1,000 guns and aircraft for a loss of 1,900 men killed and wounded—about 10 percent of their infantry. British and other Commonwealth forces attacked Italian forces in western Egypt and Cyrenaica, the eastern province of Libya, from December 1940 to February 1941, with great success. The British were unable to continue beyond El Agheila, due to broken down and worn out vehicles.

When war was declared, the Fifth Army was in Tripolitania the western Libyan province and the Tenth Army was in Cyrenaica to the east. XXII Corps had the 61st Infantry Division Sirte and XXIII Corps had the 4th Blackshirt Division 3 January and the 64th Infantry Division Catanzaro.[2]

The Western Desert Force was commanded by Lieutenant General Richard O'Connor with the 4th Indian Infantry Division and the 7th Armored Division.

The new group of Libyan divisions had the Maletti Group, the 1st Libyan Division Sibelle and the 2nd Libyan Division Pescatori.[3] From December 14, troops of the 6th Australian Infantry Division, replaced the 4th Indian Division, which was sent to East Africa, less one brigade. On August 29, as more tanks arrived from Italy, the Libyan Tank Command was formed under the command of Colonel Valentini, with three groups. The Maletti Group was formed at Derna on July 8, 1940, with seven Libyan motorized infantry battalions, a company of Fiat M11/39 tanks, a company of L3/33 tankettes, and motorized artillery and supply units as the main motorized unit of the Tenth Army. Operation Compass was the first large Allied military operation of the Western Desert Campaign. The British had some fast Cruiser Mk I, Cruiser Mk II, and Cruiser Mk III tanks with Ordnance QF 2-pounderguns, which were superior to Fiat M11/39 tanks. Group with the 1st Medium Tank Battalion and the 31st, 61st, and 62nd Light Tank Battalions, Group Trivioli, with the 2nd Medium Tank Battalion, less one company and the 9th, 10th, and 61st Light Tank Battalions and Maletti Group with the 60th light tank battalion and the remaining M11/39 company from the 2nd Medium Tank Battalion.[4] Maletti Group became part of the Royal Corps of Libyan Colonial Troops, with the 1st Libyan Division Sibelle and the 2nd Libyan Division Pescatori.[5]

Middle East Command under General Archibald Wavell had about 36,000 soldiers, 120 guns, 275 tanks, and 142 aircraft, in two squadrons of Hurricanes, one of Gloster Gladiators, three of Bristol Blenheims, three of Vickers Wellingtons, and one of Bristol Bombays—about forty-six and 116 bombers.[6] The only non-infantry formation was the partially motorized and lightly armored Maletti Group. The British also had a battalion of Matilda II infantry tanks that, while slow, were also equipped with 2-pounders; the armor of the Matildas could not be penetrated by Italian anti-tank guns or field guns.[7]

During the next few months, there were raids and skirmishes between Italian forces in Libya and British and Commonwealth forces in Egypt. Italy declared war on Britain and France on June 10, 1940. The force included the cruisers HMS *Liverpool* and HMS *Gloucester* also exchanged fire with the Italian cruiser *San Giorgio*. The Italians dug in and awaited reinforcements and supplies along the Via della Vittoria, an extension of the Via Balbia being built from the frontier. On June 12, 1940, the Mediterranean Fleet bombarded Tobruk. RAF Blenheim bombers from No. 45, No. 55, and No. 211 Squadron hit the *San Giorgio* with one bomb.[8]

The *San Giorgio*'s role was then to support the local anti-aircraft units and claimed forty-seven British aircraft shot down or damaged. The *San Giorgio* also shot down the Savoia-Marchetti SM.79 aircraft carrying Italo Balbo, the Governor-General of Libya and Commander-in-chief of Italian forces in North Africa.[9]

On June 19, the British submarine HMS *Parthian* fired two torpedoes at the *San Giorgio* but missed. As the Italians advanced, the small British force at

Sollum withdrew to the main defensive position east of Mersa Matruh.[10] The Italian advance was harassed by the 3rd Coldstream Guards, attached artillery and other units.[11] After recapturing Fort Capuzzo, the Italians advanced approximately 95 kilometers in three days and on September 16, the advance stopped at Maktila, 16 kilometers beyond Sidi Barrani.

On September 13, 1940, the Italian Tenth Army advanced into Egypt in Operation Zone "E." Five fortified camps were built around Sidi Barrani from Maktila, 24 kilometers east along the coast, south to Tummar East, Tummar West, and Nibeiwa and Sofafi on the escarpment to the south-west.[12]

Late on December 8, an Italian reconnaissance aircrew reported that attack on Maktila and Nibeiwa was imminent but Maletti was not informed. Following the Italian advance, Wavell ordered the commander of British Troops Egypt, Lieutenant General Sir Henry Maitland Wilson, to plan a limited operation to push the Italians back. Operation Compass, for administrative reasons, was originally planned as a five-day raid but consideration was given to continuing the operation to exploit success.[13, 14] On November 28, Wavell wrote to Wilson: "I do not entertain extravagant hopes of this operation but I do wish to make certain that if a big opportunity occurs we are prepared morally, mentally and administratively to use it to the fullest."[15]

Selby Force, consisting of the 3rd Battalion Coldstream Guards plus some artillery from the Matruh garrison, was to contain the enemy camp at Maktila on the coast and the Royal Navy would bombard Maktila and Sidi Barrani.[16] Preparations were kept secret and only a few officers knew during the training exercise held from November 25–26, that the objectives marked out near Matruh were replicas of Nibeiwa and Tummar. The troops were also told that a second exercise was to follow and did not know that the operation was real until December 7, as they arrived at their jumping-off points.[17]

The headquarters of the Italian XXIII Corps and the 2nd Blackshirt Division 28 October were in Sollum and Halfaya Pass respectively and the 62nd Infantry Division Marmarica was at Sidi Omar, south of Sollum.[18] The 1st Blackshirt Division 23 March and the Tenth Army Headquarters were far back at Bardia.[19]

The 7th Support Group was to observe the Italian camps on the escarpment around Sofafi, to prevent the garrisons from interfering, while the rest of the division and 4th Indian Division passed through the Sofafi–Nibeiwa gap. Once Nibeiwa was captured, a second Indian brigade and the 7th Royal Tank Regiment would attack the Tummars. The Maletti Group was at Nibeiwa and the 4th Blackshirt Division 3 January and the headquarters of the Libyan Corps were at Sidi Barrani. On December 9, the 1st Libyan Division Sibelle was at Maktila and the 2nd Libyan Division Pescatori was at Tummar. The 63rd Infantry Division Cirene and the headquarters of XXI Corps were at Sofafi and the 64th Infantry Division Catanzaro was at Buqbuq. The RAF made attacks on Italian airfields and destroyed or damaged twenty-nine aircraft on the ground.

An Indian brigade and Infantry tanks of 7th Royal Tank Regiment would attack Nibeiwa from the west, as the 7th Armored Division protected their northern flank. Maktila had been bombarded by the monitor HMS *Terror* and the gunboat HMS *Aphis*; Sidi Barrani had been shelled by the gunboat HMS *Ladybird*.[20]

Operation Compass began on the night of December 7–8. The Western Desert Force with the 7th Armored Division, 4th Indian Division, and 16th Infantry Brigade advanced 113 kilometers to their start line. Selby Force with 1,800 men moved up from Matruh, set up a brigade of dummy tanks in the desert and reached a position south-east of Maktila by dawn on December 9.

The tanks moved on to Tummar East, the greater part of which was captured by nightfall. When the British attacked again at dawn on December 11, mass surrenders began everywhere, except at Point 90 where troops of the 2nd Libyan Division Pescatori held out for a short time, after which 2,000 troops surrendered. The 4th Armored Brigade had advanced to 'Aziziya, where the garrison of 400 men surrendered and light patrols of the 7th Hussars pushed forward to cut the road from Sidi Barrani to Buqbuq, while armored cars of the 11th Hussars ranged further west. By 8.30 a.m., Nibeiwa had been captured; Maletti Group commander had been killed in the fighting along with 818 men and 1,338 wounded; and 2,000 Italian and Libyan soldiers were taken prisoner.[21] Large quantities of supplies were captured for British casualties of fifty-six men.[22]

At 5 a.m. on December 9, a detachment of artillery commenced diversionary fire from the east on the fortified camp at Nibeiwa for an hour, which was held by the Maletti Group, and at 7.15 a.m., the divisional artillery began a preliminary bombardment. Cruiser tanks of the 6th Royal Tank Regiment arrived in a sandstorm and overran the Italians in the dunes at about 5.15 p.m., then joined Selby Force to continue the pursuit. While moving across exposed ground, some casualties were incurred but with support from artillery and the 7th Royal Tank Regiment, it was in position barring the south and south western exits to Sidi Barrani by 1.30 p.m. The tanks of 7th Armored Brigade were held in reserve ready to intercept an Italian counterattack.[23] The 2nd Libyan Division lost twenty-six officers and 1,327 men killed, thirty-two officers and 804 men wounded, with the survivors being taken prisoner.[24] Unaware of the situation at the Tummars, Selby sent units to cut the western exits from Maktila but the 1st Libyan Division Sibelle filtered through and escaped.[25]

A patrol from the 7th Support Group entered Rabia and found it empty; the 63rd Division Cirene had withdrawn from Rabia and Sofafi overnight. Italian casualties were 2,184 men killed, 2,287 troops wounded, and 38,000 prisoners.[26]

On December 10, the 16th Infantry Brigade was brought forward from 4th Indian Division reserve and with part of the 11th Indian Brigade under command, advanced in trucks to attack Sidi Barrani. On December 11, Selby Force and some tanks attacked and overran the 1st Libyan Division Sibelle and by the evening, the 4th Blackshirt Division 3 January had also surrendered. The defenders held out for longer than the Nibeiwa garrison, but by 4 p.m., Tummar West was overrun except for the north-eastern corner. An order to the 4th Armored Brigade to cut them off west of Sofafi arrived too late and the Italians were able to retire along the escarpment and join Italian forces at Halfaya. The 11th Indian Infantry Brigade, with 7th Royal Tank Regiment under command, attacked Nibeiwa from the north-west, which reconnaissance had established as the weakest sector. The British attacked at 4 p.m. supported by the divisional artillery and the town fell by nightfall; the remains of the two Libyan Divisions and the 4th Blackshirt Division 3 January were trapped between the 16th Infantry Brigade and Selby Force.

Selby Force followed up the retreat as the 1st Libyan Division Sibelle moved the 24 kilometers from Maktila to Sidi Barrani and drove part of the column into sand dunes north of the coast road. Another north-west approach was made; the tanks broke through the perimeter and were followed twenty minutes later by the infantry. On December 11, the 7th Armored Brigade was ordered out of reserve to relieve the 4th Armored Brigade in the Buqbuq area, mop up and capture large numbers of men and guns.[27]

The attack on Tummar West began at 1.50 p.m., after the 7th Royal Tank Regiment had refueled and artillery had bombarded the defenses for an hour. The Italian defenders were caught at Sidi Barrani, in a pocket 16 × 8 kilometers backing on to the sea.

The 6th Australian Division attacked the Italian XXIII Corps Bardia from January 3–5, 1941, assisted by air support, naval gunfire, and artillery barrages. On the third day, the 19th Australian Infantry Brigade advanced south from Bardia, supported by artillery and the remaining six Matilda tanks. Fort Capuzzo, 64 kilometers inland at the end of the frontier wire, was captured by 7th Armored Division in December 1940, as it advanced westwards to Bardia. The Italians forces sustained 38,289 casualties, most taken prisoner, seventy-three tanks, and 237 guns, against 634 British casualties.[28] The Western Desert Force paused to reorganize and then moved quickly west along the Via della Vittoria, through Halfaya Pass and recaptured Fort Capuzzo in Libya.[29]

On December 7, Wellington bombers from Malta and Blenheim bombers from Egypt carried out raids on the Italian air bases at Castel Benito, Benina, and El Adem, the attack on Castel Benito being particularly successful, with hits on five hangars and strafing runs which hit many Italian aircraft; the attacks continued until the end of the year.[30]

By this time, the Western Desert Force had taken 38,300 prisoners and captured 237 guns and seventy-three tanks, while suffering casualties of 133 killed, 387 wounded, and eight missing.[31] The Australian infantry and twenty-three Matilda II tanks of the 7th Royal Tank Regiment overran the Italian defenses and took 8,000 prisoners.[32] The 17th Australian Infantry Brigade exploited the breach made in the perimeter and pressed south, as far as a secondary line of defenses known as the Switch Line. Thousands of prisoners were taken and the remnants of the Italian garrison held only the northern and southernmost parts of the fortress.

Exploitation continued by the two armored brigades and the 7th Support Group, with the infantry of 16th Infantry Brigade (which had been detached from the 4th Indian Division) following up. Italian forces crowded along the coast road and retreating from Sidi Barrani and Buqbuq, were bombarded by HMS *Terror* and the two gunboats, which fired on the Sollum area all day and most of the night of December 11. The 7th Armored Division concentrated south-west of Bardia, waiting for the arrival of 6th Australian Division. Late on December 12, the only Italian positions left in Egypt were the approaches to Sollum and the area of Sidi Omar. The 17th Australian Infantry Brigade attacked and the two brigades reduced the southern sector of the fortress. The 16th Australian Infantry Brigade attacked at dawn from the west, where the defenses were known to be weak. On the second day, the 16th Australian Infantry Brigade captured Bardia, cutting the fortress in two. Italian casualties also included 1,703 killed and 3,740 men wounded.[33]

At dawn, Major General Della Mura, commander of the 61st Infantry Division Sirte, surrendered with several thousand troops. The Italian attack was repulsed by the infantry, two anti-tank guns and two captured Italian tanks. More resistance was met near Pilastrino, which held out until 9.30 p.m. and the area around Solaro was captured along with Mannella.[34]

By 3.45 p.m., 20,000 prisoners, 208 guns, and eighty-seven tanks had been captured for the loss of 400 men—355 of them Australian. The 2/8th Australian Battalion was held up at the Bardia–El Adm crossroads, by a force of dug-in tanks and machine-gun nests, but at 2 p.m., the Australians attacked again and broke through on the right. The 16th Australian Brigade fanned out at 8.40 a.m. and the 19th Australian Brigade advanced north, behind an artillery barrage and counter-battery fire on the Italian artillery. Half of the Tobruk area had been captured by nightfall and the Italians began demolitions at the harbor. The 2/3rd Australian Battalion attacked at 5.40 a.m. on January 21 and after an hour, the 16th Australian Brigade and eighteen captured Italian tanks broke through to a depth of 1.6 kilometers on a 1.6-kilometer front. The armored cruiser *San Giorgio*, having been ordered to stay and help with the defense until the end, fired on the advancing Australian troops until the naval base fell; then she was blown up by her crew to avoid capture.[35, 36]

Sappers blew gaps in the barbed wire with Bangalore torpedoes, then filled in and broke down the sides of the anti-tank ditch with picks and shovels. By December 15, Sollum and the Halfaya Pass had been captured and the British bypassed Italian garrisons further south in the desert. The Italian garrisons in the north surrendered to the 16th Australian Infantry Brigade and the 7th Support Group outside the fortress; about 25,000 prisoners were taken, along with 400 guns, 130 light and medium tanks, and hundreds of motor vehicles. Over the next few days, the 4th Armored Brigade on top of the escarpment and the 7th Armored Brigade on the coast attempted a pursuit, but supply problems and the large number of prisoners impeded the advance.

The 6th Australian Cavalry Regiment reached the port and took the surrender of Admiral Massimiliano Vietina and the naval garrison. On the left, the Australians were counterattacked by seven tanks and infantry behind an artillery barrage. Italian casualties were eighteen officers and 750 men killed, thirty officers and 2,250 men wounded.[37] Most of the demolitions conducted by the Italians had been of stores rather than installations; the Inshore Squadron began mine sweeping and opened the port on January 24.[38]

During the day, Blenheims of 55 and 113 squadrons flew fifty-six sorties against Tobruk; the Gladiators and Hurricanes of 3 Squadron RAF and 73 and 274 Squadrons RAF patrolled to the west. To the north, the 2/11th Australian Battalion engaged the 60th Infantry Division Sabratha and Bersaglieri companies of the Babini Group at Derna airfield, making slow progress against determined resistance. The 60th Infantry Division Sabratha held a line from Derna, along Wadi Derna to Mechili, with the Babini Group at Mechili, Giovanni Berta and Chaulan (south of Wadi Derna), to guard the flank and rear of the infantry.[39, 40]

The British swiftly retired, calling for help from the 2nd Royal Tank Regiment, which ignored the signals through complacency. The British lost several tanks and knocked out two M13s; eventually the 2nd Royal Tank Regiment was alerted, caught the Italian tanks while sky-lined on a ridge and knocked out seven M13s, for the loss of a cruiser and six light tanks.[41, 42]

Next day, the Babini Group, with ten to fifteen M13/40s, attacked the 7th Hussars then headed west to cut the Derna–Mechili track north of Mechili. The 19th Australian Brigade began to arrive in the morning and Italian bombers and fighters attacked the Australians. The area east of the Jebel Akhdar mountains was garrisoned by the Italian XX Corps with the 60th Infantry Division Sabratha and the Babini Group, which had 120 tanks, but these included eighty-two that needed ten days to be made battle-worthy but had been rushed forward anyway. The Italians swept the flat ground with field artillery and machine-guns, stopping the Australian advance 2,700 meters short of the objective.[43] On January 26, the 2/4th Australian Battalion cut the Derna–Mechili road and a company crossed Wadi Derna during the night against bold Italian counterattacks.[44]

The Italians disengaged on the night of January 28–29, before the garrison was trapped and rearguards of the Babini Group cratered roads, planted mines and booby-traps and managed to conduct several skillful ambushes, which slowed the British pursuit.[45] Derna was occupied unopposed on 29 January and the Australians began a pursuit along the Via Balbia, closing on Giovanni Berta during 31 January.[46]

Italian garrisons held Giarabub (now Jaghbub), 240 kilometers south of Sollum, Kufra Oasis, Jalo at the west end of the Great Sand Sea, and Murzuk,

800 kilometers south of Tripoli. Further south, on the far side of the Sand Sea, the oasis of Kufra was attacked by Free French from French Equatorial Africa, in concert with Long Range Desert Group (LRDG) patrols. The base was the closest Italian outpost to the East African Empire and a raid from Uweinat on Wādī Ḥalfā in Sudan was possible.

The oasis of Giarabub was attacked in January 1941 and captured in March by the 6th Australian Cavalry Regiment and an Australian infantry battalion. The British were strafed by aircraft and attacked by armored cars of the Italian Auto-Saharan Company, which destroyed several trucks. The terrain slowed the British tanks and Combe Force, a column of wheeled vehicles, was sent ahead.[47]

The success of such columns against the Italians led to exaggerated expectations, which were confounded when better-equipped and trained German troops arrived in Libya. The 7th Armored Division was dispatched to intercept the remnants of the Tenth Army by moving through the desert, south of the Jebel Akhdar via Msus and Antelat, as the 6th Australian Division pursued the Italians along the coast road, north of the Jebel. From Benghazi to Ajdabiya, the British took 25,000 prisoners and captured 107 tanks and ninety-three guns.[48]

On January 23, the Tenth Army Commander, General Giuseppe Tellera ordered a counterattack against the British, to avoid an envelopment of XX Corps from the south.

Late on February 5, Combe Force arrived at the Via Balbia south of Benghazi and set up road blocks near Sidi Saleh, about 32 kilometers north of Ajdabiya and 48 kilometers south-west of Antelat; the leading elements of the Tenth Army arrived thirty minutes later. Further west, on the border with Chad, the Italian base at Murzuk was raided in January, when a patrol of the new Long Range Patrol Unit and a local sheikh travelled 2,100 kilometers to rendezvous near Kayugi, with a small Free French detachment.[49] The raiders then shot up three forts and departed.[50]

The lack of cover in the desert encouraged dispersion to avoid air attack but this reduced firepower at the decisive point. Leclerc decided that an attack on Kufra was not possible and the remaining British returned to Cairo, after a forty-five-day journey of 6,900 kilometers. Destruction of the dockyards and railway workshops and the sinking of vessels on the Nile could cut the link between Khartoum and Cairo.[51] The force attacked Murzuk and destroyed three aircraft and a hangar; the French commander was killed, most of the Italians surrendered, and several prisoners were taken. In late January, the British learned that the Italians were retreating along the Litoranea Balbo from Benghazi.[52, 53]

The success of the 7th Armored Division encouraged a belief in the Royal Tank Regiment that maneuver could win battles, then the engagement with the Babini Group on January 24, led to a conclusion that armored divisions needed more artillery. Next day, the Italians attacked to break through the road block and continued to attack into February 7. With British reinforcements arriving and the

Australians pressing down the road from Benghazi, the Tenth Army surrendered. The 7th Armored Division concluded that the defensive mentality of the Italians had justified the taking of exceptional risks, which would be unjustified against German troops.[54] British patrols visited Faya and met another French detachment with General Philippe Leclerc for an attack on Kufra. No integration of tanks with infantry or the use of anti-tank guns offensively was considered necessary.

The 2nd Support Group had only one motor battalion, a field artillery regiment, one anti-tank battery and a machine-gun company; most of the divisional transport had been sent to Greece. The 6th Australian Division went to Greece in March, with an armored brigade group of the 2nd Armored Division; the remainder of the division and the new 9th Australian Division, minus two brigades and most of its transport sent to Greece, were replaced by two under-equipped brigades of the 7th Australian Division. The Western Desert Force lost 500 killed, fifty-five missing, and 1,373 wounded. The RAF lost twenty-six aircraft, comprising six Hurricanes, five Gladiators, three Wellingtons, one Valentia, and eleven Blenheims.[55]

The Sirte, Tmed Hassan, and Buerat strongholds were reinforced from Italy, which brought the 10th and 5th armies up to about 150,000 men. German reinforcements were sent to Libya to form a blocking detachment under Directive 22, these being the first units of the *Afrika Korps*. The Italian Tenth Army lost at least 5,500 men killed, about 10,000 wounded, 133,298 men taken prisoner, 420 tanks, and 845 guns.[56]

The 7th Armored Division had been operating for eight months, had worn out its mechanical equipment and was withdrawn to refit. In the Western Desert Force (now XIII Corps), the 6th Australian Division was fully equipped and had few losses to replace. The division took over in Cyrenaica, on the assumption that the Italians could not begin a counteroffensive until May, even with German reinforcements.[57]

The 2nd Armored Division in Cyrenaica had the 3rd Armored Brigade, with an under strength light tank regiment, a second regiment using captured Italian tanks and a cruiser tank regiment from mid-March, also with worn-out tanks.[58] Two regiments of the 2nd Armored Division with the WDF were also worn out, leaving the division with only four tank regiments. A few thousand men of the Tenth Army escaped the disaster in Cyrenaica but the Fifth Army in Tripolitania had four divisions.[59]

A week after the Italian surrender at Beda Fomm, the Defense Committee in London, ordered Cyrenaica to be held with the minimum of forces and the surplus sent to Greece. A far larger number of aircraft became non-operational due to damage, which could not be repaired quickly for lack of spare parts, a problem made worse by the increased use of explosive bullets by the Italians. On March 25, 1941, Graziani was replaced by Gariboldi.[60]

The Germans Arrive in Africa

The *Afrika Korps* was formed on January 11, 1941 and one of Hitler's favorite generals, Lieutenant General Erwin Rommel, was designated as commander. The German Armed Forces High Command had decided to send a blocking force to Libya to support the Italian Army. The Italian army group had been routed by the British Commonwealth Western Desert Force in Operation Compass (December 9, 1940 to February 9, 1941). This was the birth of the German Africa Corps. Operation *Sonnenblume* (Sunflower) (February–March 1941) was the codename for the initial movement of German troops to North Africa, after the Italians had been forced out of Cyrenaica and appeared to be struggling to hold on to Tripolitania.[1]

On February 11, Rommel visited the Italian High Command in Rome, where he got approval for his plan to defend a line running south from Buerat, at the western end of the Gulf of Sirte. The Italians were prepared to abandon the Sirte area and make a standard around Tripoli, but unknown to them the British offensive had now run out of steam. General Wavell, the British commander-in-chief in the Middle East, had been ordered to send troops to Greece and the troops that had taken part in the advance were now exhausted.[2] Hitler feared the worst and in order to prevent a total collapse of the Italian position in Africa, decided to send a small German force to help defend Tripolitania.[3]

The new force was limited to two divisions: the 5th Light Division, which would arrive first, and the 15th Panzer Division, which would follow on. General Erwin Rommel, who had served as the commander of Hitler's escort battalion before the war and commanded the 7th Panzer Division during the invasion of France, was chosen to command the new force.[4]

The 15th Panzer Division did not complete its movement until May, but by then, Rommel's First Offensive was well under way. This gave Rommel 155 German tanks: twenty-five Panzer I Model A, forty-five Panzer II, sixty-one

Panzer III, seventeen Panzer IV, and seven command tanks (Rommel wrote that this gave him 120 tanks, perhaps suggesting that he did not count the Panzer Is or command tanks). When Italy entered the war, the front line in North Africa ran along the Egyptian–Libyan border. On this date, the situation appeared to be very critical, with the British about to take Benghazi and showing no signs of stopping.[5]

The German plan was for the first units of the light division to arrive in February 1941, with the movement to be completed by mid-April. The Germans and Italians were unaware of this. Rommel then flew to Sicily, where he ordered the first German raids on Benghazi, to harass the British supply lines.[6] Gariboldi had not been very supportive earlier, but by the time Rommel returned, new orders had arrived from Italy, and he cooperated with the Germans.[7]

Rommel had been given clear orders not to go onto the offensive until his entire force was present, and then only to make a limited move.[8] When Rommel arrived in Africa, Sirte was only defended by one Italian infantry regiment. The British were badly outnumbered, but the Italians were unable to take advantage of this. At this point, Rommel officially took command of the front line, sending Major General Johannes Streich, the commander of the 5th Light Division, to represent him.[9] On February 12, Rommel flew to Tripoli. At first, it operated alongside the Italians, and later, when more German forces arrived, it became one part of a larger army, but for their opponents, the name would soon come to stand for all of the Axis forces in North Africa.[10]

Over the next month, the rest of 5th Panzer Regiment arrived, completing its movement on March 11. This carried the 3rd Reconnaissance Battalion of the light division, commanded by Major Baron von Wechmar, and an anti-tank battalion. After visiting the new Italian commander, General Italo Gariboldi, Rommel then flew over the Sirte area and decided to make his stand there. They did advance across the Egyptian border, but a British counterattack, originally carried out with limited objectives, soon developed into a major offensive (Operation Compass). In just over a month, the Italians were forced back from their positions across the Egyptian border all the way to El Agheila, on the Gulf of Sirte. The Armored Division Ariete was ordered to move to a position further west, although its tanks were not terribly impressive.

The first troop ship reached Tripoli on February 14. British troops captured Tobruk (January 21–22), Benghazi (February 7), and El Agheila (February 9), and fresh troops with little or no desert experience replaced them. The unit was then rushed to the front, arriving on February 16. The British stopped at El Agheila and rotated most of their experienced troops back to Egypt to rest. Rommel insisted that this ship should be unloaded non-stop and overnight. The British were forced out of Cyrenaica nearly as quickly as they had advancing, setting a pattern of advance and retreat that would dominate the Desert War for the next two years.[11]

At about this time, Hitler decided to name the new unit the *Deutsches Afrika Korps*, and on February 21, 1941, Rommel's headquarters officially became Headquarters DAK (*Deutsches Afrika Korps*). Rommel was impressed by these troops when he visited them, but reinforcements were urgently needed. The sixty-one Panzer IIIs were the most potent anti-tank weapons, and ended the reign of the British Matilda II as "Queen of the Desert."

On February 6, Rommel met with Field Marshal von Brauchitsch, who outlined his new role, and then with Hitler, who gave him a detailed outline of the position in North Africa and explained that he had been selected for the role as he was believed to be the man most able to quickly adapt to the new circumstances. At no point did this unit contain all of the Axis forces in Africa. The 15th Panzer would follow by the end of May. By 11 a.m. on February 15, the unit was ready to be paraded through Tripoli. Two Italian divisions, Brescia and Pavia, were ordered up to the front, with the first moving on February 14.[12]

The British Eighth Army Campaign to Relieve the Siege of Tobruk

The British XIII Corps comprised 4th Indian Infantry Division, the newly arrived 2nd New Zealand Division and the 1st Army Tank Brigade. The Eighth Army also included the Tobruk garrison with the 32nd Army Tank Brigade and the Australian 9th Division, which in late 1941 was in the process of being replaced by the British 70th Infantry Division and the Polish Carpathian Brigade. By November, the Australian 20th Brigade remained in Tobruk. In reserve, the Eighth Army had the South African 2nd Infantry Division, making a total equivalent of about seven divisions with 770 tanks, including many of the new Crusader Cruiser tanks, after which the operation was named. Operation Crusader was intended to relieve the 1941 Siege of Tobruk; the Eighth Army tried to destroy the Axis Armored force before advancing its infantry. The plan failed when, after a number of inconclusive engagements, the British 7th Armored Division was defeated by the *Afrika Korps* at Sidi Rezegh.

Lieutenant General Erwin Rommel ordered German Armored divisions to the Axis fortress positions on the Egyptian border but failed to find the main body of the Allied infantry, which had bypassed the fortresses and headed for Tobruk. Rommel had to withdraw from the frontier to Tobruk and achieved some tactical success in costly fighting. The need to preserve his remaining forces from destruction prompted Rommel to withdraw his army to the defensive line at Gazala, west of Tobruk and then all the way back to El Agheila. It was the first victory over the German ground forces by British forces in the war.[1]

The British XXX Corps was made up of 7th Armored Division, the understrength South African 1st Infantry Division with two brigades of the Sudan Defense Force, and the independent 22nd Guards Brigade. Air support was provided by up to 724 combat airplanes of the Commonwealth air forces in the Middle East and Malta, with direct support under the command of Air Headquarters Western Desert.[2]

Opposing them were the German and Italian soldiers of Panzer Group Africa under General Erwin Rommel, with the *Afrika Korps* under Lieutenant General Ludwig Crüwell comprising the 15th Panzer Division, 21st Panzer Division (total of 260 tanks), the Division z.b.V (special use) Afrika, which had been formed in Africa as a composite formation and was renamed the 90th Light Africa Division in late November, and the Italian 55th Infantry Division Savona.[3]

The Italian XXI Army Corps consisted of the 17th Infantry Division Pavia, 102nd Motorized Division Trento, 27th Infantry Division Brescia, and 25th Infantry Division Bologna.[4] Following the costly failure of Operation Battleaxe, General Archibald Wavell was relieved as Commander-in-Chief Middle East Command and replaced by General Claude Auchinleck. The Eighth Army comprised two Corps: XXX Corps and XIII Corps.

Directly under the Italian High Command remained Italian XX Corps and XXI Corps. The Italian XX Corps consisted of the 132nd Armored Division Ariete with 146 medium tanks M13/40 and 101st Motorized Division Trieste. Rommel had to withdraw from the frontier to Tobruk and achieved some tactical success in costly fighting. The need to preserve his remaining forces from destruction prompted Rommel to withdraw his army to the defensive line at Gazala, west of Tobruk and then all the way back to El Agheila. The Western Desert Force was reorganized and renamed the Eighth Army.

In November, a five-ship convoy was sunk during Operation Crusader and ground attacks on road convoys stopped journeys in daylight. From February–May 1941, a surplus of 45,000 tons was delivered; attacks from Malta had some effect, but in May, the worst month for ship losses, 91 percent of supplies arrived. Elements of the 21st Panzer and the Savona divisions manned these defenses while Rommel kept the rest of his forces grouped near or around the Tobruk perimeter where a planned attack on November 14 had been put back to November 24 due to supply difficulties.[5] Axis initial air support consisted of about 120 German and 200 Italian serviceable airplanes but these could be reinforced quickly by transfer of units from Greece and Italy.

A German motorized division needed 350 tons per day and moving the supplies 480 kilometers took 2-ton trucks.[6] With seven Axis divisions, air and naval units, 70,000 tons of supplies per month were needed. A record amount of supplies arrived in June, but at the front, shortages worsened.[7]

There were fewer Axis attacks on Malta from June and sinking of ships increased from 19 percent in July to 25 percent in September, when Benghazi was bombed and ships diverted to Tripoli; air supply in October made little difference. Deliveries averaged 72,000 tons per month from July–October, but the consumption of 30–50 percent of fuel deliveries by road transport and a truck serviceability rate of 35 percent reduced deliveries to the front. Lack of deliveries and the Eighth Army offensive forced a retreat to El Agheila from 4 December, crowding the Via Balbia, where British ambushes destroyed about half of the remaining Axis transport.[8]

The Axis forces had built a defensive line of strong points along the escarpment running from near the sea at Bardia and Sollum and further along the border wire to Fort Capuzzo. Lack of transport in Libya left German supplies in Tripoli and the Italians had only 7,000 trucks for deliveries to 225,000 men.

Bizerte in Tunisia was canvassed as a supply port, but this was in range of RAF aircraft from Malta and was another 800 kilometers west of Tripoli.[9]

The plan was to engage the *Afrika Korps* with the 7th Armored Division while the South African Division covered their left flank. Meanwhile, on their right, XIII Corps, supported by 4th Armored Brigade, detached from 7th Armored Division, would make a clockwise flanking advance west of Sidi Omar and hold position threatening the rear of the line of Axis defensive strong points, which ran east from Sidi Omar to the coast at Halfaya. Convoys to Tripoli resumed and sinkings increased, but by December 16, the supply situation had eased, except for the fuel shortage and in December, the Luftwaffe was restricted to one sortie per day. There was also a deception plan to persuade the Axis that the main Allied attack would not be ready until early December and would be a sweeping outflanking move through Giarabub, an oasis on the edge of the Great Sand Sea, more than 240 kilometers to the south of the real point of attack.

The Vichy French sold 3,600 tons of fuel, U-boats were ordered into the Mediterranean and air reinforcements sent from Russia in December. The use of an armada for 20,000 tons of cargo ships depleted the navy fuel reserve and only one more battleship convoy was possible. Four battleships, three light cruisers and twenty destroyers escorted four ships to Libya. The Italian Navy used warships to carry fuel to Derna and Benghazi, and then made a maximum effort from December 16–17. This proved successful to the extent that Rommel, refusing to believe that an attack was imminent, was not in Africa when it came.[10] Central to the plan was the destruction of the Axis armor by 7th Armored Division to allow the relatively lightly Armored XIII Corps to advance north to Bardia on the coast whilst XXX Corps continued north-west to Tobruk and link with a break-out by 70th Division.

In his original battle plan, British Eighth Army Commander, Lieutenant General Cunningham had hoped for this so that he would be able to bring his own larger tank force to bear and defeat the *Afrika Korps* armor. Before dawn on November 18, the Eighth Army launched a surprise attack, advancing west from its base at Mersa Matruh and crossing the Libyan border near Fort Maddalena, some 80 kilometers south of Sidi Omar, and then pushing to the north-west. The Eighth Army were relying on the Desert Air Force to provide them with two clear days without serious air opposition but torrential rain and storms the night before the offensive resulted in the cancellation of all the air raids planned to interdict the Axis airfields and destroy their aircraft on the ground.[11] However, initially all went well for the Allies. The 4th Armored fought a second engagement with 21st Panzer pitting their Stuart tanks' greater speed against the enemy's heavier guns.

The Eighth Army were fortunate at this time that 15th Panzer Division had been ordered to Sidi Azeiz, where there was no British armor to engage. XIII Corps and New Zealand Division made its flanking advance with 4th Armored Brigade on its left and 4th Indian Division's 7th Infantry Brigade on its right flank at Sidi Omar. On the first day, no resistance was encountered as the Eighth Army closed on the enemy positions.

On the morning of November 19, at the First Battle of Bir el Gubi, the advance of the 22nd Armored Brigade was blunted by the Ariete division, which continued to take a major toll of British armor in the opening phase of the battle.[12] In the center of the division, the 7th Armored Brigade and the 7th Support Group raced forward almost to within sight of Tobruk and took Sidi Rezegh airfield, while on the right flank 4th Armored Brigade came into contact that evening with a force of 60 tanks supported by 88-mm gun batteries and anti-tank units from 21st Panzer Division (which had been moving south from Gambut) and became heavily engaged.[13, 14]

On November 20, the 22nd Armored Brigade fought a second engagement with the Ariete division and 7th Armored repulsed an infantry counterattack by the 90th Light and Bologna divisions at Sidi Rezegh. The 7th Armored Division's 7th Armored Brigade advanced north-west towards Tobruk with 22nd Armored Brigade to their left. By attaching the 4th Armored Brigade to XIII Corps, allowing the 22nd Armored Brigade to be sidetracked fighting the Ariete division, and letting the 7th Armored Brigade forge towards Tobruk, his armored force was by this time hopelessly dispersed. The 22nd Armored Brigade were therefore disengaged from the Ariete and ordered to move east and support the 4th Armored Brigade, while infantry and artillery elements of the 1st South African Division were to hold the Ariete, and the 4th Armored were released from their role of defending XIII Corps' flank.[15] However, the 4th Armored soon started to receive intelligence that the two German Panzer divisions were linking up.

The Polish Carpathian Brigade mounted a diversion just before dawn to pin the Division Pavia. The 70th Division attack surprised the Axis, Rommel having underestimated the size and armored strength of the garrison. The New Zealand Division exploited the decline of the 21st and 15th Panzer and advance 48 kilometers northeast to the Sidi Azeiz area, overlooking Bardia. The 22nd Armored arrived at dusk, too late to have an impact, and during the night of November 20, Rommel pulled all his tanks north-west for an attack on Sidi Rezegh.[16]

On November 21, another fierce action was fought with high casualties by elements of the German 155th Rifle Regiment, Artillery Group Böttcher, the 5th Panzer Regiment, and the British 4th, 7th, and 22nd Armored Brigades for possession of Sidi Rezegh and the surrounding height in the hands of Italian infantry and anti-tank gunners of the Bologna. The 2nd York and Lancaster Regiment, with tank support, took strongpoint Tiger leaving a 6,400-meter gap between the corridor and Ed Duda, but efforts to clear the "Tugun" and "Dalby

Square" strong points were repelled. On the evening of November 20, Scobie ordered a break-out on November 21 by the 70th Division.[17]

The 7th Armored advanced from Sidi Rezegh to link with them and roll up the Axis positions around Tobruk. The central attack by the Black Watch involved a murderous charge under heavy machine gun fire, attacking and taking various strong points, until they reached a strongpoint named Tiger. During the operation, 100 guns were to bombard the Bologna, Brescia, and Pavia positions on the Tobruk perimeter with 40,000 rounds.[18]

Fighting was intense as the three pronged attack, consisting of the 2nd King's Own on the right flank, the 2nd Battalion, Black Watch as the central force and the 2nd Queen's Own on the left flank, advanced to capture a series of prepared strong points leading to Ed Duda.[19] Initially, the Italians were stunned by the massive fire and a company of the Pavia was overrun in the predawn darkness, but resistance in the Bologna gradually stiffened.[20]

By mid-afternoon, elements of the 70th Division had advanced some 5.6 kilometers towards Ed Duda on the main supply road when they paused as it became clear that the 7th Armored would not link up. The Black Watch lost an estimated 200 men and their commanding officer.[21] The British renewed their advance but the attack petered out when the infantry involved were unable to capture the Bologna defenses around the Tugun strongpoint.

The Eighth Army plans for November 21 were for the 70th Division to break out from Tobruk and cut off the Germans to the southeast. On November 22, General Scobie ordered the position to be consolidated and the corridor widened in the hope that the Eighth Army would link up. In the afternoon of November 20, the 4th Armored were engaged with 15th Panzer Division (21st Panzer having temporarily withdrawn for lack of fuel and ammunition). In the fighting on the 22nd, the "Tugun" defenders brought down devastating fire, reducing the strength in one attacking British company to just thirty-three all ranks.[22] It was too late in the day for a decisive action but the 4th Armored nevertheless lost some forty tanks and by this time were down to less than two-thirds their original force.

Without armored support, the northward attack by the Support Group failed and by the end of the day, the 7th Armored Brigade had lost all but twenty-eight of its 160 tanks and was relying by that time mainly on the artillery of the Support Group to hold the enemy at arm's length. The South African Brigade meanwhile were dug in southeast of Bir el Haiad, but had the German armor between them and Sidi Rezegh. However, at 7.45 a.m., patrols reported the arrival from the south-east of a mass of enemy armor, some 200 tanks in all. On November 23, the 70th Division in Tobruk attacked the 25th Bologna in an attempt to reach the area of Sidi Rezegh, but elements of the Pavia soon arrived and broke up the British attack. On November 26, Scobie ordered a successful attack on the Ed Duda ridge, and in the early morning hours of November 27 the Tobruk garrison linked up with a small force of New Zealanders.[23]

Overnight Rommel once again split his forces with the 21st Panzer taking up a defensive position alongside the Africa Division between Sidi Rezegh and Tobruk and the 15th Panzer moving 24 kilometers west to Gasr el Arid to prepare for a battle of maneuver that General Ludwig Crüwell believed would favor the *Afrika Korps*. The 7th Armored Brigade, together with a battery of field artillery turned to meet this threat leaving the four companies of infantry and the artillery of the Support Group to carry through the attack to the north in anticipation of being reinforced by the 5th South African Infantry Brigade, which had been detached from the 1st South African Division at Bir el Gubi facing the Ariete division and was heading north to join them.[24] However, by the evening of November 21, the 4th Armored was 13 kilometers south east of Sidi Rezegh and the 22nd Armored Brigade were in contact with the German armor at Bir el Haiad, some 19 kilometers south-west of Sidi Rezegh.[25]

The 7th Armored had planned its attack northward to Tobruk to start at 8.30 a.m. on November 21. This presented a clear opportunity for a breakthrough to Tobruk with the whole of the 7th Armored Division concentrated and facing only the weakened 21st Panzer. However, XXX Corps commander Norrie, aware that the 7th Armored Division was down to 200 tanks, decided on caution.[26]

The most memorable action during the North African campaign of the 3rd Field Regiment was during the battle of Sidi Rezegh on November 23, 1941. However, the 21st Panzer, despite being considerably weaker in armor, proved superior in its combined arms tactics, pushing the 7th Armored Division back with a further fifty tanks lost, mainly from the 22nd Brigade.[27] The artillerymen of the 3rd Field Regiment managed to save five of their twenty-four guns from the battlefield. The 7th Armored Brigade withdrew with all but four of their 150 tanks out of commission or destroyed.[28] In four days, the Eighth Army had lost 530 tanks against Axis losses of about 100.[29]

Many of the gun crews were captured. In many places, the South African soldiers could only dig down to around 23 centimeters deep due to the solid limestone underneath their positions.[30] The Transvaal Horse Artillery engaged German tanks from the 15th and 21st Panzer divisions, the gunners firing over open sights as they were overrun. To the south, the 7th Indian Brigade captured Sidi Omar and most of the Libyan Omar strong points, the two westernmost strong points of the Axis border defenses. As darkness fell, those that could escape back to Allied lines under cover of darkness.[31]

They later recovered a further seven guns.[32] After the Battle of Sidi Rezegh, Acting Lieutenant General Sir Charles Willoughby Moke Norrie stated that the South African's "sacrifice resulted in the turning point of the battle, giving the Allies the upper hand in North Africa at that time."[33, 34]

On the XIII Corps front on November 22, the 5th New Zealand Brigade advanced north-east to capture Fort Capuzzo on the main Sollum–Bardia road.[35] The South Africans were surrounded on all sides by German armor and artillery, and were subjected to a continuous barrage. Losses in its supporting tank units caused a delay in attacks on the other strong points until replacements arrived.[36] One of the New Zealand military unit's historians described the fighting days as the 7th Indian Brigade's most difficult, with the men of the 4/16th Punjab Battalion having fought all morning to overcome resistance and the German 12th Oasis Company having formed the backbone of the defense of the whole position.[37]

The brigade attacked Bir Ghirba, south of Fort Capuzzo and the headquarters of the Savona Division but was repulsed. It tried to take cover in shallow slit trenches. Instead, in the early afternoon, Rommel attacked Sidi Rezegh with the 21st Panzer and captured the airfield. An attempt to recapture it failed and the Axis counteroffensive began to gain momentum. This continued until many of the officers were dead and the gunners had run out of ammunition.

The fighting at Sidi Rezegh continued through November 22, with South African Division's 5th Brigade by that time engaged to the south of the airfield. Fighting was desperate and gallant: for his actions during these two days of fighting, Brigadier Jock Campbell, commanding 7th Support Group, was awarded the Victoria Cross.

On November 24, the *Afrika Korps* and Ariete division headed for Sidi Omar, causing chaos and scattering the mainly rear echelon support units in their path, splitting XXX Corps and almost cutting off XIII Corps. The 6th New Zealand Brigade Group on the left flank at Bir el Hariga had been ordered north-west along the Trigh Capuzzo (Capuzzo-El Adem) to reinforce the 7th Armored Division at Sidi Rezegh.[38] The brigade arrived at Bir el Chleta, some 24 kilometers east of Sidi Rezagh, at first light on November 23, where they stumbled on the *Afrika Korps* headquarters and captured most of its staff (Crüwell was absent); no supplies reached either panzer division that day.[39] Later in the day, the 4th New Zealand Brigade Group was sent north of the 6th New Zealand Brigade to apply pressure on Tobruk and the 5th New Zealand Brigade covered Bardia and the Sollum–Halfaya positions.

On November 23, Rommel gathered his two panzer divisions in an attack with the Ariete armored division to cut off and destroy the rest of XXX Corps. By the end of the day, the 5th SA Brigade was destroyed and what remained of the defending force broke out of the pocket, heading south towards Bir el Gubi.[40] The Italian Supreme Command in Rome agreed to put the Italian XX Mobile Corps, including the Armored Ariete and the Motorized Division Trieste, under Rommel's command.[41]

British losses from November 19–23 were around 350 tanks destroyed and 150 severely damaged.[42] The *Afrika Korps* was down to forty tanks ready to be committed and Rommel ordered the relief of the frontier garrisons.[43] By November 23, the Ariete, Trieste, and Savona had knocked out about 200 British tanks and a similar number of vehicles were disabled or destroyed. On November 23, the 5th New Zealand Brigade continued its advance south-east, down the main road from Fort Capuzzo towards Sollum and cut off of the Axis positions from Sidi Omar to Sollum and Halfaya from Bardia and its supply route.

Rommel hoped to relieve the siege of Bardia and pose a large enough threat to the British rear echelon to complete the defeat of Operation Crusader. In the pocket were the remains of the 7th Armored Division, the 5th South African Infantry Brigade, and elements of the recently arrived 6th New Zealand Brigade. South of the border, the 5th Panzer Regiment of the 21st Panzer attacked the 7th Indian Brigade at Sidi Omar and were repulsed by the 1st Field Regiment Royal Artillery, firing over open sights at a range of 500 meters; a second attack left the 5th Panzer Regiment with few operational tanks.[44] The rest of the 21st Panzer had headed north-east, south of the border, to Halfaya.

By the evening of November 25, the 15th Panzer were west of Sidi Azeiz (where 5th New Zealand Brigade was headquartered) and down to fifty-three tanks, practically the entire remaining tank strength of the *Afrika Korps*.[45] The Axis column had only a tenuous link to its supply dumps on the coast between Bardia and Tobruk and supply convoys had to find a way past the 4th and 6th New Zealand Brigade Groups.

On November 26, the 15th Panzer, bypassing Sidi Azeiz headed for Bardia to resupply, arriving around midday. During the night, the 115th Regiment got to within 732 meters of Capuzzo but was disengaged to switch its attack towards Upper Sollum to meet the 21st Panzer coming from the south. In the early hours of November 27, Rommel met with the commanders of the 15th and 21st Panzer at Bardia. Meanwhile, the remains of the 21st Panzer attacked northwest from Halfaya towards Capuzzo and Bardia and the division who were approaching Bir Ghirba (24 kilometers northeast of Sidi Omar) from the west, were ordered towards Fort Capuzzo to clear any opposition and link with the 21st Panzer.[46] They were to be supported by the 15th Panzer's depleted 115th Infantry Regiment, which was ordered to advance with some artillery southeast from Bardia towards Fort Capuzzo.[47]

On November 25, in the 102nd Infantry Division Trento's sector, the 2nd Battalion Queens Royal Regiment attacked the "Bondi" strongpoint but was repelled.[48] The "Tugun" defenders, down to half their strength, exhausted and low on ammunition, food, and water, surrendered on the evening of November 25, after having defeated a British attack the previous night.[49]

On November 25, the 15th Panzer set off north-east for Sidi Azeiz and found the area empty and were constantly attacked by the Desert Air Force. It was necessary for the *Afrika Korps* to return to the Tobruk front where the 70th and New Zealand Divisions had gained the initiative. The two battalions of 5th New Zealand Brigade positioned between Fort Capuzzo and Sollum Barracks were engaged by the converging elements of the 15th and 21st Panzer at dusk on November 26.

Neumann-Silkow, however, felt the plan had little chance of success and resolved to advance to Sidi Azeiz (where he believed there was a major British supply dump), before heading to Tobruk.[50] Defending the 5th Brigade Headquarters at Sidi Azeiz was a company of the 22nd Infantry Battalion and the armored cars of the divisional cavalry plus some field artillery, anti-tank, anti-aircraft, and machine-gun units. Some 700 prisoners were taken, although the armored cars escaped.[51]

The 21st Panzer, while heading west to Tobruk from Bardia, ran into 5th New Zealand Brigade 22nd Battalion at Bir el Menastir and after an exchange lasting most of the day had been forced to detour south via Sidi Azeiz, delaying their return to Tobruk by a day.[52] By early afternoon, it became clear to Eighth Army Headquarters through radio intercepts that both *Afrika Korps* divisions were heading west to Tobruk, with the Ariete Division on their left.[53] The audacious maneuver by *Afrika Korps* had failed 6.4 kilometers of the main supply base of the Eighth Army.[54]

The dash of the *Afrika Korps* to the south removed a severe threat to the New Zealand Division left flank. The New Zealanders had not known of the threat because news of 7th Armored Division losses had not reached XIII Corps and German tank losses had been wildly overestimated.

Rommel ordered the 21st Panzer back to Tobruk and the 15th Panzer was to attack forces thought to be besieging the border positions between Fort Capuzzo and Sidi Omar. The New Zealand Division engaged elements of the *Afrika Korps*, Trieste, Bologna and Pavia Divisions, advancing west to retake Sidi Rezegh airfield and the overlooking positions to the north leading to Tobruk.[55] The 70th Division offensive was resumed on November 26 and next day elements had linked with the advancing New Zealanders of the 4th New Zealand Brigade at Ed Duda on the Tobruk bypass road; the 6th New Zealand Brigade cleared the Sidi Rezegh escarpment in a mutually-costly engagement.[56]

The New Zealanders were overrun early on November 27. Rommel was present to congratulate Brigadier James Hargest on the determined conduct of his men's defense. While Böttcher Group contained the British tank attacks in the Bologna sector, a battalion of Bersaglieri from the Trieste Division counterattacked the British break-out from Tobruk. The 15th Panzer would first have to capture Sidi Azeiz to provide space for this ambitious maneuver.

By November 27, things were therefore once more looking better for the Eighth Army: XXX Corps had more or less got itself reorganized after the chaos of the breakthrough and the New Zealand Division had linked up with the Tobruk garrison. By mid-afternoon, the 22nd Armored were under pressure but holding and the 4th Armored Brigade, with seventy tanks, had arrived on the 15th Panzer's left flank having dashed over 32 kilometers north-east cross country and was causing confusion in the panzer division's rear echelons. Auchinleck had spent three days during the period of the breakthrough at Cunningham's headquarters. At midday on November 27, the 15th Panzer reached Bir el Chleta and came into head-on contact with the reorganized 22nd Armored Brigade, now a composite regiment of under fifty tanks. The panzer division was also suffering heavy casualties from bombing.[57]

Once again, the New Zealand Division engaged in heavy fighting on the southeast end of the tenuous corridor into Tobruk, would be under direct threat from the *Afrika Korps*.[58] As night fell, the British tanks disengaged to replenish but inexplicably moved south to do this, leaving the route west open for the 15th Panzer. Cunningham had wanted to halt the offensive and withdraw but Auchinleck had handed Cunningham written orders on November 25 which included the sentence "There is only one order, attack and pursue."[59] On returning to Cairo on November 26, after conferring with his superiors, Auchinleck relieved Cunningham and appointed to command the Eighth Army his deputy Chief of Staff, Major General Neil Ritchie, whom he now promoted to acting lieutenant-general.

From November 26–27, in a determined attack, the 70th Division killed or forced out the defenders of several Italian concrete pillboxes before reaching Ed Duda. The New Zealand Brigade managed to link up with the 32nd Tank Brigade at Ed Duda and the 6th and 32nd Brigades secured a small bridgehead on the Tobruk front, but this was to last for five days. On November 27, the 6th New Zealand Brigade fought a fierce battle with a battalion of the Italian 9th Bersaglieri Regiment, which, having dug in among the Prophet's Tomb, used its machine guns very effectively. By November 28, the Bologna division had regrouped largely in the Bu Amud and Belhamed areas and the division was now stretched out along 13 kilometers from the Via Balbia to the Bypass Road, fighting in several places. The Reuters correspondent with the Tobruk garrison wrote on November 28:

The division holding the perimeter continues to fight with utmost bravery and determination. They are stubbornly holding small isolated defense pits, surrounded with barbed wire. On the night of November 27–28, Rommel had discussed with Crüwell plans for the next day, indicating that his priority was to cut the Tobruk corridor and destroy the enemy forces fighting there. Crüwell wanted to eliminate the threat of the 7th Armored Division tanks to the south and felt this needed attention first. 15th Panzer spent most of November 28 once more engaged with 4th and 22nd Armored and dealing with supply problems. Despite being outnumbered by two to one in tanks and at times immobile because of lack of fuel, 15th Panzer succeeded in pushing the British tank force southwards, while moving westwards.[60]

The Italian Bersaglieri captured 1,000 patients and 700 medical staff.[61] They also freed some 200 Germans being held captive in the enclosure on the grounds of the hospital.[62] The New Zealand Official History mentions the capture of 1,000 patients and implies that they were captured by Germans.

It had not been possible to create a firm communications link between the 70th and the New Zealand Divisions, making coordination between the two somewhat difficult. "They're Jerries!" echoed many as the German infantrymen ran down into the *wadi* and, as if to show that they did not intend to be trifled with, fired a few bullets into the sand.[63] At 6 p.m., the Australian 2/13th Battalion moved to reinforce Ed Duda, where some platoons took severe casualties from intense shelling.[64]

On the night of November 28, Rommel rejected Crüwell's plan for a direct advance towards Tobruk, having had no success with head-on attacks on Tobruk during all the months of the siege. When two Italian motorized battalions of Bersaglieri together with supporting tanks, anti-tank guns and artillery moved towards Sidi Rezegh, they overran a New Zealand field hospital. He decided on a circling movement to attack Ed Duda from the south-west and carry on through to cut off the enemy forces outside the Tobruk perimeter and destroy them.[65]

The cooks were preparing the evening meal on November 28, when over the eastern ridge of the *wadi* appeared German tracked troop-carrying vehicles, from which sprang men in slate-grey uniforms and knee boots, armed with Tommy guns, rifles, and machine guns. The remnants of the 21st Panzer were supposed to be moving up on their right to form a pincer but were in disarray when von Ravenstein failed to return from a reconnaissance that morning, having been captured. Fierce fighting continued through November 28 around the Tobruk corridor with the battle ebbing and flowing. In the afternoon, to the east of Sidi Rezegh, the 21st Battalion of New Zealanders was overrun on the much contested Point 175 by elements of the Ariete Division.[66] The New Zealanders were caught off-guard, having mistaken the attackers for reinforcements from the 1st South African Brigade, which had been due to arrive from the southwest to reinforce XIII Corps.[67]

During the morning, the 7th Armored Division were ordered to advance to provide direct assistance. According to Lieutenant Colonel Howard Kippenberger, who later rose to command the New Zealand 2nd Division:

> About 1730 pm, damned Italian Motorized Division [Ariete] turned up. 1st SA Brigade were to all intents and purposes tied to the armored brigades, unable to move in open ground without them because of the threat from the panzer divisions. They passed with five tanks leading, twenty following, and a huge column of transport and guns, and rolled straight over our infantry on Point 175.[68]

The 24th and 26th Battalions met a similar fate at Sidi Rezegh. A German armored attack on Belhamed practically destroyed the 20th Battalion.[69] The New Zealanders suffered heavily in the attacks: 879 dead, 1,699 wounded, 2,042 captured.[70]

On the morning of November 29, the 15th Panzer set off west travelling south of Sidi Rezegh.

However, a counterattack by 4th Royal Tank Regiment supported by Australian infantry recaptured the lost positions and the German units fell back 914 meters to form a new position.[71]

Meanwhile, the leading elements of the 15th Panzer reached Ed Duda, but made little progress before nightfall against determined defenses. Meanwhile, radio intercepts had given the Eighth Army to believe that the 21st Panzer and Ariete were in trouble and Lieutenant General Ritchie ordered the 7th Armored Division to stick to them like hell.[72]

Following the resistance at Ed Duda Rommel decided to withdraw the 15th Panzer to Bir Bu Creimisa, 8 kilometers to the south, and relaunch his attack northeast from there on November 30, aiming between Sidi Rezegh and Belhamed while leaving Ed Duda outside his encircling pocket. On the evening of November 29, the 1st South African Brigade was placed under command of the 2nd New Zealand Division and ordered to advance north to recapture Point 175.

Eight British Matilda tanks provided the preliminary bombardment for a counterattack by two companies of the 2/13th Australian Infantry Battalion on the night of November 29–30. At 6.15 a.m. on December 1, the 15th Panzer renewed their attack towards Belhamed, supported by a massive artillery effort, and once again, the New Zealand Division came under intense pressure. In a bayonet charge against German positions, the 2/13th lost two killed and five wounded, but took 167 prisoners.[73] The weakened 24th Battalion was overrun as were two companies of 26th Battalion, although on the eastern flank of the position, the 25th Battalion repelled an attack from the Ariete moving from Point 175.[74]

By mid-afternoon, the New Zealand 6th Brigade was being heavily pressed on the western end of the Sidi Rezegh position. The 4th Armored Brigade arrived at Belhamed and may have had the opportunity for a decisive intervention since they outnumbered the forty or so 15th Panzer Division tanks attacking the position, but they believed their orders were to cover the withdrawal of the remains of 6th New Zealand Brigade, which precluded an offensive operation.[75]

By December 3, the 11th Indian Brigade was heavily engaged in action against a strongpoint near Bir el Gubi, some 25 miles south of Ed Duda. It reached the XXX Corps lines with little further interruption and, in the early hours, the 3,500 men and 700 vehicles that had emerged were heading back to Egypt.[76]

Once again, Rommel became concerned with the cut off units in the border strong points, and on December 2, believing that he had won the battle at Tobruk, he sent the Geissler Advance Guard and the Knabe Advanced Guard battalion groups to open the routes to Bardia and to Capuzzo and thence Sollum.[77] Orders were issued by Freyberg to be ready to move east at 5.30 p.m. However, Rommel soon realized he could not deal with the situation at Tobruk and also send a strong force east, and the Ariete went no further than Gasr el Arid.

On December 4, Rommel launched a renewed attack on Ed Duda, which was repulsed by the 70th Division's 14th Infantry Brigade. The 15th Panzer, which had been resupplying, renewed its attack at 4.30 p.m. and the Trieste cut the tenuous link established with Tobruk. The New Zealanders became involved in a desperate fighting withdrawal from its western positions. Nevertheless, the division, showing admirable discipline, was formed up by 5.30 p.m., and having paused an hour for the tanks and artillery to join them from the west, set off at 6.45 p.m. Rommel drew the inference that army headquarters had given up hope of holding the Tobruk corridor and signaled mid-morning that, without the South Africans, his position would be untenable and that he was planning a withdrawal. The 1st and 2nd Battalions of the Italian 136th Giovani Regiment Fascisti from this hilltop position successfully fought off repeated attacks by the British armor and Indian infantry units during the first week of December.

During the morning of December 1, Freyberg, commanding the 2nd New Zealand Division, saw a signal from the Eighth Army indicating that the South African Brigade were now to be under command of the 7th Armored Division. When it was clear that the attack would fail, Rommel resolved to withdraw from the eastern perimeter of Tobruk to allow him to concentrate his strength against the growing threat from XXX Corps to the south.

The remains of the 2nd New Zealand Division were now concentrated near Zaafran, 5 miles east of Belhamed and slightly further north-east of Sidi Rezegh. On December 3, the Geissler Advance Guard was heavily defeated by elements of the 5th New Zealand Brigade on the Bardia road near Menastir. All *Afrika Korps* tanks were undergoing overhaul, so Rommel ordered the rest of the 15th Panzer and the Italian Mobile Corps eastwards on December 4, which caused considerable alarm at Eighth Army Headquarters.

Following the withdrawal of the 2nd New Zealand Division, Ritchie had reorganized his rear echelon units to release to the front line 4th Indian Infantry Division's 5th and 11th Brigades as well as 22nd Guards Brigade. To the south, the Knabe force at the same time fared slightly better on the main track to Capuzzo, coming up against "Goldforce" (based on the Central India Horse reconnaissance regiment) and retiring after an artillery exchange.[78] Rommel insisted once again on trying to relieve the frontier forts.[79] One British historian reported:

> Although Norrie had an overwhelming superiority in every arm in the area of Bir Gubi, the failure to concentrate them and co-ordinate the action of all arms in detail had allowed one Italian battalion group to frustrate the action of his whole corps and inflict heavy casualties on one brigade. Once again the Allied infantry were exposed to a possible armored attack as Army HQ had ordered Norrie to send 4th Armored Brigade east to cover against the developing threat to Bardia and Sollum.[80]

On December 4, the Pavia and Trento Divisions launched counterattacks against the 70th Division in an attempt to contain them within the Tobruk perimeter, and reportedly recaptured the "Plonk" and "Doc" strong points. Rommel had been told on December 5 by the Italian Supreme Command that supply could not improve until the end of the month when the paratroopers supply from Sicily would start. By December 7, the 4th Armored Brigade had closed up and the opportunity lost. However, he hesitated until too late in the day and was unable to strike a conclusive blow before dark.[81]

On December 5, the 11th Indian Brigade continued its attack against Point 174. The Indian Brigade was broken and had to be withdrawn to refit and arrangements made to bring the 22nd Guards Brigade into their place.[82] Despite the German 90th Light Division pulling out of the Tobruk sector on December 4, the Bologna Division held out until the night of December 8–9, when trucks were finally assigned to give them some support. Crüwell was unaware that the 4th Armored Brigade, now with 126 tanks, was over 32 kilometers away and he withdrew to the west. Worse, the 15th Panzer's skillful commander, Neumann-Silkow was mortally wounded late on the 6th.[83]

Crüwell still had the opportunity to strike a heavy blow on December 6 as the 4th Armored Brigade made no move to close up to the 22nd Guards Brigade. The 4th Armored continued to fight for another month and a half. Realizing that success was now unlikely at Bir el Gubi, Crüwell decided to narrow his front and shorten his lines of communication by abandoning the Tobruk front and withdrawing to the positions at Gazala, 16 kilometers to his rear, which had been in preparation by Italian rear echelon units and which he had occupied by December 8.[84] The weakened Italian Mobile Corps anchored the southern end of the line at Alem Hamza while the *Afrika Korps* were placed behind the southern flank ready to counterattack.[85]

Rommel ordered his divisions to retreat westwards, leaving the Savona to hold out as long as possible in the Sollum, Halfaya, and Bardia area. As dusk approached, the *Afrika Korps* and Armored Division Ariete intervened to relieve the Young Fascist garrison at Point 174 and cause mayhem in 11th Indian Brigade. That night, the 70th Division captured the German-held "Walter" and "Freddie" strong points without any resistance; however, one Pavia battalion made a stand on Point 157, inflicting heavy casualties on the 2nd Durham Light Infantry with its dug-in infantry before being overcome after midnight.[86] He placed Italian X Corps at the coastal end of the line and Italian XXI Corps inland. In a final action on the part of the British 70th Division, the Polish Carpathian Brigade attacked elements of the Brescia covering the Axis retreat and captured the White Knoll position.[87] The Tobruk defenders were finally relieved as a result after a nineteen-day battle. Rommel also sent forward to XIII Corps the 4th Indian Infantry Division and 5th New Zealand Infantry Brigade.[88]

On December 14, the Polish Independent Brigade was brought forward to join the New Zealanders and prepare a new attack for the early hours of December 15. They were thus left in a vulnerable salient, and the 7th Indian Infantry Brigade to their left were ordered to send northwards the 4th Battalion 11th Sikh Regiment, supported by guns from the 25th Field Regiment and twelve Valentine tanks from the 8th Royal Tank Regiment, to ease their position.[89] This force found itself confronted by the *Afrika Korps*, fielding thirty-nine tanks together with 300 trucks of infantry and guns.[90]

The 4th Armored Brigade engaged the 15th Panzer, disabling eleven more tanks. The attack took the defenders by surprise. In the hope of getting better coordination between his infantry and armor, Ritchie transferred the 7th Armored Division to XIII Corps and directed XXX Corps Headquarters to take South African 2nd Division under command and conduct a siege of the border fortresses. Taking heavy casualties, they nevertheless managed to knock out fifteen German tanks and stall the counterattack.[91]

Godwin-Austen ordered Gott to get the British armor to a position where it could engage the *Afrika Korps*, unaware that Gott and his senior commanders were no longer confident they could defeat the enemy directly, despite their superiority in numbers; as the Germans had superior tactics and anti-tank artillery, Gott and his commanders favored making a wide detour to attack the enemy's soft-skinned elements and lines of supply to immobilize them.[92] Once again, the 7th Armored Division was not in place to intervene and it was left to the force's artillery and supporting tanks to face the threat. The 5th New Zealand Brigade attacked along an 8-mile front from the coast while the 5th Indian Infantry Brigade made a flanking attack at Alem Hamza. The two brigades made good progress but narrowly failed to breach the line.[93] The Eighth Army launched its attack on the Gazala line on December 13. Although the Trieste division successfully held Alem Hamza, 1st Battalion Buffs from the 5th Indian Infantry succeeded in taking Point 204, some miles west of Alem Hamza.

Meanwhile, on December 14, to the south, there was little activity from the *Afrika Korps* and the 7th Indian Infantry Brigade were limited to patrolling through a shortage of ammunition as supply problems multiplied.[94] At Alem Hamza, the 5th Indian Brigade renewed its attack but made no progress against determined defense, and at Point 204, the 5th Indian Brigade's battalion of the Royal East Kent Regiment supported by ten I tanks, an armored car squadron of the Central India Horse, a company of Bombay Sappers and Miners, and the artillery of the 31st Field Regiment and elements of 73rd Anti-Tank Regiment and some anti-aircraft guns, were attacked by ten or twelve tanks, the remnants of the Armored Division Ariete, which they beat off.[95]

On December 15, the Brescia and Pavia, with Trento in close support, repelled a strong Polish-New Zealand attack, thus freeing the German 15th Panzer Division that had returned to the Gazala Line to be used elsewhere. In *Crusader: Eighth Army's Forgotten Victory, November 1941–January 1942*, author Richard Humble wrote:

> The Poles and New Zealanders made good initial progress, but the Italians rallied well, and by noon it was clear to [General Alfred] Godwin-Austen that his two brigades lacked the weight to achieve a breakthrough on the right flank. It was the same story in the center, where the Italians of "Trieste" continued to repulse 5th Indian Brigade's attack on Point 208. By mid-afternoon the III Corps attack had been fought to a halt all along the line.[96]

By the afternoon of December 15, the 4th Armored, having looped round to the south, was at Bir Halegh el Eleba, some 48 kilometers northwest of Alem Hamza, and ideally placed both to strike at the rear of the *Afrika Korps* and advance north to cut Panzer Group *Afrika*'s main lines of communication along the coast, which Godwin-Austen was urging them to do.[97]

Fortunately for the rest of the 5th Indian Brigade, it was by then too late in the day for the attacking force to collect itself and advance further to intervene at Alem Hamza.[98] The attackers too had suffered heavily in the engagement: the German commander was heard on a radio intercept to report the inability of his force to exploit his success because of losses sustained.[99]

In the afternoon, the 15th Panzer moving west were able to pass by the 4th Armored's rear and block any return move to the north. Despite the vehement objections of the Italian generals as well as Crüwell, he ordered an evacuation of the Gazala line on the night of the 15th.[100]

As his lines of supply shortened and supplies to El Agheila improved, he was able to rebuild his tank force while correspondingly the Eighth Army lines of supply became more and more stretched. While the mere presence of the British armor had tipped Rommel's hand to withdraw from Gazala, the opportunity to gain a decisive victory had been missed.[101]

Auchinleck's determination and Ritchie's aggression had removed the Axis threat to Egypt and the Suez Canal for the time being. This allowed the Axis forces to fall back to a tactically more desirable defensive line at El Agheila during the first two weeks of January without having to deal with pressure from the enemy.[102]

By December 15, the *Afrika Korps* was down to eight working tanks, although the Ariete still had some thirty. Rommel considered Point 204 a key position and so great a part of the available neighboring armored and infantry units were committed to attack it on December 15, and in fierce and determined fighting, the attacking force, the Ariete and the 15th Panzer Division, with the 8th Bersaglieri Regiment and the 115th Truck Infantry Regiment, overran the Royal East Kent Regiment and its supporting elements during the afternoon. Rommel, who had greater respect for the capabilities of the 7th Armored at this time than either Crüwell (or apparently even Gott), became very concerned about a perceived flanking move to the south by the British Armor. However, early on December 16, only a small detachment was sent north, which caused serious confusion among Panzer Group Africa's rear echelon but was not decisive, while the rest of the brigade headed south to meet its petrol supplies. Over the following ten days, Rommel's forces withdrew to a line between Ajdabiya and El Haseia, maintaining his lines of communication and avoiding being cut off and surrounded as the Italians had been the previous year.

On December 27, he was able in a three-day tank battle at El Haseia to inflict heavy damage on the 22nd Armored Brigade forcing the leading echelons of the Eighth Army to withdraw. The Royal East Kent Regiment lost over 1,000 men killed or captured with only seventy-one men and a battery of field artillery escaping.

Although the action had originally been a reconnaissance in force, finding the Eighth Army forward elements to be dispersed and tired, in his typical manner he took advantage of the situation and drove the Eighth Army back to Gazala where they took up defensive positions along Rommel's old line. The 5,000 defenders, mainly 55th Infantry Division Savona's troops, were already desperately short of food and water and after this had to rely on meagre supplies from air drops. However, Rommel had failed to relieve the isolated German–Italian strongholds on the Libya–Egypt border and the 7,000 strong garrison at Bardia surrendered on January 2, 1942 after an attack by the 2nd South African Division.[103] Sollum fell to the South Africans on January 12 after a small fiercely fought engagement. This completed the surrounding of the heavily fortified Halfaya position, which included the escarpment, the plateau above it, and the surrounding ravines, and cut it off from the sea and any potential seaborne supply. Here, a stalemate set in as both sides regrouped, rebuilt, and reorganized.

While it may have proved a limited success, Operation Crusader showed Rommel's *Afrika Korps* could be beaten and is a fine illustration of the dynamic, back and forth fighting that characterized the North African Campaign. The carefully prepared positions allowed the defenders to hold out obstinately against the heavy artillery and aerial bombardment with relatively few casualties, but hunger and thirst forced a capitulation on January 17.[104] Of the commander of the Italian division, General Fedele de Giorgis, Rommel reported: "Superb leadership was shown by the Italian General de Giorgis, who commanded this German–Italian force in its two months' struggle."[105]

On January 21, Rommel launched from El Agheila a surprise counterattack. Geoffrey Cox wrote: "Sidi Rezegh was the forgotten battle of the Desert War. Crusader was won by a hair's breadth by the newly designated Eighth Army, but had we lost it, we would have had to fight the battle of El Alamein six months or a year earlier, without the decisive weapon of the Sherman tank."[106]

The First Battle of El Alamein

General Ritchie had decided not to hold the defenses on the Egyptian border because the defensive plan there relied on his infantry holding defended localities, while a strong armored force was held back in reserve to foil any attempts to penetrate or outflank the fixed defenses. The Mersa defense plan also included an armored reserve, but in its absence, Ritchie believed he could organize his infantry to cover the minefields between the defended localities to prevent Axis engineers from having undisturbed access.[1]

Since General Ritchie had virtually no armored units left fit to fight, the infantry positions would be defeated in detail. Axis positions near El Alamein, only 106 kilometers from Alexandria, were dangerously close to the ports and cities of Egypt, the base facilities of the Commonwealth forces and the Suez Canal, and the Axis forces were too far from their base at Tripoli in Libya to remain at El Alamein indefinitely, which led both sides to accumulate supplies for more offensives against the constraints of time and distance. Following its defeat at the Battle of Gazala in Eastern Libya in June 1942, the British Eighth Army, commanded by Lieutenant General Neil Ritchie, had retreated east from the Gazala line into north-western Egypt as far as Mersa Matruh, roughly 160 kilometers inside the border.

Only 64 kilometers to the south of El Alamein, the steep slopes of the Qattara Depression ruled out the possibility of Axis armor moving around the southern flank of his defenses and limited the width of the front Ritchie had to defend. He concluded that his inferiority in armor after the Gazala defeat meant he would be unable to prevent Rommel either breaking through his center or enveloping his open left flank to the south in the same way he had at Gazala. He decided instead to employ delaying tactics while withdrawing a further 160 kilometers or more east to a more defensible position near El Alamein on the Mediterranean coast. To defend the Matruh line, Ritchie placed the 10th Indian Infantry

Division and 50th Northumbrian Infantry Division, 24 kilometers down the coast at Gerawla under X Corps Headquarters, newly arrived from Syria.[2] Inland from X Corps would be XIII Corps with the 5th Indian Infantry Division (with only one infantry brigade, 29th Indian, and two artillery regiments) around Sidi Hamza, about 32 kilometers inland, and the newly arrived 2nd New Zealand Division (short one brigade, the 6th, which had been left out of combat in case the division was captured and it would form the nucleus of a new division) at Minqar Qaim, on the escarpment 48 kilometers inland, and the 1st Armored Division in the open desert to the south.[3] The 1st Armored Division had taken over the 4th and 22nd Armored Brigades from the 7th Armored Division, which by this time had only three tank regiments between them.[4]

On June 25, General Claude Auchinleck, Commander-in-Chief Middle East Command, relieved Ritchie and assumed direct command of the Eighth Army himself. He decided not to seek a decisive confrontation at the Mersa Matruh position.[5] Auchinleck had planned a second delaying position at Fukah, some 48 kilometers east of Matruh, and at 9.20 p.m., he issued the orders for a withdrawal to Fukah. Rommel ordered the 90th Light Division to resume its advance, requiring it to cut the coast road behind the 50th Division by the evening.[6] The late change of orders resulted in some confusion in the forward formations of X Corps and XIII Corps between the desire to inflict damage on the enemy and the intention not to get trapped in the Matruh position but retreat in good order. While preparing the Alamein positions, Auchinleck fought strong delaying actions, first at Mersa Matruh on June 26–27 and then Fukah on June 28. It succeeded in breaking out on the night of June 27 without serious losses and withdraw east.[7] As the 21st Panzer moved on Minqar Qaim, the 2nd New Zealand Division found itself surrounded. Early on June 27, resuming its advance, the 90th Light was checked by British 50th Division's artillery. Confusion in communication led the division withdrawing immediately to the El Alamein position.[8] The 15th Panzer were blocked by the 4th Armored and 7th Motor Brigades, but the 21st Panzer were ordered on to attack Minqar Qaim. Meanwhile, the 15th and 21st Panzer Divisions advanced east above and below the escarpment. The result was poor coordination between the two forward corps and units within them. Late on June 26, the 90th Light and 21st Panzer Divisions managed to find their way through the minefields in the center of the front.

The Qattara Depression lay 32 kilometers to the south. In the process, the 5th Indian Division in particular sustained heavy casualties, including the destruction of the 29th Indian Infantry Brigade at Fukah.[9] Axis forces captured more than 6,000 prisoners, in addition to forty tanks and an enormous quantity of supplies.[10]

Alamein itself was an inconsequential railway station on the coast. In the darkness, there was considerable confusion as they came across enemy units made camp for the night. They were ordered to break out southwards into the desert and then make their way east. The British Army in Egypt recognized this before the war and had the Eighth Army begin construction of several "boxes" (dug-outs and surrounded by minefields and barbed wire), the most developed being around the railway station at Alamein.[11] Only then did they discover that the withdrawal order had been given. X Corps, having made an unsuccessful attempt to secure a position on the escarpment, were out of touch with the Eighth Army from 7.30 p.m. until 4.30 a.m. Ruweisat Ridge lay 16 kilometers to the south; this is a low stony ridge that nonetheless gave excellent observation for many miles over the surrounding desert. Most of the line, however, was just open, empty desert.[12]

Lieutenant General William Norrie organized the position and started to construct three defended "boxes." The first and strongest, at El Alamein on the coast, had been partly wired and mined by the 1st South African Division. At 9 p.m. on June 28, X Corps, organized into brigade groups, headed south. The line the British chose to defend stretched between the sea and the Qattara Depression, which meant that Rommel could outflank it only by taking a significant detour to the south and crossing the Sahara Desert. The withdrawal of XIII Corps had left the southern flank of X Corps on the coast at Matruh exposed and their line of retreat compromised by the cutting of the coastal road 27 kilometers east of Matruh. Auchinleck ordered XIII Corps to provide support but they were in no position to do so. The Bab el Qattara box—some 32 kilometers from the coast and 13 kilometers south-west of the Ruweisat Ridge—had been dug but had not been wired or mined, while at the Naq Abu Dweis box, on the edge of the Qattara Depression, 55 kilometers from the coast, very little work had been done.[13]

On June 29, the order came for XXX Corps, the 1st South African, 5th, and 10th Indian divisions to take the coastal sector on the right of the front and XIII Corps, the 2nd New Zealand Division, and 4th Indian divisions to be on the left. Supplies remained a problem because the Axis staff had originally expected a pause of six weeks after the capture of Tobruk. Defensive positions were constructed west of Alexandria and on the approaches to Cairo, while considerable areas in the Nile delta were flooded. On June 30, Rommel's Panzer Army Africa approached the Alamein position. Auchinleck, although believing he could stop Rommel at Alamein, felt he could not ignore the possibility that he might once more be out maneuvered or out fought.[14] The Axis, too, believed that the capture of Egypt was imminent. Italian leader Benito Mussolini, sensing an historic moment, flew to Libya to prepare for his triumphal entry into Cairo.[15]

Rommel had driven them forward ruthlessly, being confident that, provided he struck quickly before the Eighth Army had time to settle, his momentum would take him through the Alamein position and he could then advance to the Nile with little further opposition. The remains of the 1st Armored Division and the 7th Armored Division were to be held as a mobile army reserve.[16] His intention was for the fixed defensive positions to channelize and disorganize the enemy's advance while mobile units would attack their flanks and rear.[17] The scattering of X Corps at Mersa Matruh disrupted Auchinleck's plan for occupying the Alamein defenses. German air units were also exhausted and providing little help against the Royal Air Force's all-out attack on the Axis supply lines that, with the arrival of United States Army Air Forces heavy bombers, could reach as far as Benghazi.[18] Although captured supplies proved useful, water and ammunition were constantly in short supply, while a shortage of transport impeded the distribution of the supplies that the Axis forces did have.[1]

During the early afternoon, the 90th Light had extricated itself from the El Alamein box defenses and resumed its move eastward. An Italian division was to attack the Alamein box from the west and another was to follow the 90th Light Division. The Italian XX Corps was to follow the *Afrika Korps* and deal with the Qattara box, while the 133rd Littorio Armored Division and German reconnaissance units would protect the right flank.[20]

The British position in Egypt was desperate: the rout from Mersa Matruh had created a panic in the British headquarters at Cairo, something later called "the Flap." On what came to be referred to as "Ash Wednesday," at British headquarters, rear echelon units, and the British Embassy, the British frantically burned confidential papers in anticipation of the fall of the city. The Axis forces were exhausted and under strength. He therefore believed that, to maintain his army, plans must be made for the possibility of a further retreat while maintaining morale and retaining the support and co-operation of the Egyptians.

The British ran into the 15th Panzer Division just south of Deir el Shein and drove it west. The 90th Light Division was then to veer north to cut the coastal road and trap the defenders of the Alamein box (which Rommel thought was occupied by the remains of the 50th Infantry Division) and the *Afrika Korps* would veer right to attack the rear of XIII Corps. Rommel's plan was for the 90th Light Division and the 15th and 21st Panzer divisions of the *Afrika Korps*—to penetrate the Eighth Army lines between the Alamein box and Deir el Abyad. On June 30, the 90th Light Division was still 24 kilometers short of its start line, the 21st Panzer Division was immobilized through lack of fuel, and the promised air support had yet to move into its advanced airfields.[21]

At 3 a.m. on July 1, the 90th Light Infantry Division advanced east but strayed too far north and ran into the 1st South African Division's defenses and became pinned down.[22, 23] The 15th and 21st Panzer Divisions of the *Afrika Korps* were delayed by a sandstorm and then a heavy air attack. It was broad daylight by the time they circled round the back of Deir el Abyad where they found the feature to the east of it occupied by the 18th Indian Infantry Brigade that, after a hasty journey from Iraq, had occupied the exposed position just west of Ruweisat Ridge and east of Deir el Abyad at Deir el Shein to create one of Norrie's additional defensive boxes.[24]

At about 10 a.m. on July 1, the 21st Panzer Division attacked Deir el Shein. The 18th Indian Infantry Brigade, supported by twenty-three 25-pounder gun-howitzers, sixteen of the new 6-pounder anti-tank guns, and nine Matilda tanks, held out the whole day in desperate fighting, but by evening, the Germans succeeded in over-running them.[25] The time they bought allowed Auchinleck to organize the defense of the western end of Ruweisat Ridge.[26] The 1st Armored Division had been sent to intervene at Deir el Shein. By the end of the day's fighting, the *Afrika Korps* had thirty-seven tanks left out of its initial complement.[27] Rommel had planned to attack on June 30, but supply and transport difficulties had resulted in a day's delay, vital to the defending forces reorganizing on the Alamein line. It came under artillery fire from the three South African brigade groups and was forced to dig in.[28]

Italian X Corps, meanwhile was to hold El Mreir. Robcol—in line with normal British Army practice for *ad hoc* formations—was named after its commander, Brigadier Robert Waller, the Commander Royal Artillery of the 10th Indian Infantry Division.[29] Robcol was able to buy time, and by late afternoon the two British Armored brigades joined the battle with the 4th Armored Brigade engaging the 15th Panzer and 22nd Armored Brigade 21st Panzer respectively.[30] They drove back repeated attacks by the Axis armor, who then withdrew before dusk. The British defense of Ruweisat Ridge relied on an improvised formation called "Robcol," comprising a regiment each of field artillery and light anti-aircraft artillery and a company of infantry. Once again, the 90th Light failed to make progress, so Rommel called the *Afrika Korps* to abandon its planned sweep southward and instead join the effort to break through to the coast road by attacking east toward Ruweisat Ridge. The now enlarged Robcol became "Walgroup."[31] Meanwhile, the RAF made heavy air attacks on the Axis units.[32]

The British reinforced Ruweisat on the night of July 2. That same day, Rommel ordered the resumption of the offensive. By this stage, the *Afrika Korps* had only twenty-six operational tanks.[33] There was a sharp armored exchange south of Ruweisat ridge during the morning and the main Axis advance was held.[34] The next day, July 3, Rommel ordered the *Afrika Korps* to resume its attack on the Ruweisat ridge with the Italian XX Motorized Corps on its southern flank. On July 3, the RAF flew 780 sorties.

To the south, on July 5, the New Zealand group resumed its advance northwards towards El Mreir, intending to cut the rear of the Ariete Division. The plan was that the New Zealand 2nd Division, with the remains of the Indian 5th Division and 7th Motor Brigade under its command, would swing north to threaten the Axis flank and rear.[35]

Meanwhile, the Eighth Army was reorganizing and rebuilding, benefiting from its short lines of communication. Rommel reported to the German High Command that his three German divisions numbered just 1,200–1,500 men each and resupply was proving highly problematic because of enemy interference from the air. The Italian commander ordered his battalions to fight their way out independently, but the Ariete lost 531 men (about 350 were prisoners), thirty-six pieces of artillery, six tanks, and fifty-five trucks.[36] By the end of the day, the Ariete Division had only five tanks.[37] The day ended once again with the *Afrika Korps* and Ariete Division coming off second best to the superior numbers of the British 22nd Armored and 4th Armored Brigades, frustrating Rommel's attempts to resume his advance.[38] The RAF once again played its part, flying 900 sorties during the day.[39]

Heavy fire from the Italian Motorized Division Brescia at El Mreir, however, 8 kilometers north of the Qattara box, checked their progress and led XIII Corps to call off its attack.[40] By July 4, the Australian 9th Division had entered the line in the north, and on July 9, the Indian 5th Infantry Brigade also returned, taking over the Ruweisat position. He expected to have to remain on the defensive for at least two weeks.[41]

At this point, Rommel decided his exhausted forces could make no further headway without resting and regrouping. The Allied Desert Air Force was concentrating fiercely on his fragile and elongated supply routes while British mobile columns moving west and striking from the south were causing havoc in the Axis rear echelons.[42] Rommel could afford these losses even less since shipments from Italy had been substantially reduced. In June, he received 5,000 tons of supplies compared with 34,000 tons in May and 400 vehicles compared with 2,000 in May.[43]

This force encountered the Armored Division Ariete's artillery, which was driving on the southern flank of the division as it attacked Ruweisat. At the same time, the fresh Indian 161st Infantry Brigade reinforced the depleted Indian 5th Infantry Division.[44]

By early afternoon, the feature was captured and was then held against a series of Axis counterattacks throughout the day. A small column of armor, motorized infantry, and guns then set off to raid Deir el Abyad and caused a battalion of Italian infantry to surrender. Meanwhile, XIII Corps would prevent the Axis from moving troops north to reinforce the coastal sector.[45]

The raiding parties were to be provided by 1st Armored Division.[46] On July 8, Auchinleck ordered the new XXX Corps commander, Lieutenant General William Ramsden, to capture the low ridges at Tel el Eisa and Tel el Makh Khad and then to push mobile battle groups south toward Deir el Shein and raiding parties west toward the airfields at El Daba. The bombardment was the heaviest barrage yet experienced in North Africa, which created panic in the inexperienced soldiers of the Italian 60th Infantry Division Sabratha who had only just occupied sketchy defenses in the sector.[47] Following a bombardment, which started at 3.30 a.m. on July 10, the Australian 26th Brigade launched an attack against the ridge north of Tel el Eisa station along the coast. The Australian attack took more than 1,500 prisoners, routed an Italian Division, and overran the German Signals Intercept Company 621.[48] Meanwhile, the South Africans had by late morning taken Tel el Makh Khad and were in covering positions.[49]

Elements of the German 164th Light Division and Italian 101st Motorized Division Trieste arrived to plug the gap torn in the Axis defenses.[50] That afternoon and evening, tanks from the German 15th Panzer and Italian Division Trieste launched counterattacks against the Australian positions, the counterattacks failing in the face of overwhelming Allied artillery and the Australian Anti-tank guns.[51] Rommel was by this time suffering from the extended length of his supply lines. To relieve the pressure on the right and center of the Eighth Army line, XIII Corps on the left advanced from the Qattara box, known to the New Zealanders as the Kaponga box. At first light on July 11, the Australian 2/24th Battalion supported by tanks from 44th Royal Tank Regiment attacked the western end of Tel el Eisa hill.[52]

Ramsden tasked the Australian 9th Division with the 44th Royal Tank Regiment under command with the Tel el Eisa objective and the South African 1st Division with eight supporting tanks, Tel el Makh Khad. Its progress was checked at the Miteirya ridge and it was forced to withdraw that evening to the El Alamein box.[53] During the day, more than 1,000 Italian prisoners were taken.[54]

After seven days of fierce fighting, the battle in the north for Tel el Eisa salient petered out. Rommel was still determined to drive the British forces from the northern salient. On July 12, the 21st Panzer Division launched a counterattack against Trig 33 and Point 24, which was beaten off after a two-hour and thirty-minute fight, with more than 600 German dead and wounded left strewn in front of the Australian positions.[55] The next day, the 21st Panzer Division launched an attack against Point 33 and South African positions in the El Alamein box.[56] Although the Australian defenders had been forced back from Point 24, heavy casualties had been inflicted on the 21st Panzer Division.[57] On July 16, the Australians, supported by British tanks, launched an attack to try to take Point 24, but were forced back by German counterattacks, suffering nearly 50 percent casualties.[58, 59]

The Australian 9th Division estimated at least 2,000 Axis troops had been killed and more than 3,700 prisoners of war taken in the battle.[60] Possibly the most important feature of the battle, however, was that the Australians had captured Signals Intercept Company 621. That source of intelligence was now lost to Rommel.[61]

The attack was halted by intense artillery fire from the defenders. This unit had provided Rommel with priceless intelligence, gleaned from intercepting British radio communications. The attack commenced at 11 p.m. on July 14. As the Axis forces dug in, Auchinleck, having drawn a number of German units to the coastal sector during the Tel el Eisa fighting, developed a plan—codenamed Operation Bacon—to attack the Italian Pavia and Brescia Divisions in the center of the front at the Ruweisat ridge.[62] His policy was to hit the Italians wherever possible in view of their low morale and because the Germans cannot hold extended fronts without them.[63] Meanwhile, the 22nd Armored Brigade had been engaged at Alam Nayil by the 90th Light Division and the Armored Division Ariete advancing from the south. The two New Zealand brigades, shortly before dawn on July 15 took, their objectives, but minefields and pockets of resistance created disarray among the attackers. On the left, the 22nd Armored Brigade would be ready to move forward to protect the infantry as they consolidated on the ridge.[64] Signals intelligence was giving Auchinleck clear details of the Axis order of battle and force dispositions. At first light, a detachment from the 15th Panzer Division's 8th Panzer Regiment launched a counterattack against New Zealand's 4th Brigade's 22nd Battalion.

As a result, the New Zealand brigade occupied exposed positions on the ridge without support weapons except for a few anti-tank guns.[65] More significantly, communications with the two British armored brigades failed, and the British armor did not move forwards to protect the infantry. About 350 New Zealanders were taken prisoner.[66] The intention was for the 4th New Zealand Brigade and 5th New Zealand Brigade, on 4th Brigade's right, to attack north-west to seize the western part of the ridge and on their right the Indian 5th Infantry Brigade to capture the eastern part of the ridge in a night attack. With the help of the armor and artillery, the Indians were able to take their objectives by early afternoon.[67]

By 7 a.m., word finally reached 2nd Armored Brigade, which started to move north-west. Then, the 2nd Armored Brigade would pass through the center of the infantry objectives to exploit toward Deir el Shein and the Miteirya Ridge. While—with help from mobile infantry and artillery columns from the 7th Armored Division—it pushed back the Axis probe with ease, the brigade was prevented from advancing north to protect the New Zealand flank.[68] Early on July 16, Nehring renewed his attack. By 3 p.m., the 3rd Reconnaissance Regiment and part of the 21st Panzer Division from the north and 33rd Reconnaissance Regiment and the Baade Group comprising elements from 15th Panzer Division from the south were in place under Lieutenant Walther Nehring.[69]

The 4th New Zealand Brigade was still short of support weapons and also, by this time, ammunition. Once again, the anti-tank defenses were overwhelmed and about 380 New Zealanders were taken prisoner, including Captain Charles Upham, who gained a second Victoria Cross for his actions, including destroying a German tank and several guns and vehicles with grenades despite being shot through the elbow by a machine gun bullet and having his arm broken.[70] When Nehring's renewed attack came late in the afternoon, it was repulsed. The Indian 5th Infantry Brigade pushed them back, but it was clear from intercepted radio traffic that a further attempt would be made. Seeing the Brescia and Pavia under pressure, Rommel rushed German troops to Ruweisat. At about 6 p.m., the brigade headquarters was overrun. At about 6.15 p.m., the 2nd Armored Brigade engaged the German armor and halted the Axis eastward advance. At dusk, Nehring broke off the action.[71] Accordingly, strenuous preparations to dig in anti-tank guns were made, artillery fire plans organized, and a regiment from the 22nd Armored Brigade was sent to reinforce the 2nd Armored Brigade.[72]

While the 2nd New Zealand Division attacked the western slopes of Ruweisat Ridge, the Indian 5th Brigade made small gains on Ruweisat ridge to the east. A sharp exchange knocked out the anti-tank guns and the infantry found themselves exposed in the open with no alternative but to surrender. A number of pockets of resistance were left behind the forward troops' advance, which impeded the move forward of reserves, artillery, and support arms. Two regiments became embroiled in a minefield, but the third was able to join Indian 5th Infantry 5th Brigade as it renewed its attack. After the battle, the Indians counted twenty-four destroyed tanks, as well as armored cars and numerous anti-tank guns left on the battlefield.[73] At 5 p.m., Nehring launched his counterattack.

In three day's fighting, the Allies captured more than 2,000 Axis soldiers, mostly from the Italian Brescia and Pavia Divisions; the New Zealand division suffered 1,405 casualties.[74] The fighting at Tel el Eisa and Ruweisat had seen the destruction of three Italian divisions and forced Rommel to redeploy his armor from the south and made it necessary to lay minefields in front of the remaining Italian divisions and stiffen them with detachments of German troops.[75]

To relieve pressure on Ruweisat ridge, Auchinleck ordered the Australian 9th Division to make another attack from the north. In the early hours of July 27, the Australian 24th Brigade—supported by 44th Royal Tank Regiment and strong fighter cover from the air—assaulted Miteirya ridge, known as "Ruin ridge" to the Australians.[76]

The initial night attack went well, with 736 prisoners taken, mostly from the Italian Trento and Motorized Division Trieste. Once again, however, a critical situation for the Axis forces was retrieved by vigorous counterattacks from hastily assembled German and Italian forces, which forced the Australians to withdraw back to their start line with 300 casualties.[77] Although the Australian Official History of the 24th Brigade's 2/32nd Battalion describes the counterattack force as Germans, the Australian historian Mark Johnston reports that German records indicate that it was the Trento Division that overran the Australian battalion.[78, 79]

The Eighth Army now enjoyed a massive superiority in material over the Axis forces: the 1st Armored Division had 173 tanks and more in reserve or in transit, including sixty-one Grants, while Rommel possessed only thirty-eight German tanks and fifty-one Italian tanks, although his armored units had some 100 tanks awaiting repair.[80, 81, 82, 83] The plan was complicated and ambitious.[84] The attack by Indian 161st Brigade had mixed fortunes. The New Zealand attack took the objectives in the El Mreir depression, but, once again, many vehicles failed to arrive and they were short of support arms in an exposed position.[85]

The brigade found itself mired in minefields and under heavy fire. On the left, the initial attempt to clear the western end of Ruweisat failed, but at 8 a.m., a renewed attack by the reserve battalion succeeded. At daylight, two British armored brigades—the 2nd Armored Brigade and the fresh 23rd Armored Brigade—swept through the gap created by the infantry. At daybreak on July 22, Nehring's 5th and 8th Panzer Regiments responded with a rapid counterattack that quickly overran the New Zealand infantry in the open, inflicting more than 900 casualties on the New Zealanders.[86] The 2nd Armored Brigade sent forward two regiments to help, but they were halted by mines and anti-tank fire.[87] On the right, the attacking battalion broke into the Deir el Shein position but was driven back in hand-to-hand fighting.[88] At 5 p.m., Gott ordered the 5th Indian Infantry Division to execute a night attack to capture the western half of Ruweisat ridge and Deir el Shein. Major General Gatehouse—commanding the 1st Armored Division—had been unconvinced that a path had been adequately cleared in the minefields and had suggested the advance be cancelled.[89]

Compounding the disaster at El Mreir, at 8 a.m., the commander of the 23rd Armored Brigade ordered his brigade forward, intent on following his orders to the letter. They were then counterattacked by the 21st Panzer at 11 a.m. and forced to withdraw.[90] The 23rd Armored Brigade was destroyed, with the loss of forty tanks destroyed and forty-seven badly damaged.[91] The 3/14th Punjab Regiment from 9th Indian Infantry Brigade attacked at 2 a.m. on July 23, but failed as they lost their direction. At daybreak on July 22, the British armored brigades again failed to advance. A further attempt in daylight succeeded in breaking into the position, but intense fire from three sides resulted in control being lost as the commanding officer was killed, and four of his senior officers were wounded or went missing.[92] Meanwhile, the 50th Royal Tank Regiment supporting the Australians was having difficulty locating the minefield gaps made by the Australian 2/24th Battalion. At 6 a.m. on July 22, the Australian 26th Brigade attacked Tel el Eisa and the Australian 24th Brigade attacked Tel el Makh Khad toward Miteirya Ridge.[93]

On July 26–27, Auchinleck launched Operation Manhood in the northern sector in a final attempt to break the Axis forces. However, the supporting anti-tank units became lost in the darkness or delayed by minefields, leaving the attackers isolated and exposed when daylight came. The 69th Infantry Brigade would pass through the minefield gap created by the South Africans to Deir el Dhib and clear and mark gaps in further minefields. The fighting for Tel el Eisa was costly, but by the afternoon, the Australians controlled the feature.[94]

By 1 a.m. on July 27, the 24th Australian Infantry Brigade was to have captured the eastern end of the Miteirya ridge and would exploit toward the north-west. The plan was to break the enemy line south of Miteirya ridge and exploit north-west. XXX Corps was reinforced with the 1st Armored Division, minus the 22nd Armored Brigade, 4th Light Armored Brigade, and 69th Infantry Brigade. The result was that the infantry and armor advanced independently, and having reached the objective, the 50th Royal Tank Regiment lost twenty-three tanks because they lacked infantry support.[95]

However, XIII Corps commander, Lieutenant General William Gott, rejected this and ordered the attack but on a center line, 1.6 kilometers south of the original plan, which he incorrectly believed was mine-free. Auchinleck's plan was for the Indian Infantry 161st Brigade to attack along Ruweisat ridge to take Deir el Shein, while the New Zealand 6th Brigade attacked from south of the ridge to the El Mreir depression. These orders failed to get through and the attack went ahead as originally planned.

They failed to find a route through and in the process were caught by heavy fire and lost thirteen tanks. On the other hand, for Rommel, the situation continued to be grave as, despite successful defensive operations, his infantry had suffered heavy losses and he reported that the situation is critical in the extreme.[96] To the south, the British 69th Brigade set off at 1.30 a.m. and managed to take their objectives by about 8 a.m. The tank unit had not been trained in close infantry support and failed to coordinate with the Australian infantry. The South Africans were to make and mark a gap in the minefields to the south-east of Miteirya by midnight of July 26–27.[97] It was during this fighting that Arthur Stanley Gurney performed the actions for which he was posthumously awarded the Victoria Cross. To the north, Australian 9th Division continued its attacks. There followed a period during which reports from the battlefront regarding the minefield gaps were confused and conflicting. The 2nd Armored Brigade would then pass through to El Wishka and would be followed by the 4th Light Armored Brigade, which would attack the Axis lines of communication.[98] This was the third attempt to break through in the northern sector, and the Axis defenders were expecting the attack.[99] Like the previous attacks, it was hurriedly and therefore poorly planned.[100]

The Australian 24th Brigade managed to take their objectives on Miteirya Ridge by 2 a.m. on July 27.[101] That evening, the Australian 24th Brigade attacked Tel el Makh Khad with the tanks of the 50th RTR in support. As a consequence, the advance of the 2nd Armored Brigade was delayed.[102] Rommel launched an immediate counterattack and the German Armored battle groups overran the two forward battalions of the 69th Brigade.[103] The 69th Brigade suffered 600 casualties and the Australians 400 for no gain.[104]

Once more, the Eighth Army had failed to destroy Rommel's forces, despite its overwhelming superiority in men and equipment. The unsupported 2/28th Australian battalion on the ridge was overrun. Rommel was later to blame the failure to break through to the Nile on how the sources of supply to his army had dried up and how then the power of resistance of many Italian formations collapsed. The Eighth Army was exhausted, and on July 31, Auchinleck ordered an end to offensive operations and the strengthening of the defenses to meet a major counteroffensive. He wrote:

The duties of comradeship, for me particularly as their Commander-in-Chief, compel me to state unequivocally that the defeats which the Italian formations suffered at Alamein in early July were not the fault of the Italian soldier. The Italian was willing, unselfish and a good, and, considering the conditions under which he served, had always given better than average. There is no doubt that the achievement of every Italian unit, especially of the motorized forces, far surpassed anything that the Italian Army had done for a hundred years. Many Italian generals and officers won our admiration both as men and as soldiers. The cause of the Italian defeat had its roots in the whole Italian military state and system, in their poor armament and in the general lack of interest in the war by many Italians, both officers and statesmen. This Italian failure frequently prevented the realization of my plans.[105]

Rommel complained bitterly about the failure of important Italian convoys to get through to him desperately needed tanks and supplies, always blaming the Italian Supreme Command, never suspecting British codebreaking.[106] Gott was killed on the way to take up his command when his aircraft was shot down. The Eighth Army had suffered over 13,000 casualties in July, including 4,000 in the 2nd New Zealand Division, 3,000 in the 5th Indian Infantry Division, and 2,552 battle casualties in the 9th Australian Division, but had taken 7,000 prisoners and inflicted heavy damage on Axis men and machines.[107]

The battle was a stalemate, but it had halted the Axis advance on Alexandra, Cairo, and, ultimately, the Suez Canal. Auchinleck therefore made plans for a defensive battle.[108, 109] In early August, Winston Churchill and General Sir Alan Brooke, the Chief of the Imperial General Staff, visited Cairo on their way to meet Joseph Stalin in Moscow.[110] They decided to replace Auchinleck, appointing the XIII Corps commander, William Gott, to the Eighth Army command and General Sir Harold Alexander as Middle East Command.[111] Persia and Iraq were to be split from Middle East Command as a separate Persia and Iraq Command and Auchinleck was offered the post of Commander-in-Charge, which he refused.[112]

Auchinleck believed that because Rommel understood that with the passage of time the Allied situation would only improve, he was compelled to attack as soon as possible and before the end of August, when he would have superiority in armor. In his appreciation of July 27, Auchinleck wrote that the Eighth Army would not be ready to attack again until mid-September at the earliest.[113]

The Second Battle of El Alamein

In early August, British Prime Minister Winston Churchill and General Sir Alan Brooke-the Chief of the Imperial General Staff appointed Lieutenant General Bernard Montgomery commander of the Eighth Army. The two armored divisions of the *Afrika Korps*, together with a force made up of the reconnaissance units of Panzer Army Africa, led the attack but the Allies stopped them at the Alam el Halfa ridge and Point 102 on August 30, 1942.

Faced with long supply lines and lacking reinforcements, and well aware of massive Allied reinforcements in men and materiel on the way, Rommel decided to strike the Allies while their build-up was incomplete. The attack failed in this second battle at the Alamein line, better known as the Battle of Alam el Halfa; expecting a counterattack by Montgomery's Eighth Army, the Panzer Army Africa dug in.

The factors that had favored the Eighth Army's defensive plan in the First Battle of El Alamein, the short front line and the secure flanks, now favored the Axis defense.[1] Rommel, furthermore, had plenty of time to prepare his defensive positions and lay extensive minefields, laying approximately 500,000 mines and barbed wire.[2] Alexander and Montgomery were determined to establish a superiority of forces sufficient not only to achieve a breakthrough but also to exploit it and destroy the Panzer Army Africa. The Eighth Army counteroffensives during July failed, as Rommel had dug in to allow his exhausted troops to regroup. In all the previous swings of the pendulum in the Western Desert Campaign since 1941, neither side had ever had the strength after achieving victory in an offensive battle to exploit it decisively: the losing side had always been able to withdraw and regroup closer to its main supply bases.

A reorganization of the intelligence function in Africa in July had also improved the integration of intelligence received from all sources and the speed of its dissemination.[3] With rare exceptions, intelligence identified the supply ships destined for North Africa, their location or routing, and, in most cases their cargoes, allowing them to be attacked.[4] By October, the Panzer Army fuel stocks were down to three days' supply, of which only two days' worth were east of Tobruk. British Intelligence determined that the Panzer Army did not possess the operational freedom of movement that was absolutely essential in consideration of the fact that the British offensive could be expected to start any day.[5] Submarine and air transport somewhat eased the shortage of ammunition, and by late October, stocks amounting to sixteen days' supply were held in forward areas.[6] After six more weeks, the Eighth Army was ready: 195,000 men and 1,029 tanks began the offensive against the 116,000 men and 547 tanks of Panzer Army Africa. The British had an intelligence advantage: signals intelligence from Ultra and local sources exposed the Axis order of battle, its supply position, force disposition, and intentions. They would rally and consolidate their position just west of the infantry positions, blocking an Axis tank counterattack. Montgomery's plan was for a main attack to the north of the line and a secondary attack to the south, involving XXX Corps and XIII Corps, while X Corps was to exploit the success.[7]

One corridor was to run south-west through the 2nd New Zealand Division sector towards the center of Miteirya Ridge, while the second was to run west, passing 3.2 kilometers north of the west end of the Miteirya Ridge across the 9th Australian and 51st Division sectors.[8]

With Operation Lightfoot, Montgomery intended to cut two corridors through the Axis minefields in the north. Montgomery expected a twelve-day battle in three stages: the break-in, the dogfight, and the final breaking of the enemy.[9] Tanks would then pass through and defeat the German armor. The British tanks would then advance to Skinflint, astride the north-south Rahman Track deep in the Axis defensive system, to challenge the Axis Armor.[10] The infantry battle would continue as the Eighth Army infantry crumbled the deep Axis defensive fortifications (three successive lines of fortification had been constructed) and destroy any tanks that attacked them.[11]

It was wrongly assumed that German paratroopers had manned the defenses and been responsible for the British reverse. In a reverse feint, the tanks destined for battle in the north were disguised as supply trucks by placing removable plywood superstructures over them.[12] On the other hand, the British Commonwealth forces were being resupplied with men and materials from the United Kingdom, India, Australia, and New Zealand, as well as with trucks and the newly-introduced Sherman tanks from the United States. To further the illusion, dummy tanks consisting of plywood frames placed over jeeps were constructed and deployed in the south. This allowed the Eighth Army to build up supplies in the forward area unnoticed by the Axis, by replacing the rubbish with ammunition, petrol, or rations at night. The *Afrika Korps'* war diary notes that the Italian paratroops bore the brunt of the attack. The Commonwealth forces practiced a number of deceptions in the months before the battle to confuse the Axis command, not only as to the exact whereabouts of the forthcoming battle, but as to when the battle was likely to occur. The Italian paratroopers repelled the attack, killing or capturing over 300 of the attackers.[13]

For the first night of the offensive, Montgomery planned for four infantry divisions of XXX Corps to advance on a 26-kilometer front to the Oxalic Line, over-running the forward Axis defenses. Engineers would clear and mark the two lanes through the minefields, through which the armored divisions from X Corps would pass to gain the Pierson Line. Diversions at Ruweisat Ridge in the center and also the south of the line would keep the rest of the Axis forces from moving northwards.

In September, they dumped waste materials under camouflage nets in the northern sector, making them appear to be ammunition or ration dumps. The German and Italian supply lines were overstretched and had been relying on captured Allied supplies and equipment that had long since been consumed. It fought well and inflicted heavy losses on the enemy.[14]

With the failure of their offensive at Alam el Halfa, the Axis forces were now on the defensive, but losses had not been excessive. The Axis naturally noticed these, but, as no offensive action immediately followed and the dumps did not change in appearance, they were subsequently ignored. Despite these warnings, Rommel pressed ahead with his advance to Alamein and as predicted, the supply echelons could not deliver the required supplies from the ports to the front.[15]

The Axis laid around half a million mines, mostly Teller anti-tank mines with some smaller anti-personnel types. Using this delay, Rommel hoped to convince the German High Command to reinforce his forces for the eventual link-up between the Panzer Army Africa and the German armies battling their way through southern Russia, enabling them to finally defeat the British and Commonwealth armies in North Africa. His only hope now relied on the German forces fighting in the Battle of Stalingrad to quickly defeat the Soviet forces, move south through the Trans-Caucasus, and threaten Iran and the Middle East. Before he left for Germany on September 23, Rommel organized the planned defense and wrote a long appreciation of the situation to the German High Command, once again setting out the essential needs of the Panzer Army.[16]

As a preliminary, the 131st Infantry Brigade of the 44th Infantry Division, supported by tanks from the 4th Armored Brigade, launched Operation Braganza, attacking the 185th Paratroopers Division Folgore on the night of September 29–30 in an attempt to capture the Deir el Munassib area. Rommel had been advised by both the German and Italian staffs that his army could not be properly supplied so far from the ports of Tripoli and Benghazi. Rommel continued to request equipment, supplies, and fuel, but the main focus of the German war machine was on the Eastern Front, and very limited supplies reached North Africa. This operation was codenamed Operation Bertram. Meanwhile, a dummy pipeline was built, hopefully leading the Axis to believe the attack would occur much later than it, in fact, did and much further south.

In early September, arrangements were made for him to return to Germany on sick leave and for *General der Panzertruppe* Georg Stumme to transfer from the Russian front to take his place. Furthermore, Rommel was ill. To lure enemy vehicles into the minefields, the Italians had a trick of dragging an axle and tires through the fields using a long rope to create what appeared to be well-used tracks.

Many of these mines were British and had been captured at Tobruk. The front face of each box was lightly held by battle outposts and the rest of the box was unoccupied but sowed with mines and explosive traps and covered by enfilading fire.[17] These became known as the "Devil's Gardens." This would require large numbers of British Commonwealth forces to be sent from the Egyptian front to reinforce British forces in Iran, leading to the postponement of any offensive against his army.

In the meantime, his forces dug in and waited for the eventual attack by the British Commonwealth forces or the defeat of the Soviet Army at Stalingrad. The main defensive positions were built to a depth of at least 2 kilometers behind the second mine belt.[18] Rommel knew full well that the British Commonwealth forces would soon be strong enough to launch an offensive against his army. Rommel added depth to his defenses by creating at least two belts of mines about 5 kilometers apart that were connected at intervals to create boxes, which would restrict enemy penetration and deprive British armor of room for maneuver. As a result of their intelligence advantage, the British were well aware that Rommel would be unable to mount a defense based on his usual battle-of-maneuver tactics. The 15th Panzer Division had 125 operational tanks.[19] However, having concentrated his defense, he would not be able to move his forces again because of lack of fuel.[20]

The effect, however, was that a significant proportion of his armored reserve was dispersed and held unusually far forward. As the Allied deception measures had confused the Axis as to their likely point of attack, Rommel departed from his usual practice of holding his armored strength in a single concentrated reserve and split it into a northern group (the 15th Panzer and Littorio Divisions) and a southern group (the 21st Panzer and Ariete Divisions), each organized into battle groups in order to be able to make a quick armored intervention wherever the blow fell and so prevent any narrow breakthroughs from being enlarged. Rommel believed that when the main thrust came, he could maneuver his troops faster than the Allies to concentrate his defenses at the battle's center of gravity. He therefore had to try to restrict the battle to his defended zones and counter any breakthrough both quickly and vigorously. However, no clear picture emerged of how he would fight the battle and, in the event, British plans seriously underestimated the Axis defenses and the Panzer Army's power of resistance.[21] Anti-tank mines would not be tripped by soldiers stepping on them since they were too light. Then at 9.40 p.m. on October 23 on a calm, clear evening under the bright sky of a full moon, Operation Lightfoot began, not with a 1,000-gun barrage, the fire plan had been arranged so that the first rounds from the 882 guns from the field and medium batteries would land along the 64-kilometer front at the same time.[22]

The minefields were deeper than anticipated and clearing paths through them was impeded by Axis defensive fire. The Battle of El Alamein is usually divided into five phases, consisting of the break-in (October 23–24), the crumbling (October 24–25), the counter (October 26–28), Operation Supercharge (November 1–2), and the break-out (November 3–7). The engineers had to clear an 8-kilometer route through the Devil's Gardens. The shelling plan continued for five and a half hours, by the end of which each gun had fired about 600 rounds—about 529,000 shells in total.[23]

Further back, however, Rommel did have the 90th Light and Motorized Division Trieste in reserve near the coast. Rommel therefore stiffened his forward lines by alternating German and Italian infantry formations. Rommel was concerned with not letting the British armor break out into the open because he had neither the strength of numbers nor fuel to match them in a battle of maneuver.

The objective was to establish a bridgehead before dawn at the imaginary line in the desert where the strongest enemy defenses were situated, on the far side of the second mine belt. As the infantry advanced, engineers had to clear a path for the tanks coming behind. Once the infantry reached the first minefields, the mine sweepers, including Reconnaissance Corps troops and sappers, moved in to create a passage for the armored divisions of X Corps. Only about half of the infantry attained their objectives and none of the tanks broke through.[24] After twenty minutes of general bombardment, the guns switched to precision targets in support of the advancing infantry. It was a difficult task that was not achieved because of the depth of the Axis minefields.

At 10 p.m., the four infantry divisions of XXX Corps began to move. The attack met determined resistance, mainly from the 185th Paratroopers Division Folgore, part of the Ramcke Parachute Brigade and the Keil Group.[25, 26] The 7th Armored Division with one Free French Brigade under command from XIII Corps made a secondary attack to the south. By 4 a.m., the lead tanks were in the minefields, where they stirred up so much dust that there was no visibility at all, traffic jams developed and tanks bogged down. No name is given to the period from October 29–31, when the battle was at a standstill.

Prior to the main barrage, there was a diversion by the 24th Australian Brigade, which involved the 15th Panzer Division being subjected to heavy fire for a few minutes. The main attack aimed to achieve a breakthrough, engage and pin down the 21st Panzer Division and the Armored Division Ariete around Jebel Kalakh, while the Free French on the far left were to secure Qaret el Himeimat and the El Taqa plateau. The right flank of the attack was to be protected by the 44th Infantry Division with the 131st Infantry Brigade. Progress was slower than planned, but at 2 a.m., the first of the 500 tanks crawled forward. Each gap was to be 7.3 meters wide, which was just enough to get tanks through in single file. By dawn on October 24, paths still had not been cleared through the second minefield to release the 22nd and 4th Light Armored Brigades into the open to make their planned turn north into the rear of enemy positions 8 kilometers west of Deir el Munassib.

Further north along the XIII Corps front, the 50th Infantry Division achieved a limited and costly success against determined resistance from the Pavia Division, Brescia Division, and elements of the 185th Paratroopers Division Folgore.[27] The 4th Indian Infantry Division, on the far left of the XXX Corps front at Ruweisat Ridge, made a mock attack and two small raids intended to deflect attention to the center of the front.[28] Operation Lightfoot alluded to the infantry attacking first.

There was little activity during the day pending more complete clearance of paths through the minefields. The lifting of mines on the Miteirya Ridge and beyond took far longer than planned and the leading unit, 8th Armored Brigade, was caught on their start line at 10 p.m.—Zero Hour—by an air attack and were scattered. Dawn aerial reconnaissance showed little change in Axis disposition, so Montgomery gave his orders for the day: the clearance of the northern corridor should be completed and the New Zealand Division supported by the 10th Armored should push south from Miteirya Ridge. Over 100 tanks were involved and half were destroyed by dark. Panzer units counterattacked the 51st Highland Division just after sunrise, only to be stopped in their tracks.[29]

Rommel flew to Rome early on October 25 to press the Italian Supreme Command for more fuel and ammunition and then on to North Africa to resume command that night of the Panzer Army Africa, which that day was renamed the German–Italian Panzer Army.[30] The thrust that night by the 10th Armored Division from Miteirya Ridge failed. The reports that Stumme had received that morning showed the attacks had been on a broad front but that such penetration as had occurred should be containable by local units. Artillery and the Allied Desert Air Force, making over 1,000 sorties, attacked Axis positions all day to aid the "crumbling" of the Axis forces. Rommel went forward himself to observe the state of affairs and, finding himself under fire, suffered a heart attack and died. The 9th Australian Division in the north should plan a crumbling operation for that night, while in the southern sector the 7th Armored should continue to try to break through the minefields with support, if necessary, from the 44th Division. Temporary command was given to Major General Wilhelm Ritter von Thoma. By 4 p.m., there was little progress.[31] The morning of Saturday October 24 brought disaster for the German headquarters. Neither position was altered. At around 10 a.m., Axis aircraft had destroyed a convoy of twenty-five Allied vehicles carrying petrol and ammunition, setting off a night-long blaze; Lumsden wanted to call off the attack, but Montgomery made it clear that his plans were to be carried out.[32]

Hitler had already decided that Rommel should leave his sanatorium and return to North Africa. By the time they had reorganized, they were well behind schedule and out of touch with the creeping artillery barrage. By daylight, the brigade was out in the open taking considerable fire from tanks and anti-tank guns. Meanwhile, the 24th Armored Brigade had pushed forward and reported at dawn they were on the Pierson line, although it turned out that, in the dust and confusion, they had mistaken their position and were well short.[33]

By early morning, the Axis forces launched a series of attacks using the 15th Panzer and Littorio Divisions. The Australian 26th Brigade attacked at midnight, supported by artillery and thirty tanks of the 40th Royal Tank Regiment. Fighting continued in this area for the next week, as the Axis tried to recover the small hill that was so important to their defense. The attack in the XIII Corps sector to the south fared no better. When the sun set, the Allied infantry went on the attack. The Panzer Army was probing for a weakness, but without success. The Allies had advanced through the minefields in the west to make a 9.7-kilometer-wide and 8-kilometer-deep inroad. Meanwhile, the 1st Armored Division—on the Australians' left—would continue to attack west and north-west, and activity to the south on both corps' fronts would be confined to patrolling. The division took the position and 240 prisoners. Allied air activity that night focused on Rommel's northern armored group, where 135 tons of bombs were dropped. To prevent a recurrence of the 8th Armored Brigade's experience from the air, attacks on Axis landing fields were also stepped up.[34] The initial thrust had ended by Sunday.

At dusk, with the sun at their backs, Axis tanks from the 15th Panzer Division and Italian Littorio Division swung out from the Kidney feature (also known to the Germans and Italians as Hill 28), often wrongly called a ridge as it was actually a depression, to engage the 1st Armored Division and the first major tank battle of El Alamein began. The armor was held at Oxalic.

Axis forces were firmly entrenched in most of their original battle positions and the battle was at a standstill. Pandemonium and carnage ensued, resulting in the loss of over 500 Allied troops, and leaving only one officer among the attacking forces.

This was the new northern thrust Montgomery had devised earlier in the day, and was to be the scene of heated battle for some days. The 44th Division's 131st Infantry Brigade cleared a path through the mines, but when the 22nd Armored Brigade passed through; they came under heavy fire and were repulsed, with thirty-one tanks disabled. They now sat atop Miteirya Ridge in the south-east. Around midnight, the 51st Division launched three attacks, but no one knew exactly where they were. Montgomery decided that the planned advance southward from Miteirya Ridge by the New Zealanders would be too costly and instead decided that XXX Corps—while keeping firm hold of Miteirya—should strike northward toward the coast with 9th Australian Division. The battle would be concentrated at the Kidney feature and Tel el Eisa until a breakthrough occurred.[35] While the 51st Highland Division was operating around Kidney, the Australians were attacking Point 29, a 6.1-meter-high Axis artillery observation post south-west of Tel el Eisa, in an attempt to surround the Axis coastal salient containing the German 164th Light Division and large numbers of Italian infantry.[36]

Meanwhile, the air force night bombers dropped 115 tons of bombs on targets in the battlefield and 14 tons on the Stuka base at Sidi Haneish, while night fighters flew patrols over the battle area and the Axis forward landing grounds.[37] In the south, the 4th Armored Brigade and 69th Infantry Brigade attacked the 187th Folgore at Deir Munassib, but lost about twenty tanks gaining only the forward positions.[38, 39] Casualties, particularly in the north, as a result of incessant artillery and air attack, had been particularly heavy. He found that the Italian Division Trento had lost 50 percent of its infantry and most of its artillery, the 164th Light Division had lost two battalions, and although the 15th Panzer and Littorio Divisions had held off the Allied Armor, this had proved costly— the 15th Panzer had a mere thirty-one tanks remaining. Most other units were understrength, all men were on half rations, a large number were sick, and the entire Axis army had only enough fuel for three days.[40]

Rommel was convinced by this time that the main assault would be in the north and was determined to retake Point 29.[41] He ordered a counterattack against it by the 15th Panzer, 164th Light Division, and elements of Italian XX Corps to begin at 3 p.m., but (according to the British official history) under heavy artillery and air attack, this came to nothing.[42] Rommel, on his return to North Africa on the evening of October 25, immediately assessed the battle. According to Rommel, this attack did meet some success, with the Italians recapturing part of what he calls Hill:

> Attacks were now launched on Hill 28 by elements of the 15th Panzer Division, the Littorio and a Bersaglieri Battalion, supported by the concentrated fire of all the local artillery and A.A.…. In the evening part of the Bersaglieri Battalion succeeded in occupying the eastern and western edges of the hill.[43]

The bulk of the Australian 2/17th Battalion, which had defended the position, was in fact forced to pull back.[44] During the day, Rommel reversed his policy of distributing his armor across the front, ordering the 90th Light Division forward from Ed Daba and the 21st Panzer north along with one-third of the Ariete Division and half the artillery from the southern sector to concentrate with the 15th Panzer and Littorio in the north at what was becoming the focal point of the battle.[45] He therefore decided that over the next two days, while continuing the process of attrition, he would thin out his front line to create a reserve with which to restore his momentum. The 21st Panzer and the Ariete made slow progress during the night as they were heavily bombed. Rommel was aware that having moved the 21st Panzer north, he would be unable to move it back south because of a lack of fuel.[46]

Churchill railed: "Is it really impossible to find a general who can win a battle?"[47] On a brighter note for the British, three Vickers Wellington torpedo night bombers of No. 38 Squadron destroyed the oil tanker *Tergestea* at Tobruk and Bristol Beaufort torpedo bombers of No. 42 Squadron RAF, attached to No. 47 Squadron, sank the tanker *Proserpina* at Tobruk, removing the last hope for refueling Rommel's army.[48]

Back at the Kidney feature, the British failed to take advantage of the missing tanks. Each time they tried to move forward, they were stopped by anti-tank guns. Although by October 26, XXX Corps' infantry had completed the capture of the planned bridgehead west of the second mine belt, the armor of X Corps, although established just beyond the infantry, had failed to break through the enemy's anti-tank defenses. The Allied offensive was stalled. Rommel himself noted in his diary that with the sinking of *Tergestea* and *Proserpina*, the battle was lost.[49]

Montgomery was concerned that the impetus of the offensive was waning. The reserve was to include the New Zealand Division (with the 9th Armored Brigade under command), 10th Armored Division, and 7th Armored Division. The Trieste Division was ordered from Fukah to replace the 90th Light at Ed Daba. The attacks in the south, which lasted three days and caused considerable losses without achieving a breakthrough, was suspended.[50] At Snipe, mortar and shellfire was constant all day long. The attack was to be supported by all the available artillery of both X and XXX Corps.[51] Both battalions had difficulty finding their way in the dark and dust. The plan was for the 2nd Armored Brigade to pass round the north of Woodcock the following dawn and the 24th Armored Brigade round the south of Snipe. The 2nd Rifle Brigade had had better fortune and after following the shell bursts of the supporting artillery dug in when they concluded they had reached their objective having encountered little opposition.[52]

At 6 a.m., the 2nd Armored Brigade commenced its advance and ran into such stiff opposition that, by noon, it had still not linked with the Royal Rifle Corps. Some hours of confused fighting ensued, involving tanks from the Littorio and troops and anti-tank guns from the 15th Panzer, which managed to keep the British armor at bay in spite of the support of the Rifle Brigade battle group's anti-tank guns.[53] The 90th Light Division was to make a fresh attempt to capture Point 29 and the 21st Panzer were targeted at Snipe (the Ariete detachment had returned south).[54] At dawn, the Royal Rifle Corps had not reached its objective and was forced to find cover and dig in some distance from Woodcock. Its commander, Lieutenant Colonel Victor Buller Turner, was awarded the Victoria Cross.[55] Only one anti-tank gun, from 239 Battery, was brought back.[56]

Rommel had decided to make two counterattacks using his fresh troops. Against them, the Rifle Brigade had thirteen 6-pounder anti-tank guns along with six more from the supporting 239th Anti-tank Battery, Royal Artillery. The 24th Armored Brigade started a little later and was soon in contact with the Rifle Brigade, having shelled them in error for a while. German and Italian tanks moved forward. An attack was planned on these areas using two battalions from the 7th Motor Brigade.

At 11 p.m. on October 26, the 2nd Battalion Rifle Brigade attacked Snipe and the 2nd Battalion King's Royal Rifle Corps would attack Woodcock. At 4 p.m., Rommel launched his major attack. By this time, the main battle was concentrated around Tel el Aqqaqir and the Kidney feature at the end of the 1st

Armored Division's path through the minefield. A mile north-west of the feature lay Outpost Woodcock and roughly the same distance south-west lay Outpost Snipe. The Germans gave up, but in error, the British battle group was withdrawn without being replaced that evening. Although on the point of being overrun more than once, they held their ground, destroying twenty-two German and ten Italian tanks.

By 1.30 a.m. on October 28, the 4th Battalion Royal Sussex Regiment judged they were on Woodcock and dug in. When it was discovered that neither Woodcock nor Snipe was in Eighth Army hands, the 133rd Truck Infantry Brigade was sent to capture them. At dawn, the 2nd Armored Brigade moved up in support, but before contact could be made, the 4th Royal Sussex were counterattacked and overrun with heavy losses.[57] Meanwhile, the Truck Brigade's two other battalions had moved on Snipe and dug in, only to find out the next day that they were in fact well short of their objective.[58]

Further north, the 90th Light Division's attack on Point 29 during the afternoon of October 27 failed under heavy artillery and bombing, which broke up the attack before it had closed with the Australians.[59] The action at Snipe was an episode of the Battle of El Alamein described by the regiment's historian as the most famous day of the regiment's war. Lucas-Phillips, in *Alamein*, records:

> The desert was quivering with heat. The gun detachments and the platoons squatted in their pits and trenches, the sweat running in rivers down their dust-caked faces. There was a terrible stench. The flies swarmed in black clouds upon the dead bodies and excreta and tormented the wounded. The place was strewn with burning tanks and carriers, wrecked guns and vehicles, and over all drifted the smoke and the dust from bursting high explosives and from the blasts of guns.[60]

On the night of October 28–29, the 9th Australian Division was ordered to make a second set-piece attack. In the afternoon, they paused to regroup to attack again, but they were bombed for two and a half hours and were prevented from even forming up.[61] This proved to be Rommel's last attempt to take the initiative and, as such, his defeat here represented a turning point in the battle.[62]

The 20th Brigade took its objectives with little trouble, but the 26th Brigade had more trouble. On October 28, the 15th and 21st Panzer made a determined attack on the X Corps front but was halted by sustained artillery, tank, and anti-tank gun fire. The 20th Australian Infantry Brigade with 40th Royal Rifle Corps in support would push north-west from Point 29 to form a base for the 26th Australian Infantry Brigade with 46th Royal Rifle Corps in support to attack north-east to an Axis location south of the railway known as Thompson's Post and then over the railway to the coast road, where they would advance south-east to close on the rear of the Axis troops in the coastal salient. Due to the distances involved, the troops were riding on the 46th Royal Rifle Corps Valentine tanks as well as carriers, which mines and anti-tank guns soon brought to grief, forcing the infantry to dismount. The British 133rd Brigade was sent forward to recover lost positions, but the next day, a good part of this force was overrun by German and Italian tanks from the Littorio and supporting 12th Bersaglieri Regiment and several hundred British soldiers were captured.[63] The German and Italian forces that had participated in the counterattack formed an outpost and held on until the arrival of German reinforcements on November 1.

An attack by the third brigade would then be launched on the salient from the south-east.[64] Montgomery ordered the X Corps formations in the Woodcock–Snipe area to go over to defense while he focused his army's attack further to the north. The infantry and tanks lost touch with each other in fighting with the 125th *Panzergrenadier* Regiment and a battalion of the 7th Bersaglieri Regiment sent to reinforce the sector and the advance came to a halt.[65] These actions by the Australians and British had alerted Montgomery that Rommel had committed his reserve in the form of the 90th Light Division to the front and that its presence in the coastal sector suggested that Rommel was expecting the next major Eighth Army offensive in this sector. It became clear that there were no longer enough hours of darkness left to reform, continue the attack, and see it to its conclusion, so the operation was called off.[66] The night of October 30 saw a continuation of previous Australian plans, their third attempt to reach the paved road. With the help of signals intelligence information, the *Proserpina*, carrying 4,500 tons of fuel, and the *Tergestea*, carrying 1,000 tons of fuel and 1,000 tons of ammunition, had been destroyed on October 26 and the tanker *Luisiano*, carrying 2,500 tons of fuel, had been sunk off the west coast of Greece by a torpedo from a Wellington bomber on October 28.[67] Rommel told his commanders:

> It will be quite impossible for us to disengage from the enemy. Although not all the objectives were achieved, by the end of the night they were astride the road and the railway, making the position of the Axis troops in the salient precarious. Montgomery determined therefore that it would take place further south on a 3,700 meter front south of Point 29. Rommel brought up a battle group from 21. We have only one choice and that is to fight to the end at Alamein.[68]

The Australians suffered 200 casualties in that attack and suffered twenty-seven killed and 290 wounded. To keep Rommel's attention on the coastal sector, Montgomery ordered the renewal of the 9th Australian Division operation on the night of October 30–31.[69] By the end of these engagements in late October, the British had 800 tanks still in operation, while the Panzer Army Day Report, intercepted and read by the Eighth Army the following evening, recorded eighty-one serviceable German tanks and 197 Italian. There was no gasoline for such a maneuver. The attack was to take place on the night of October 31–November 1 as soon as he had completed the reorganization of his front line to create the reserves needed for the offensive, although in the event, it was postponed by twenty-four hours. Rommel brought up a battle group from the 21st Panzer Division, and on October 31, launched four successive attacks against Thompson's Post. The fighting was intense and often hand-to-hand, but no ground was gained by the Axis forces. One of the Australians killed was Sergeant William Kibby (2/48th Infantry Battalion) who, for his heroic actions from the 23rd until his death on the 31st—including a lone attack on a machine-gun position at his own initiative—was awarded the Victoria Cross.[70] He did, however, regain contact with Panzergrenadier Regiment 125 in the nose of the salient and the supporting the 10th Battaglione Bersaglieri—that fought well according to German and Allied sources.[71] The Bersaglieri had resisted several Australian attacks even though they were, in the words of military historian Niall Barr, "surrounded on all sides, short of ammunition, food and water, and unable to evacuate their many wounded."[72]

On November 1, two more supply ships, the *Tripolino* and the *Ostia*, had been torpedoed and sunk from the air northwest of Tobruk. This phase of the battle began at 1 a.m. on November 2, with the objective of destroying enemy armor, forcing the enemy to fight in the open, reducing the Axis stock of petrol, attacking and occupying enemy supply routes, and causing the disintegration of the enemy army. Rommel's fuel state continued to be critical. The shortage forced him to rely increasingly on fuel flown in from Crete on the orders of Albert Kesselring, Luftwaffe Supreme Commander South, despite the restrictions imposed by heavy bombing of the airfields in Crete and the Desert Air Force's efforts to intercept the transport aircraft.[73]

By now, it had become obvious to Rommel that the battle was lost. The division's commander, Lieutenant General Sir Bernard Freyberg, had tried to free them of this task, as they had lost 1,405 men in just three days at El Ruweisat Ridge in July. However, in addition to its own 5th New Zealand Infantry Brigade and 28th Infantry Battalion, the division was to have had placed under its command the 151st Durham Brigade from the 50th Division, 152nd Brigade from the 51st Division, and the 133rd Royal Sussex Truck Infantry Brigade. Ironically, large amounts of fuel arrived at Benghazi after the German forces had started to retreat, but little of it reached the front, a fact Kesselring tried to change by delivering it more closely to the fighting forces.[74]

Rommel began to plan a retreat anticipating retiring to Fukah, some 80 kilometers west, as he had only ninety tanks remaining in stark contrast with the Allies' 800. The objective of this operation was Tel el Aqqaqir, the base of the Axis defense roughly 4.8 kilometers north-west of the Kidney feature and situated on the Rahman lateral track.[75] The initial thrust of Supercharge was to be

Above: Italian anti-tank rifle team in North Africa using a German Solothum 20 mm. (*WWII History*)

Below: Italian artillerymen prepare to fire a 105-mm gun in North Africa. (*istpravda.ru/pictures*)

Above: Italians on abandoned British Mk V light tank. (*istpravda.ru/pictures*)

Below: Italian Bersaglieri motorcycle soldiers in Africa 1942. (*Italian Army Archives*)

Above: Italian soldiers being transported by truck during the Italo–Ethiopian War in Ethiopia. (*Library of Congress, Washington, D.C.*)

Below: Italians celebrating a victory near Sidi Barrani in 1940. (*istpravda.ru/pictures*)

Above: Erwin Rommel shortly after his arrival in North Africa. (*Bundesarchiv*)

Below: 185th Parachute Division Folgore soldiers in North Africa. (*lrdg.hegewisch.net*)

Right: General Italo Gariboldi awards *Afrika Korps* Commander Lieutenant General Erwin Rommel the Italian silver medal for bravery. (*Bundesarchiv*)

Below: The artillery of the Italian Celere division. (*The General Staff Archive*)

Above: North Africa Italian soldiers on the march. (*Bundesarchiv*)

Below: An Italian 47-mm anti-tank gun manned by Bersagliere. (*Avalanche Press*)

Right: General Annibale
Bergonzoli, commander
the Italian X Army in 1941.
(*know.cf/enciclopedia*)

Below: Italian M13/40s
of the 132nd Armoured
Division Ariete during
the Battle of Gazala,
June 1942.
(*Italian Army Archive*)

Left: Italian Generals Nicolini, Baldassarre, and Lombardi before the Battle of Gazala. (*archivio central dello stato*)

Below: The 6th Army (Wehrmacht) arriving in Tobruk. (*Bundesarchiv*)

Above: A British gun crew digging in. (*legacy.history.co.uk*)

Below: The Special Air Service (SAS) in North Africa during World War II. A heavily-armed patrol of "L" Detachment SAS in their jeeps, January 18, 1943. (*http://imgur.com*)

Above: A group of Axis prisoners are taken during the Allied assault on German positions near Tunisia, 1943. (*Life Magazine*)

Below: When Italy invaded Ethiopia, it met surprisingly strong resistance, including local women soldiers. (*Italian Army Archive*)

Above: Hitler and Mussolini in Munich after the Abyssinian Crisis. (*Everett Historical Shutterstock*)

Below: Four Italian soldiers taking aim in Ethiopia in 1935 during the Second Italo–Abyssinian War. (*AP Photo*)

Above left: An Italian soldier conducting artillery training. (*Italian Federal Archieve*)

Above right: Napoleone Bartoli, an Italian Bersaglieri (sharpshooter) in North Africa. (*Italian Federal Archive*)

Above left: Italian Bersaglieri on a motorcycle with a Breda 30 light machine gun during the Western Desert Campaign. (*Italian Federal Archive*)

Above right: German and Italian prisoners captured during recent fighting in Libya, June 1, 1942. (*Italian Army Archive*)

Right: Italian Parachute Corps lined up for inspection in Libya in 1940. (*Italian Army Archive*)

Below: Italian infantry on the march through the wilderness in British Somalia. (*Bundesarchive*)

Left: An Italian soldier with FIAT Revelli machine gun operating in North Africa. (*Bundesarchive*)

Below: An Italian soldier in North Africa with his Motorguzzi bike. (*Italian Army Archive*)

Above: Members of the Italian *Camicie Nere* (Blackshirts) taking possession of the railway station at Dire Dawa, Ethiopia, in May 1936. (*Bundesarchive*)

Below: Standing by their battle flag, officers of the 225th Infantry Regiment of the 14th Italian Expeditionary Force prepare to depart for East Africa in 1935. (*Italian Army Archive*)

Left: An Italian soldier in desert uniform.
(*Rai Cultura*)

Below: Italian soldiers in North Africa manning a Brenda 200 anti-aircraft gun.
(*Historical Society of German Military History*)

carried out by the 2nd New Zealand Division. The intensity and the destruction in Supercharge were greater than anything witnessed so far during this battle. Again, on Sunday November 1, Rommel tried to dislodge the Australians, but the brutal, desperate fighting resulted in nothing but lost men and equipment. In addition, the division was to have the British 9th Armored Brigade under command.[76]

Once the 9th Armored Brigade reached its objectives, 3,700 meters distant, it would pass through supported by a heavy artillery barrage and break open a gap in the Axis defenses on and around the Rahman track, some 1,800 meters further forward, which the 1st Armored Division, following behind, would pass through into the open to take on Rommel's armored reserves.[77] Rommel had ordered the 21st Panzer Division from the front line to form a mobile counterattacking force. As in Operation Lightfoot, it was planned that two infantry brigades, the 151st on the right and 152nd on the left, each this time supported by a regiment of tanks—the 8th and 50th Royal Tank Regiments—would advance and clear a path through the mines. The division had left behind a Panzergrenadier regiment that would bolster the Trieste Division, which had been ordered forward to replace it. On November 1, the two German armored divisions had 102 effective tanks to face Supercharge and the Littorio and Trieste Divisions had sixty-five tanks between them.[78]

Supercharge started with a seven-hour aerial bombardment focused on Tel el Aqqaqir and Sidi Abd el Rahman, followed by a four-and-a-half-hour barrage of 360 guns firing 15,000 shells. The two assault brigades started their attack at 1.05 a.m. on November 2 and gained most of their objectives to schedule and with moderate losses.[79] On the right of the main attack, the 28th Battalion captured positions to protect the right flank of the newly formed salient and the 133rd Truck Infantry did the same on the left. Rommel had also interspersed formations from the Trieste and the 15th Panzer Divisions to bolster his weaker forces in the front line. New Zealand engineers cleared five lines through the mines, allowing the Royal Dragoons Armored car regiment to slip out into the open and spend the day raiding the Axis communications.[80]

The 9th Armored Brigade had started its approach march from El Alamein railway station with around 130 tanks and arrived at its start line with only ninety-four operational tanks.[81] The brigade was to have started its attack towards Tel el Aqqaqir at 5.45 a.m. behind a barrage, but the attack was postponed for thirty minutes while the brigade regrouped on Currie's orders.[82] At 6.15 a.m., thirty minutes before dawn, the three regiments of the brigade advanced towards the gunline.[83]

The brigade had sacrificed itself upon the gun line and caused great damage but had failed to create the gap for the 1st Armored Division to pass through; however, soon after dawn, the 1st Armored Division started to deploy and the remains of the 9th Armored Brigade came under its command. The Axis gun screen started to inflict a steady amount of damage upon the advancing tanks but was unable to stop them; over the course of the next thirty minutes, around thirty-five guns were destroyed and several hundred prisoners taken. Brigadier Currie had tried to get the brigade out of doing this job, stating that he believed the brigade would be attacking on too wide a front with no reserves and that they would most likely have 50 percent losses.[84] After the brigade's action, Brigadier Gentry of the 6th New Zealand Brigade went ahead to survey the scene. German tanks, which had penetrated between the Warwickshire Yeomanry and Royal Wiltshire Yeomanry, also caused many casualties.[85]

On seeing Brigadier Currie asleep on a stretcher, he approached him saying, "Sorry to wake you, John, but I'd like to know where your tanks are." Currie waved his hand at a group of tanks around him replying, "There they are." Gentry was puzzled. The 9th Armored Brigade had started the attack with ninety-four tanks and was reduced to only twenty-four, and of the 400 tank crew involved in the attack, 230 were killed, wounded, or captured.[86]

British tanks attacking the Folgore sector were fought off with petrol bombs and mortar fire, as well as with the obsolete Italian 47-mm cannon. "I don't mean your headquarters tanks, I mean your Armored regiments. 2nd Armored Brigade came up behind the 9th, and by mid-morning 8th Armored Brigade had come up on its left, ordered to advance to the south-west. But there are no more infantry available. Where are they?" Currie waved his arm and again replied, "There are my armored regiments, Bill."[87] In heavy fighting during the day the British armor made little further progress. The counterattack failed under a blanket of shells and bombs, resulting in a loss of some 100 tanks.[88]

Montgomery was aware of the risk and had accepted the possibility of losing 100 percent of the 9th Armored Brigade to make the break, but in view of the promise of immediate breakthrough of the 1st Armored Division, the risk was not considered as great as all that. The German and Italian anti-tank guns, mostly Pak38 and Italian 47-mm guns, along with twenty-four of the formidable 88-mm flak guns, opened fire upon the charging tanks silhouetted by the rising sun. At 11 a.m. on November 2, the remains of the 15th Panzer, 21st Panzer, and Littorio Armored Divisions counterattacked the 1st Armored Division and the remains of the 9th Armored Brigade, which by that time had dug in with a screen of anti-tank guns and artillery, together with intensive air support.

Fighting continued throughout November 3, but the 2nd Armored was held by elements of the *Afrika Korps* and tanks of the Littorio Division. The heavy artillery concentration that accompanied their advance suppressed the opposition from the Trieste Division and the operation succeeded with few casualties.[89] Meanwhile, in the late afternoon and early evening, the 133rd Truck and 151st Infantry Brigades—by this time back under command of the 51st Infantry Division—attacked respectively the Snipe and Skinflint positions in order to form a base for future operations. His mobile forces, XX Corps,

Afrika Korps, 90th Light Division, and 19th Flak Division were ordered to make a fighting withdrawal while his other formations were to withdraw as best they could with the limited transport available.[90]

Although tank losses were approximately equal, this represented only a portion of the total British Armor, but most of Rommel's tanks; the *Afrika Korps* strength of tanks fit for battle fell by seventy, while in addition to the losses of the 9th Armored Brigade, the 2nd and 8th Armored Brigades lost fourteen tanks in the fighting, with another forty damaged or broken down. This combined with stiff resistance led to the failure of their attack. He called up Ariete from the south to join the mobile Italian XX Corps around Tel el Aqqaqir. The fighting was later termed the "Hammering of the Panzers."

At 8.30 p.m. on November 2, Lumsden decided that one more effort by his X Corps would see the gun screen on the Rahman track defeated and ordered the 7th Motor Brigade to seize the track along a 3.2-kilometer front, north of Tell el Aqqaqir. He also reinforced X Corps by moving the 7th Armored Division from army reserve and sending the 4th Light Armored Brigade from XIII Corps in the south. Rommel concluded that to forestall a breakthrough and the resulting destruction of his whole army, he would have to start withdrawing to the planned position at Fukah. Although X Corps had failed in its attempt to break out, it had succeeded in its objective of finding and destroying enemy tanks. General von Thoma's report to Rommel that night said he would have at most thirty-five tanks available to fight the next day and his artillery and anti-tank weapons had been reduced to one-third of their strength at the start of the battle. As a consequence, the orders for the armor were changed and the 2nd Armored Brigade was tasked to support the forward battalion of the 133rd Truck Brigade (2nd King's Royal Rifle Corps) and the 8th Armored Brigade was to push south-west. On the morning of November 3, the 7th Armored Division would pass through and swing north heading for the railway at Ghazal station.[91]

Montgomery once again reshuffled his infantry in order to bring four brigades—the 5th Indian, 151st, 5th New Zealand, and 154th—into reserve under XXX Corps to prepare for the next thrust. The 2nd and 8th Armored Brigades would then pass through the infantry to a distance of about 5.6 kilometers. Further south, the 8th Armored Brigade was held off by anti-tank units helped later by tanks of the arriving Ariete Division.[92] On 2 November, Rommel informed Hitler the following:

> The army's strength was so exhausted after its ten days of battle that it was not now capable of offering any effective opposition to the enemy's next break-through attempt.... With our great shortage of vehicles an orderly withdrawal of the non-motorized forces appeared impossible.... In these circumstances we had to reckon, at the least, with the gradual destruction of the army.[93]

At 1.30 p.m. on November 3, Rommel received a reply:

> To Field Marshal Rommel, it is with trusting confidence in your leadership
> and the courage of the German–Italian troops under your command that
> the German people and I are following the heroic struggle in Egypt. In the
> situation which you find yourself there can be no other thought but to stand
> fast, yield not a yard of ground and throw every gun and every man into
> the battle. Considerable air force reinforcements are being sent to C-in-C
> [Commander in Chief] South. The Duce and the *Comando Supremo* are also
> making the utmost efforts to send you the means to continue the fight. Your
> enemy, despite his superiority, must also be at the end of his strength. It would
> not be the first time in history that a strong will has triumphed over the bigger
> battalions. As to your troops, you can show them no other road than that to
> victory or death. Adolf Hitler.[94]

Rommel thought the order, similar to one that had been given at the same time
by Benito Mussolini through the Italian Supreme Command, demanded the
impossible. He stated:

> We were completely stunned, and for the first time in the African campaign I
> did not know what to do. A kind of apathy took hold of us as we issued orders
> for all existing positions to be held on instructions from the highest authority.[95]

On the night of November 3, Montgomery launched at the Rahman track three
of the infantry brigades he had gathered into reserve as a prelude to a massive
armored breakout. The paths through the minefields were very congested and
broken up, which delayed matters further. He then replied to Hitler confirming
his determination to hold the battlefield.[96]

The 1st and 7th Armored Divisions' plan to trap the 90th Light Division also
hit trouble. By the time the 5th Indian Brigade set off, the defenders had started
to withdraw and their objective was taken with virtually no opposition. In what
was its biggest day of the battle, it flew 1,208 sorties and dropped 396 tons of
bombs in the twenty-four hours of November 3.[97] Meanwhile, the Desert Air
Force continued to apply huge pressure. By the time the 154th Brigade moved
forward, although they met some shelling, the enemy had left.[98]

On November 4, the Eighth Army's plan for pursuit was set in motion at dawn.
There were no fresh units available for the chase so the 1st and 7th Armored
Division were to swing northward to roll up the Axis units still in the forward
lines and the 2nd New Zealand Division, with two lorry-borne infantry brigades
and the 9th Armored and 4th Light Armored Brigades under command,
would head west along desert tracks to the escarpment above Fukah, some 97
kilometers away.[99]

By dark, Freyberg had leaguered his force only 24 kilometers west of the Rahman track, although the 9th Armored Brigade was still at the track and the 6th New Zealand Brigade was even further back.[100] The 5th Indian Infantry Brigade would attack the track 6.4 kilometers south during the early hours of November 4, and at 6.15 a.m., the 154th Infantry Brigade would attack Tel el Aqqaqir itself. Rommel decided to compromise. The X and XXI Italian Corps and 90th Light Division would stand firm while the *Afrika Korps* would withdraw approximately 9.7 kilometers west during the night of November 3, with XX Italian Corps and the Ariete Division conforming to their position. At 5.45 p.m., the 152nd Infantry Brigade, with 8th Royal Tank Regiment in support, attacked about 3.2 kilometers south of Tel el Aqqaqir.

The 1st Armored came into contact with the remnants of the 21st Panzer and had to spend most of the day pushing them back 13 kilometers. Failed communications compounded problems and the forward infantry elements ended up dug in well short of their objective. The first of these attacks—having been mistakenly told the enemy had withdrawn from their objectives—met stiff resistance. Meanwhile, the 7th Armored was being held up by the Armored Division Ariete, which in the course of the day was decimated while giving stout resistance.[101]

The New Zealanders got off to a bad start because the units involved were dispersed after the recent fighting and took time to concentrate. This action is described by Rommel in his diary:

Enormous dust-clouds could be seen south and south-east of headquarters [of the DAK], where the desperate struggle of the small and inefficient Italian tanks of XX Corps was being played out against the hundred or so British heavy tanks which had come round their open right flank. I was later told by Major von Luck, whose battalion I had sent to close the gap between the Italians and the *Afrika Korps*, that the Italians, who at that time represented our strongest motorized force, fought with exemplary courage. Tank after tank split asunder or burned out, while all the time a tremendous British barrage lay over the Italian infantry and artillery positions. The last signal came from the Ariete at about 1530 hours: "Enemy tanks penetrated south of Ariete. Ariete now encircled. Location 5 km north-west Bir el Abd. Ariete tanks still in action." In the Ariete we lost our oldest Italian comrades, from whom we had probably always demanded more than they, with their poor armament, had been capable of performing.[102]

This day also saw the destruction of the Littorio Armored Division and the Motorized Division Trieste. Berlin radio claimed that in this sector the British were made to pay for their penetration with enormous losses in men and material. The Italians fought to the last man.[103] The British, however, took many prisoners, since the remnants of Italian infantry divisions were not motorized and could not escape from encirclement. Private Sid Martindale, 1st Battalion Argyll and Sutherland Highlanders, wrote about the Bologna Division, which had taken the full weight of the British Armored attack:

> The more we advanced the more we realized that the Italians did not have much fight in them after putting up a strong resistance to our overwhelming advance and they started surrendering to our lead troops in droves. There was not much action to see but we came across lots of burnt out Italian tanks that had been destroyed by our tanks. I had never seen a battlefield before and the site of so many dead was sickening.[104]

The Bologna and the remainder of Trento Division tried to fight their way out of El Alamein and marched in the desert without water, food, or transport before surrendering exhausted and dying from dehydration.[105] It was reported that Colonel Arrigo Dall'Olio, commanding the 40th Infantry Regiment of the Bologna, surrendered, saying, "We have ceased firing not because we haven't the desire but because we have spent every round."[106] In a symbolic act of final defiance no one in the 40th Bologna Infantry Regiment raised their hands. Harry Zinder of *Time* magazine noted that the Italians fought better than had been expected, and commented:

> [For the Italians] it was a terrific letdown by their German allies. They had fought a good fight. In the south, the famed Parachute Division Folgore fought to the last round of ammunition. Two Armored divisions and a motorized division, which had been interspersed among the German formations, thought they would be allowed to retire gracefully with Rommel's 21st, 15th and 19th light. But even that was denied them. When it became obvious to Rommel that there would be little chance to hold anything between El Daba and the frontier, his Panzers dissolved, disintegrated and turned tail, leaving the Italians to fight a rear-guard action.[107]

By late morning on November 4, Rommel realized his situation was dire:

> The picture in the early afternoon of the 4th was as follows: powerful enemy armored forces ... had burst a 19-kilometer hole in our front, through which strong bodies of tanks were moving to the west. As a result of this, our forces in the north were threatened with encirclement by enemy formations 20 times their number in tanks.... There were no reserves, as every available man and gun had been put into the line. So now it had come, the thing we had done everything in our power to avoid—our front broken and the fully motorized enemy streaming into our rear. Superior orders could no longer count. We had to save what there was to be saved.[108]

At 5.30 p.m., unable to wait any longer for a reply from Hitler, Rommel gave orders to retreat.[109]

Due to insufficient transportation, most of the Italian infantry formations were abandoned and left to their fate.[110] Any chance of getting them away with an earlier move had been spoiled by the dictator's insistence that Rommel hold his ground, obliging him to keep the un-motorized Italian units well forward until it was too late.[111]

To deepen the armored thrusts, the 1st Armored Division was directed at El Daba, some 24 kilometers down the coast and the 7th Armored towards Galal, a further 24 kilometers west along the railway. The 1st Armored determined to make up time with a night march, but in the darkness the armor became separated from their support vehicles and as a consequence ran out of fuel at dawn on November 6, 26 kilometers short of Bir Khalda. Meanwhile, the New Zealand group had hoped to reach their objective by mid-morning on November 5, but was held up by shellfire when picking their way through what turned out to be a dummy minefield and the 15th Panzer were able to get there first.[112] By 11 a.m. on November 6, the "B" Echelon vehicles were starting to reconnect with the 1st Armored Division, but only enough to partly refuel two of the armored regiments, which set off again hoping to be in time to cut off the enemy. The 7th Armored was ordered across country to intercept the coastal road at Sidi Haneish, 105 kilometers west of the Rahman track while the 1st Armored, at that time west of El Dada, was ordered to take a wide detour through the desert to Bir Khalda, 130 kilometers west of the Rahman track, preparatory to swinging up to cut the road at Mersa Matruh.[113]

The air force continued to fly in support, but because of the wide spread of the various X Corps units, it was difficult to establish firm bomb lines demarcating areas in which troops and vehicles could be assumed to be those of the enemy and so free to be attacked.[114]

Neither move proved successful. Rommel telegraphed Hitler for permission to fall back on Fukah. As further Allied blows fell, von Thoma was captured and reports came in from the Ariete and Trento that they were encircled. The 7th Armored finished the day 32 kilometers short of its objective. However, it ran out of fuel again, 48 kilometers south-west of Mersa Matruh.[115] A fuel convoy had set out from Alamein on the evening of November 5, but progress was slow as the tracks had become very cut up. By midday on the 6th, rain had started to fall and the convoy became bogged down, still 64 kilometers from the planned meeting point, with the 1st Armored's "B" echelon support vehicles.[116] Montgomery now realized that in order to finish the enemy off, he would need to make even deeper armored thrusts.

The last rearguards left Matruh on the night of November 7–8, but were only able to hold Sidi Barrani until the evening of the 9th. Roughly 24 kilometers south-west of Sidi Haneish, the 7th Armored Division had come upon the

21st Panzer and the Voss Reconnaissance Group that morning. The division narrowly escaped encirclement, however, and escaped on wheels that evening to Mersa Matruh.[11]

Once again, it proved difficult to firmly identify targets for the air force. By the evening of November 10, the New Zealand Division, heading for Sollum, had the 4th Light Armored Brigade at the foot of the Halfaya Pass, while the 7th Armored Division was conducting another detour to the south aiming to swing round and take Fort Capuzzo and Sidi Azeiz. Churchill said: "It may almost be said, before Alamein we never had a victory. Heavy bombers attacked Tobruk, sinking the *Mars* and setting the tanker *Portofino* on fire."[118] The 10th Armored Division, with the benefit of working on the coastal road and with ample fuel, pushed its tanks on to Mersa Matruh while its infantry mopped up on the road west of Galal.[119]

Rommel intended to fight a delaying action at Sidi Barrani, 130 kilometers west of Matruh, to give his retreating forces time to get through the bottleneck through the escarpment passes at Halfaya and Sollum.[120] The Allies frequently had numerical superiority in the Western Desert but never had it been so complete in quantity and quality. Air supremacy had a huge effect on the battle and not only because of its physical impact. On the morning of November 11, the 5th New Zealand Infantry Brigade stormed the pass, taking 600 Italian prisoners.[121] By the end of the day on the 11th, the Egyptian border area was clear, but Montgomery was forced to order that the pursuit should, for the time being, be continued by armored cars and artillery only because of the difficulty in supplying larger formations west of Bardia until the supply infrastructure could catch up.[122]

El Alamein was an Allied victory, although Rommel did not lose hope until the end of the Tunisia Campaign.[123] With the arrival of Sherman tanks, 6-pounder anti-tank guns, and Spitfires in the Western Desert, the Allies gained a comprehensive superiority.[124] Montgomery envisioned the battle as an attrition operation, similar to those fought in the Great War and correctly predicted the length of the battle and the number of Allied casualties.[125] Allied artillery was superbly handled and Allied air support was excellent, in contrast to the Luftwaffe and *Regia Aeronautica*, which offered little or no support to ground forces, preferring to engage in air-to-air combat. As Montgomery later wrote:

> The moral effect of air action [on the enemy] is very great and out of all proportion to the material damage inflicted. In the reverse direction, the sight and sound of our own air forces operating against the enemy have an equally satisfactory effect on our own troops. A combination of the two has a profound influence on the most important single factor in war-morale.[126]

On December 11, Montgomery launched the 51st Highland Division along the line of the coast road with the 7th Armored Division on the inland flank. The

Axis now faced a war in Africa on two fronts with the Eighth Army approaching from the east and the British, French, and Americans from the west. Hitler was determined to retain hold of Tunisia and Rommel finally started to receive replacement men and materials. In 2005, Barr wrote that the 36,939 men Panzer Army casualties was an estimate because of the chaos of the Axis retreat. In a note to *The Rommel Papers*, Fritz Bayerlein, quoting figures obtained from *Offizieller Bericht des Oberkommandos Afrika*, instead estimated German losses in the battle as 1,100 killed, 3,900 wounded, and 7,900 taken as prisoners and Italian losses as 1,200 killed, 1,600 wounded, and 20,000 taken as prisoners.[127] According to the official history of the Italian Army, Axis losses during the battle were 4,000 to 5,000 killed or missing, 7,000 to 8,000 wounded, and 17,000 taken as prisoners; during the retreat, the losses rose to 9,000 killed or missing, 15,000 wounded, and 35,000 taken as prisoners.[128] According to the writings of General Giuseppe Rizzo, total Axis casualties included 25,000 men killed or wounded (including 5,920 Italians killed) and 30,000 prisoners (20,000 Italians and 10,724 Germans), as well as 510 tanks and 2,000 field guns, anti-tank guns, and anti-aircraft guns.[129]

Huge quantities of engineer stores had been collected to repair transport infrastructure and the railway line from El Alamein to Fort Capuzzo, despite having been blown up in over 200 places, was quickly repaired. About half of the 278 Italian tanks had been lost and most of the remainder were knocked out of action the next day by the 7th Armored Division.[130] The Eighth Army had 13,560 casualties, of whom 2,350 men had been killed, 8,950 had been wounded, and 2,260 men were missing; 58 percent of the casualties were British, 22 percent Australian, 10 percent New Zealanders, 6 percent South African, 1 percent Indian, and 3 percent were Allied forces.[131] The Highland Division made a slow and costly advance and the 7th Armored met stiff resistance from the Combat Group Ariete (the remains of the Armored Division Ariete). The artillery lost 111 guns and the Desert Air Force lost seventy-seven British and twenty American aircraft.[132] The Eighth Army was surprised by Rommel's withdrawal, and confusion caused by redeployments between the three corps meant they were slow in pursuit, failing to cut off Rommel at Fukah and Mersa Matruh.[133]

Axis tank losses were 500. On November 4, only thirty-six German tanks were left out of the 249 at the beginning of the battle. Italian losses were 971 dead, 933 wounded, and 15,552 men captured. Mussolini replied on December 19 that the Panzer Army must resist to the last man at Buerat. On January 15, 1943, General Montgomery launched the 51st Highland Division in a frontal attack while sending the 2nd New Zealand Division and the 7th Armored Division around the inland flank of the Axis line. Supply shortages and a belief that the Luftwaffe were about to get strong reinforcements led the Desert Air Force to be cautious, reduce the number of offensive sorties on November 5, and protect the Eighth Army.[134]

The Axis made a fighting withdrawal to El Agheila, but Rommel's troops found themselves exhausted and with few replacements, while Montgomery had planned to transport material over great distances to provide the Eighth Army with 2,600 tons of supplies per day.[135]

By November 11, the number of Axis prisoners had risen to 30,000 men. Benghazi handled 3,000 tons a day by the end of December, rather than the expected 800 tons.[136] Mindful of Axis counterstrokes from El Agheila, Montgomery paused for three weeks to concentrate his forces and prepare an assault.[137] About 254 Axis guns were lost, along with sixty-four German and twenty Italian aircraft.[138]

The Desert Air Force failed to make a maximum effort to bomb a disorganized and retreating opponent, which on November 5 was within range and confined to the coast road. Rommel's army had lost roughly 75,000 men, 1,000 guns, and 500 tanks since the Second Battle of El Alamein and withdrew.[139] By December 15, the New Zealanders had reached the coast road, but the firm terrain allowed Rommel to break his forces into smaller units and withdraw off road, through the gaps between the New Zealanders positions.[140] Rommel conducted a textbook retreat, destroying all equipment and infrastructure left behind and peppering the land behind him with mines and booby traps.[141] West of Sirte, the Eighth Army was forced to pause to consolidate its strung out formations, to prepare an attack at Wādī Zamzam near Buerat 370 kilometers east of Tripoli, finally reaching Sirte on December 25.[142] Rommel had, with the agreement of Field Marshal Bastico, sent a request to the Italian Supreme Command in Rome to withdraw to Tunisia, where the terrain would be better suited to defensive action and where he could link with the Axis army forming there in response to the Operation Torch landings.

The Eighth Army lost from 332–500 tanks, although by the end of the battle, 300 had had already been repaired. Rommel's German–Italian Panzer Army was renamed the Italian First Army under General Giovanni Messe, and Rommel assumed command of the new Army Group Africa, responsible for both fronts. In the month after the Eighth Army reached Capuzzo, the railway carried 133,000 tons of supplies. British figures, based on Ultra intercepts, gave German casualties as 1,149 killed, 3,886 wounded, and 8,050 men captured. The port of Tripoli, some 240 kilometers further west, was taken on January 23 as Rommel continued to withdraw to the French-built southern defenses of Tunisia, the Mareth Line.[143]

British-United States Invasion of French North Africa

By the summer of 1941, the series of Italian failures, German rescue missions, and British reactions had created a confused arrangement of deployments in and around the Mediterranean, satisfactory to neither side. Axis forces held Greece and the island of Crete, as well as Sicily, the stepping-stone to Tunisia. In North Africa, Erwin Rommel and his *Afrika Korps*, allied with an Italian army of questionable ability, had pushed the British into Egypt to a point only 60 miles from Alexandria.[1] Allied prospects were in a tenuous state. The bottleneck at Gibraltar was open, but passage depended on running a gauntlet of German submarines. Britain still held the island of Malta, though it was under frequent air attack, and the British Eighth Army was still a viable force in Egypt, though it had been on the defensive for some time. Both the Axis and Allies had invested heavily in the Mediterranean area, and to justify their presence, both would have to continue efforts there. Both would also have to deal with the question hanging over the entire theater: would overseas French forces fight with the Axis or Allies?[2]

Landings in French North Africa were proposed. Operation Torch (initially called Operation Gymnast) was the British–United States invasion of French North Africa. The Soviet Union had pressed the U.S. after the Western Allies' Combined Chiefs of Staff met in Washington on July 30. General George Marshall and Admiral Ernest King declined to approve the plan. When President Roosevelt was told of this, he was furious, calling Marshall and King to the White House and giving a direct order that Torch was to have precedence over other operations and was to take place at the earliest possible date.[3] They would also secure Allied naval control of the south-west Mediterranean, and enable an invasion of Southern Europe later in 1943. Roosevelt suspected that landings in Northwest Africa would rule out an invasion of Europe in 1943, but agreed to support British Prime Minister Winston Churchill.[2] Roosevelt wanted to get to grips with Germany as soon as possible, cabling Churchill that "last week represented a turning point in the war."[4]

Senior U.S. commanders remained strongly opposed to the landings. Landings to the west would reduce pressure on Allied forces in Egypt and enable the British to start operations in Europe and open a second front to reduce the pressure of German forces on the Soviet troops. This was one of only two direct orders Roosevelt gave to military commanders during the war.[5]

Major General George S. Patton, Jr., would lead Western Task Force into Casablanca; Major General Lloyd R. Fredendall would lead Center Task Force into Oran; and British Lieutenant General Kenneth A. N. Anderson would lead Eastern Task Force into Algiers. However, in deference to French feelings, American Major General Charles W. Ryder was selected to lead the initial landing force at Algiers. Naval support would be coordinated through the Royal Navy. Land-based air support would come from two commands, one British and one American, the latter under Brigadier General James H. Doolittle. General Eisenhower hoped to make these three landings in late October, but as planning advanced, D-day was set for November 8.[6]

On November 8, 1942, the first waves of landing craft plowed through dark swells toward beaches codenamed, from north to south, Red, Blue, Green, and Yellow. As naval gunfire pounded French batteries, the first American troops to land in French Morocco—Company "K," 47th Infantry—came ashore at 4.45 a.m. at Green Beach. Forty-five minutes later, over 600 men from all beaches returned sniper and machine-gun fire and began capturing French and Moroccan troops and key points. By daylight, American troops controlled all port facilities, the post office, telecommunications station, petroleum storage tanks, all roads leading into town, and the civil police force.[7] Reinforced by continuing waves of landing craft, American troops extended their beachhead inland against little more than sniper fire. Sunrise made more accurate naval gunfire possible, and by 10.45 a.m., all French batteries were out of action. Most resistance to infantry advancing through town came from a walled barracks—headquarters to the garrison of fewer than 1,000 men. American troops surrounded and isolated the barracks, then moved on to clear the rest of the town.[8] As artillery was offloaded, it too was trained on the barracks, but because Eisenhower and Patton hoped to gain the surrender of troops who could later fight Axis armies without a costly battle, they issued no attack order.[9]

Landings in the Algiers area met mixed success. The British 11th Infantry Brigade Group came across Beach Apples on time and without mishap, the smoothest of all Torch landings. Fortunately, landings at Apples and Beer were unopposed.[10] At Beach Charlie, however, coastal batteries fired on transports as the landing craft neared shore. Naval gunfire responded, but then high surf scattered the 39th Regimental Combat Team boats, smashing some against coastal rocks. Leaving the boats, most troops found a vertical bluff with stairs cut for sightseers, instead of gradually rising ground. Overcoming all these difficulties, the troops of the 39th Team moved 8 miles inland and took the airfield at Maison Blanche by 8.30 a.m. However, for the rest of the day, a fierce battle raged with a French marine artillery battery. Royal Navy surface and air units eventually prevailed, though Axis bombers managed to damage a transport and destroyer.[11]

Late in Center Task Force planning, the British had added another landing. Operation Reservist called for 400 men to assault Oran harbor itself to prevent sabotage and, possibly, accept the surrender of the city from surprised officials. Yet even before the troops reached shore, Reservist became the biggest disappointment of all Torch landings.[12] The troops from the 6th Armored Infantry Regiment, 1st Armored Division, boarded two British cutters. Entering the harbor, the two cutters were soon found by searchlights and by devastating fire from shore batteries and French destroyers. One cutter tried to ram a destroyer, and in a crunching sideswipe, it received pointblank fire that killed or wounded nearly half of the American troops and British crew.[13] Both cutters were reduced to burning, sinking hulks, with survivors scrambling for launches. Only forty-seven American troops eventually landed.[14]

Operation Torch gave the Allies substantial beachheads in North Africa at rather modest cost, considering the size of forces committed: 125,000 soldiers, sailors, and airmen participated in the operation, 82,600 of them U.S. Army personnel.[15] Of the 1,469 casualties, 96 percent were American, with the Army losing 526 killed, 837 wounded, and forty-one missing. Casualties varied considerably among the three task forces. Eastern Task Force lost the fewest Americans killed in action, 108; Western Task Force, with four times as many American troops, lost 142 killed; and Center Task Force lost almost twice as many killed, 276. Yet without the British-sponsored Reservist disaster at Oran, the Center Task Force KIA total would have been in the same range as that of the other task forces.[16]

Axis forces pushed on to Sbeitla and then to the Kasserine Pass on February 19, where the U.S. elements of the British First Army under Lieutenant General Kenneth Anderson came to within 64 kilometers of Tunis before a counterattack at Djedeida thrust them back. Hard fighting followed, but the Allies cut off the Germans and Italians from support by naval and air forces between Tunisia and Sicily.[17] The Axis forces again attacked eastward at Medenine on March 6, but they were easily repulsed by the Eighth Army. The First and Eighth Armies then attacked the Axis in April.[18] On May 6, as the culmination of Operation Vulcan, the British took Tunis and American forces reached Bizerte.[19] Rommel counselled Hitler to allow a full retreat to a defensible line, but he was denied, and on March 9, Rommel left Tunisia to be replaced by Hans-Jürgen von Arnim, who had to spread his forces over 160 kilometers of northern Tunisia.[20]

The setbacks at Kasserine forced the Allies to consolidate their forces and develop their lines of communication and administration so that they could support a major attack. Fredendall was replaced by George Patton.

General Sir Harold Alexander arrived in Tunisia in late February to take charge of the new 18th Army Group headquarters, which had been created to take overall control of both the Eighth Army and the Allied forces already fighting in Tunisia.[21] By May 13, the Axis forces in Tunisia had surrendered. This opened the way for the Allied invasion of Sicily in July.[22]

In the west, the forces of the First Army came under attack at the end of January, being forced back from the Faïd Pass and then suffering a reversal at Sidi Bou Zid on February 14–15.[23] In January 1943, German and Italian troops under General Field Marshall Erwin Rommel—retreating westward from Libya—reached Tunisia.[24] The British Eighth Army in the east, commanded by Lieutenant General Bernard Montgomery, stopped around Tripoli to allow reinforcements to arrive and build up the Allied advantage.[25] II Corps retreated in disarray until heavy Allied reinforcements halted the Axis advance on February 22. After consolidating in Algeria, the Allies set their sights on Tunisia.[26]

The Battle of El Agheila

By mid-morning on December 11, 1942, British patrols detected that the Axis positions were starting to thin out. In doing so, Rommel defied the "stand to the last" orders of Adolf Hitler to save the remainder of his force.[1] They had been caught out in earlier campaigns by an enemy that had drawn them on and then counterattacked. There were Anglo–American landings in Morocco and Algeria (Operation Torch), Cyrenaica was abandoned without serious resistance, and the Italians resumed their withdrawal on the same day after an Allied attack, and the Germans followed suit.[2] Montgomery rested some of his formations after their efforts at El Alamein, leading with the 4th Light Armored Brigade.[3]

By this time, all available men and equipment were being diverted to Tunis to prevent Tunisia falling to an Allied advance from Algeria following the Allied landings of Operation Torch. Facing the prospect of a large Allied force to his rear, he decided to withdraw in one bound to El Agheila.[4] Axis forces retired from Sidi Barrani and Halfaya Pass (on the Libyan–Egyptian border), the last position in Egypt. Rommel wanted to save 10,000 tons of equipment in Tobruk, but it fell to the British on November 13.[5] An attempt by Montgomery to trap the Tobruk garrison by an encirclement toward Acroma, west of Tobruk failed and the garrison retreated along the Via Balbia toward Benghazi with few losses.[6]

Rommel's supply position had not improved. Tunisia was still being prioritized for supplies, and of the ships that were sent to Tripoli to supply the Panzer Army in November, three-quarters had been destroyed. Montgomery had intended to build his army's morale by banishing the habit of defeat and retreat, and the 1st Armored Division and 2nd New Zealand Division were held at Bardia, resting and providing a defense. Rommel was short of men and equipment and very short of fuel and ammunition. His stated intention therefore was to hold out as long as possible, but to retire in the face of strong pressure. When the preliminary attacks began on December 11, Rommel took this to be the start of the Eighth Army's attack and started to withdraw. When a reconnaissance force of armored cars was sent across country, it became delayed by waterlogged ground. The maneuver was to be masked by bombardments and infantry raids on the forward positions of the *Panzerarmee*, commencing on the night of December 11–12, to divert attention. The RAF quickly occupied the airfield to provide air cover for a Malta convoy on November 18. Axis forces had withdrawn 640 kilometers in ten days.[7] Despite the importance of the Port of Benghazi to the Axis supply chain, Rommel abandoned the port to avoid a repeat of the disastrous entrapment suffered by the Italians at the Battle of Beda Fomm in February 1941.[8] Rommel ordered the demolition of port facilities and materiel in Benghazi, writing afterwards: "… in Benghazi, we destroyed the port facilities and platforms and the chaos overwhelmed the civilians in this miserable town." Benghazi was occupied by the British, and three days later, the Axis forces retreated from Ajdabiya and fell back to Mersa Brega.[9] To delay the British advance at any cost, Axis sappers laid mines in the Mersa Brega area and steel helmets were laid to mislead British mine detectors.[10]

During their withdrawal to Mersa Brega, the Axis forces faced many difficulties—including British air superiority—that allowed them to target the Axis columns, crowded on the coastal road and short of fuel. Signals intelligence revealed to the Eighth Army that the *Panzerarmee* was virtually immobilized by lack of fuel, prompting Montgomery to order a stronger force to be sent across country. The Eastern Task Force aimed at Algiers, landed with 20,000 troops, and began moving east towards Rommel. Rommel received a warning from Hitler of an expected Allied landing between Tobruk and Benghazi, but on November 8, he discovered that this was wrong. Having heard of the presence of the reconnaissance force, Rommel brought forward his retirement from Benghazi and was able to brush the Armored cars aside, untroubled by the stronger force that had yet to arrive.[11] During the eighteen days between the evacuation of Ajdabiya on November 23 and the beginning of the Battle of El Agheila on December 11, Rommel described disagreements with his political and military superiors and he engaged in fruitless bitter arguments with Hitler, Hermann Göring, General Albert Kesselring (Army Command in the South), Ugo Cavallero (the Italian chief of staff at Italian Supreme Command), and the Governor of Libya Ettore Bastico.[12]

Rommel wanted to withdraw to Tunis as soon as possible, while the others wanted him to make a stand on the El Agheila–Mersa Brega line.[13] Mussolini ordered Rommel to stand on the Agheila line to defend Tripolitania and this was supported by Hitler, who ordered that El Agheila should be held "in all circumstances."[14]

Although the Agheila position was naturally strong, being surrounded by salt marshes, soft sand, or broken ground, restricting the ability of vehicles to maneuver, Rommel's assessment was that he would be able to hold the position only if he received artillery and tank replacements, if the Luftwaffe was strengthened and his fuel and ammunition supplies were restored.[15]

The *Afrika Korps* reached the village of Fukah the next day. Italian forces had arrived earlier, having withdrawn from El Alamein from November 3–4, and formed a defensive line. By the time of Rommel's visit to Berlin at the beginning of December, Mussolini and Hitler had accepted the reality of the situation and agreed for preparations to be made for a withdrawal to Buerat, some 400 kilometers to the west and by December 3, the un-mechanized Italian infantry had begun a retirement.[16]

For much of the pursuit to El Agheila, the British were uncertain of Rommel's intentions. Supplies could be moved 710 kilometers from Alexandria to Tobruk by rail, the 630 kilometers from Tobruk to Ajdabiya was slightly shorter, but supplies had to go by road on the Via Balbia or by sea to Benghazi and then by road to Ajdabiya. Despite Rommel's concerns of entrapment by a rapid Allied advance across the Cyrenaica bulge, Montgomery was aware that an extended and isolated force could also be vulnerable, as in early 1941 and early 1942. On November 26, X Corps was taken into reserve and XXX Corps took over the Eighth Army front line with the 7th Armored Division, 51st Highland Infantry Division, and 2nd New Zealand Division.[17]

On December 13, Axis reconnaissance aircraft discovered some 300 vehicles north of Marada oasis 121 kilometers south of El Agheila (the New Zealand column), which meant for the Axis forces the danger of being outflanked. A frontal attack by the 51st Highland Division on the coast and the 7th Armored Division inland on their left would begin on the night of December 16–17, once the New Zealanders were in position behind the Axis position.[18]

Montgomery planned for the 2nd New Zealand Division, with the 4th Light Armored Brigade under command, to commence a wide outflanking movement on December 13.

The British had to supply their forces from Egypt to Ajdabiya. In response, Montgomery ordered the New Zealand Division to move immediately and brought forward the main assault to the night of December 14–15.[19] By the evening of December 12, the Axis withdrawal was under way, except for some units who were covering the extrication.[20]

Rommel wished to launch his remaining armor at this outflanking force, but he was prevented by lack of fuel and ordered the withdrawal to continue. An attack by the 7th Armored Division was repulsed in a rearguard action by the Italian Combat Group Ariete. Rain on the afternoon of November 6, impeded the British pursuit as the Axis forces continued their withdrawal and a new defense line was established at Mersa Matruh the following day, some 180 kilometers west of El Alamein. In his diary, Rommel wrote:

> Late in the morning, a superior enemy force launched an attack on Combat Group Ariete, which was located south-west of El Agheila, with its right flank

resting on the Sebcha Chebira and its left linking up with 90th Light Division. Bitter fighting ensued against 80 British tanks and lasted for nearly ten hours. The Italians put up a magnificent fight, for which they deserved the utmost credit. Finally, in the evening, the British were thrown back by a counterattack of the Centauro's armored regiment, leaving 22 tanks and 2 armored cars burnt out or damaged on the battlefield. The British intention of cutting off the 90th Light Division had been foiled. The Eighth Army change of plan had come too late and when the New Zealand Division completed their "left hook" on December 15, they were dispersed after a difficult journey across tough terrain which left them with only 17 serviceable tanks. They found 15th Panzer Division on the escarpment guarding the coast road and the 6th New Zealand Brigade further west, was ordered to form a block on the coast road, while the 5th Brigade protected the divisional supply and transport vehicles. During the night of 15–16 December, most of the remaining elements of the Panzer Army were able to withdraw towards Nofilia, moving in small fast columns through the gaps in the dispersed New Zealand units, under cover of dark. On December 18, short-lived but fierce fighting took place at Nofaliya (100mi (160km) west of El Agheila), which brought the battle of El Agheila to an end.[21]

The Battle of Tunisia

The first two years of the war in North Africa were characterized by chronic supply shortages and transport problems.[1] Control of the central Mediterranean was contested by the British and Italian navies, which were equally matched and exerted a reciprocal constraint supply through Alexandria, Tripoli, Benghazi, and Tobruk, although the British could supply Egypt via the long route through the Atlantic around the Cape of Good Hope and by the Indian Ocean into the Red Sea.[2]

The North African coast has few natural harbors and the British base at Alexandria on the Nile Delta was some 2,100 kilometers by road from the main Italian port at Tripoli in Libya. The main attack began the afternoon of December 22. With the arrival of the German *Afrika Korps*, the Axis counterattacked in Operation Sonnenblume, and in April 1941, they reached the limit of their supply capacity at the Egyptian border but failed to recapture Tobruk.[3] By November 10, French opposition to the Torch landings had ceased, creating a military vacuum in Tunisia.[4]

In July 1942, the Allies discussed relatively small-scale amphibious operations to land in northern France during 1942 (Operation Sledgehammer, which was the forerunner of Operation Roundup, the main landings in 1943), but agreed that these operations were impractical and should be deferred. Instead, it was agreed that landings would be made to secure the Vichy territories in North Africa (Morocco, Algeria, and Tunisia) and then to thrust east to take the Axis forces in the Western Desert in their rear.[5]

The Allied force initially withdrew roughly 9.7 kilometers to the high positions of Longstop Hill (Djebel el Ahmera) and Bou Aoukaz on each side of the river, but concern over the vulnerability to flanking attacks prompted a further withdrawal west so that, by the end of December 10, Allied units held a defensive line just east of Medjez el Bab. However, this came too late to affect the fighting on land because the armored elements of the 10th Panzer Division had already arrived. The Tenth Army was destroyed and the Western Desert Force occupied El Agheila, some 970 kilometers from Alexandria. On November 8, Operation Torch landed Allied forces in Algeria (at Oran and Algiers) and Morocco (at Casablanca) with the intention that, once Vichy forces in Algeria had capitulated, an advance would be made to Tunis, some 800 kilometers to the east. The Allies expected that the Axis would move to occupy the country as soon as they heard of the Torch landings.[6]

Despite some Vichy French forces, such as Barré's siding against the Axis, the position of Vichy forces remained uncertain until the North African Agreement on November 22 placed French North Africa on the Allied side, allowing the Allied garrison troops to be sent forward to the front. However, there was a limit to how far east the Torch landings could be made because of the increasing proximity of Axis airfields in Sicily and Sardinia, which at the end of October, held 298 German and 574 Italian aircraft.[7]

Two Allied brigade groups advanced toward Djebel Abiod and Beja respectively. The Western Desert Force fought a delaying action as it fell back to Mersa Matruh (Matruh), then began Operation Compass, a raid and counterattack into Libya. By the end of the month, three German divisions, including the 10th Panzer Division and two Italian infantry divisions had arrived. In 1942, the Royal Navy and Italian Navy were still disputing the Mediterranean, but the British hold on Malta allowed the RAF to sink more Italian supply ships. Once Algiers was secured, a small force (the Eastern Task Force) would be projected as quickly as possible into Tunisia in a race to occupy Tunis—some 800 kilometers distant along poor roads in difficult terrain during the winter rainy season—before the Axis could organise.[8]

Further attacks were driven back from cleverly planned interlocking defenses. This meant that, at Algiers, the disembarkation of mobile forces for an advance to Tunisia would necessarily be delayed.[9] Plans were thus a compromise, and the Allies realized that an attempt to reach Bizerte and Tunis overland before the Axis could establish themselves represented a gamble that depended on the ability of the navy and air force to delay the Axis build-up.[10] The Allies, although they had provided for the possibility of strong Vichy opposition to their landings both in terms of infantry and air force allocations, seriously underestimated the Axis appetite for and speed of intervention in Tunisia.[11] Once operations had commenced, and despite clear intelligence reports regarding the Axis reaction, the Allies were slow to respond and it was not until nearly two weeks after the landings that air and naval plans were made to interdict Axis sea transport to Tunis.[12]

The Combined Chiefs of Staff had decided that, with the forces available, Torch would not include landings close to Tunisia. This would ensure the success of the initial landings in spite of uncertainty as to how the incumbent French forces would react. The two Allied columns concentrated at Djebel Abiod and Beja, preparing for an assault on November 24. The Tunisian Campaign, also known as the Battle of Tunisia, was a series of battles that took place in Tunisia. Large quantities of supplies became available to the British from the United States and the supply situation of the Eighth Army eventually resolved. In the south, the 11th Brigade were halted by stiff resistance at Medjez. The 36th Brigade was to advance from Djebel Abiod toward Mateur and the 11th Brigade was to move down the valley of the Medjerda River to take Majaz al Bab and then to Tebourba, Djedeida, and Tunis. Night convoys resumed on completion of the extension of Axis minefields, which severely restricted the activities of Force "K" and Force "Q."[13]

On November 17, the same day Nehring arrived, the leading elements of the British 36th Brigade on the northern road met a mixed force of seventeen tanks and 400 paratroops with self-propelled guns at Djebel Abiod. Anderson needed to get his limited force east quickly before the Axis could reinforce Tunisia, but the Allies had only two brigade groups and some additional armor and artillery for the attack.[14]

Early on November 26, 1942, as the Germans withdrew, the 11th Brigade were able to enter Medjez unopposed and, by late in the day, had taken positions in and around Tebourba, which had also been evacuated by the Germans, preparatory to advancing on Djedeida. The First Army was immediately ordered to send the 36th Infantry Brigade Group, which had been the floating reserve for the Algiers landing, eastward by sea to occupy the Algerian ports of Bougie, Philippeville, and Bône and the airfield at Djidjelli, preliminary to advancing into Tunisia. The Italian invasion of Egypt by the Tenth Army in 1940, advanced 97 kilometers into Egypt and more than 1,600 kilometers in a straight line from Tripoli, 600 kilometers from Benghazi, and 320 kilometers from Tobruk. Admiral Esteva did not close airfields to either side; the Germans moved first, and by November 9, there were reports of forty German aircraft arriving at Tunis, and by November 10, aerial reconnaissance reported 100 aircraft.[15]

On November 22, tanks from the Italian 50th Brigade forced U.S. paratroopers to abandon Gafsa. Despite rain and insufficient air cover, progress was made up the lower ridges of the 270-meter Longstop Hill that controlled the river corridor from Medjez to Tebourba and thence to Tunis. The French military commander in Tunisia, General Barré, moved troops into the western mountains of Tunisia and formed a defensive line from Tebersouk through Medjez el Bab.[16] However, planners had to assume the worst case regarding the extent of Vichy opposition at Algiers and the invasion convoys were assault-loaded with a preponderance of infantry to meet heavy ground opposition. On November 11, the British 36th Infantry Brigade had landed unopposed at Bougie, but supply shortages delayed their arrival at Djidjelli until November 13.[17] At the end of November, naval Force "K" was reformed in Malta with three cruisers and four destroyers and Force "Q" formed in Bône with three cruisers and two destroyers. A parachute battalion made an unopposed drop at Youks-les-Bains, capturing the airfield and advancing to take the airfield at Gafsa on November 17.[18] Two days later, an airlift began that carried over 15,000 men and 581 tons of supplies and ships brought 176 tanks, 131 artillery pieces, 1,152 vehicles, and 13,000 tons of supplies. Walther Nehring was assigned command of the newly formed XC Corps on November 12 and flew in on November 17. The Germans attacked twice and were repulsed, but the French defensive success was costly and, lacking armor and artillery, were obliged to withdraw.[19, 20]

On November 19, German Commander Walter Nehring demanded passage for his forces across the bridge at Medjez and was refused by Barré. The Luftwaffe, happy to have local air superiority while the Allies planes had to fly from relatively distant bases in Algeria, harassed them all the way.[21]

A hasty intelligence review showed about 125,000 combat and 70,000 service troops, mostly Italian, in front of them. The German paratroopers, Luftwaffe, and Italian fire support from the 1st Mountain Infantry Division Superga knocked out eleven tanks, but their advance was halted while the fight at Djebel Abiod continued for nine days.[22] Algiers was accordingly chosen for the most easterly landings. No Axis ships sailing to Tunis were sunk in November, but the Allied naval forces had some success in early December sinking seven Axis transports. The 1st Armored Division had concentrated forward for an attack in conjunction with Blade Force planned for December 2. Blade Force, an armored regimental group was to strike across country on minor roads in the gap between the two infantry brigades towards Sidi Nsir and make flanking attacks on Tebourba and Djedeida.[23]

The Allied plan was to advance along the two roads and take Bizerte and Tunis. Smaller ports at Benghazi and Tobruk were 1,050 kilometers and 640 kilometers west of Alexandria on the Litoranea Balbo running along a narrow corridor along the coast. Blade Force passed through Sidi Nsir to reach the Chouigui Pass, north of Tebourba, and part of Blade Force infiltrated behind Axis lines to the newly activated airbase at Djedeida in the afternoon and destroyed more than twenty Axis planes, but, lacking infantry support, withdrew to Chouigui.[24] Blade Force's attack caught Nehring by surprise and he decided to withdraw from Medjez and strengthen Djedeida, only 30 kilometers from Tunis.[25] The 36th Brigade's delayed attack began on November 26, but the brigade was ambushed with the leading battalion taking 149 casualties.[26, 27]

The position remained in German hands until the last days of fighting in Tunisia the following spring.[28] The northern attack did not take place because torrential rain had slowed the build-up. Advanced guards of the 36th Infantry Brigade reached Tabarka on November 15 and Djebel Abiod on November 18, where the brigade met Axis forces. To counter the surface threat, Axis convoys were switched to daylight when they could be protected by air cover paratroopers to abandon Gafsa.

The slow build up had brought Allied force levels up to a total of 54,000 British, 73,800 American, and 7,000 French troops. However, on November 27, the Germans attacked in strength and the 11th Brigade's attempted to regain the initiative in the early hours of November 28, attacking toward Djedeida airfield with the help of U.S. armor.[29] The French governor in Tunisia, Admiral Esteva, was afraid to support the Allies or oppose the Axis. They were forestalled by an Axis counterattack led by Major-

General Wolfgang Fischer, whose 10th Panzer Division had just arrived in Tunisia.[30] By the evening of December 2, Blade Force had been withdrawn, leaving the 11th Brigade and Combat Command "B" to deal with the Axis attack.[31] This threatened to cut off the 11th Brigade and break through into the Allied rear, but desperate fighting over four days delayed the Axis advance and permitted a controlled withdrawal to the high ground on each side of the river west of Terbourba.[32] The chronic difficulty in the supply of military forces in the desert led to several indecisive victories by both sides and long fruitless advances along the coast. Here, they started a build up for another attack and were ready by late December 1942.[33]

To forestall this, it would be necessary to occupy Tunisia as quickly as possible after the landings were made. An Allied occupation of the whole of the North African coast would open the Mediterranean to Allied shipping, releasing the huge capacity required to maintain supplies around the circuitous route via the Cape of Good Hope. The Eighth Army was soon pushed back to Gazala west of Tobruk and at the Battle of Gazala in May 1942, the Axis pushed them all the way back to El Alamein, only 160 kilometers from Alexandria. After three days of to-and-fro fighting, with ammunition running low and Axis forces now holding adjacent high ground, the Longstop position became untenable and the Allies were forced to withdraw to Medjez, and by December 26, 1942, the Allies had withdrawn to the line they had set out from two weeks earlier, having suffered 20,743 casualties.

At first, the German and Italian troops were successful in defeating the Allies quickly in Tunisia, driving them back 80 kilometers through the Kasserine Pass and destroying 100 U.S. tanks in the attack commanded by Erwin Rommel. During the assaults, the Germans seized large amounts of discarded Allied equipment. Rommel's troops were badly defeated by the British Eighth Army at Tripoli, so he moved to Tunisia to join up with German General von Arnim. While the British were reworking their supply lines, U.S. II Corps failed to attack the Germans when they had a chance and the Germans launched a heavy armored assault destroying thirteen tanks, 208 vehicles, eighteen field guns, three anti-tank guns, one anti-aircraft battery, and 2,546 troops missing.

Enormous amounts of supplies finally reached the Allies and the tide quickly turned around. Rommel's 160 tanks now faced more than 400 British tanks and 500 British anti-tank guns that caused heavy losses on Rommel but not before Rommel took out most of the Allies' Valentine tanks. The failure of the Allies to defeat Rommel caused the Allies to rethink their strategic plan of attack. The new M4 Sherman tank was brought in along with expanded air support and strengthened troop movement into the region. In March 1943, the Allies were back on the offensive. Montgomery and Patton hit the south and east flanks, pushing the Axis forces into the northeast corner. It proved to be too much for the Axis as enemy troops were surrendering in masses. On May 9, over 275,000 prisoners were captured by the Allies, bringing an end to the Battle of Tunisia and effectively ending the war in North Africa.[34]

Analysis of Italian Army Performance in North Africa

Prior to World War II, the Italian Army had created a series of unit organizations that reflected the strategic needs of nation. The doctrine, tenets, and procedures of the army itself, and the strength and weaknesses of Italian society and its economy were considered. Within this organizational design, the army generally recognized two armies: the metropolitan army that would serve in Europe and a colonial army that would serve in Italy's overseas territories—primarily Africa.

Given their limitations, the army compromised and developed modified divisional organizations for use in the desert that could be equipped within Italy's limited means. These organizations were called Africa Northern. The divisional organizations that were planned were not necessarily what was seen on the battlefield. Shortages of equipment and supplies limited the actual level of motorization in these formations. All units began the process of transition to each new table of organization and equipment, but the lack of equipment and combat losses normally left the process incomplete.

Three general types of units comprised the forces under Africa Northern; Indigenous natives comprised the bulk of the forces stationed in Africa after World War I, supported by a small number of Italian volunteer units and Carabinieri units. This remained the situation until 1937, when the events set in motion by the Italian invasion of Ethiopia caused the Italian military to increase its forces in Libya. Four new metropolitan divisions were raised and stationed in Libya, organized into two corps (XX Corp with the Sabratha and Division Sirte and XXI Corp with the Cirene and Marmarica divisions). The number of Libyan units was increased at the same time. In January 1939, a new plan was developed for the defense of Libya that would increase the number of Metropolitan divisions to eight. When the war began in September 1939, the Italians mobilized and transported the four additional divisions to Africa (Bologna, Savona, Brescia, and Pavia). At the same time, four militia, commonly known as Blackshirt Divisions, were formed using units from Italy and sent south. Additionally, two Libyan divisions were formed in February 1940 using existing units in Africa

Most of the overseas forces were stationed in Ethiopia and Libya. In Ethiopia, the Italian military forces were organized as the Armed Forces of Italian Eastern Africa. This organization was, at its core, a colonial force. The bulk of the military forces stationed in Ethiopia (twenty-nine brigades) were raised from the local population. These units were supported by two divisions organized from Italian nationals. In Libya, the Italian military forces were organized under the Upper Armed Forces North Africa Command Africa. This headquarters controlled two armies; the Fifth Army in Tripolitania, facing Tunisia, and the Tenth Army in Cyrenaica, facing Egypt. Lacking a large indigenous population to create colonial formations, a total of twelve Italian divisions were stationed in the colony in 1940.

Mussolini wanted to occupy the French and British colonies in Africa and seize control of the Suez Canal from the British. In August 1940, he ordered attacks on British positions in East Africa and Egypt. Troops from the Italian colony of Ethiopia invaded British Somaliland and quickly overran its garrison made up of mostly conscripted natives. At the same time, other Italian troops began to move westward from Ethiopia into Sudan to seize the upper Nile Valley. They quickly captured Kassala and Gallabat, while more Italian troops moved south to capture Moyale, in the northern part of the British colony of Kenya. Buoyed by their successes, the Italians prepared to march from Libya across northern Egypt to seize the Suez Canal. The youngest elements of the Italian Army were indoctrinated to consider themselves invincible because they were Italians and Fascists. They were taught that their enemies were inferior and would be easily defeated. Mussolini repeatedly refused offers of assistance from Hitler during this period, convinced that his forces could vanquish the British.

Libya presented challenges for the operation of a large military force. The lack of infrastructure (power grid, roads, railways, etc.) made an army total dependent upon itself. Where pack and draught animals could support military operations in a European setting, the lack of water and forage precluded any use of animals in Libya. The answer was motorization, and this was the direction taken by the Italian Army in designing the organizations of units serving in Libya. However, Italian industry and the nation's finances limited what could be accomplished. Completely motorizing the entire force in Libya, in addition to the vehicles required by the metropolitan army, was beyond Italy's means.

The Africa type unit was basically a standard metropolitan auto-transportable organization. The auto-transportable division had limited manning and equipment changes from the infantry division to better meet the requirements of desert operations. The auto-transportable division was a semi-motorized unit that provided vehicles for the divisional artillery and services component in the place of draught and pack animals. No additional transport was provided for the infantry component; the division remained a foot-mobile infantry unit that still employed animals for the infantry heavy weapons.

The Africa type variation of auto-transportable division increased the number of vehicles in the supply services and the infantry heavy weapons, but left the infantry on foot. The intent was that the corps' transportation group would be increased in size to provide additional truck support. When properly outfitted with trucks, the corps' transportation group could provide limited transport for part of the infantry within the corps (similar to the pre-war British infantry division structure). Firepower was slightly increased due to a higher allocation of automatic weapons (262 Breda 30 sub-machine guns instead of 220 found in a metropolitan division). A replacement battalion was included as the units in Africa would have limited access to the depots in Italy.

On September 13, 1940, Marshal Rodolfo Graziani, commander of the Italian Army in North Africa, began his advance into Egypt, hoping to make a quick dash to the Suez Canal. He commanded a 236,000-strong army supported by a powerful air force. Yet, behind the overwhelming numbers facing the British were glaring weaknesses that not even Graziani's Fascist confidence could overcome. The Italian Tenth and Fifth Armies in Libya marched on foot, while the British rode in trucks. Two of the six Italian divisions were Blackshirt militia outfits, clad in fancy black uniforms, but they were poorly trained soldiers. The main characteristic of Italian tactics was a lack of flexibility. They had remained attached to one principle, which consisted of the concentration of the greatest mass possible for whatever task lay ahead of them. In addition, Italian divisions were reduced from three regiments to two. This created more Italian divisions, but weakened their strength. Further, the Italian forces relied on poor, obsolete equipment: armored cars dated back to 1909; the L3 rank mounted only two Breda machine guns; the underpowered and thinly Armored M11 tank was no better—its 37-mm gun could not traverse; the heavyweight M13 tank packed a 47-mm gun, but crawled along at 9 mph (none could match the British Matilda tank with its 50-mm armor and 40-mm gun); Italian troops were short of anti-tank guns, anti-aircraft guns, ammunition, and radio sets; artillery was light and ancient; Italian infantrymen carried the Carcano Modello 1891 rifle, which suffered from low muzzle velocity; and their Breda machine guns were clumsy to operate and jammed easily. On the other hand, the British troops used the reliable J03-caliber Lee-Enfield rifle and the very good Bren and Vickers machine guns. The Italians also had problems in the air. While they could sortie eighty-four modern bombers and 114 fighters, backed up by 113 obsolete aircraft, they were completely outclassed by the British Hawker Hurricane fighter aircraft. Furthermore, the British Army, which had trained for years in the Egyptian desert, was much better at maintaining its equipment under the extremes of the arid climate.

Four Italian divisions and an armored group under General Annibale Bergonzoli advanced slowly toward Egypt across a hostile landscape in temperatures of up to 122 degrees Fahrenheit. They succeeded in covering only 12 miles a day. Historically, the Italian Army was structured for deployment in the mountainous terrain found in Italy and its immediate neighbors. Graziani's army as a whole was not trained for desert warfare, and the heat and sand took a toll on men and equipment. British General Archibald Wavell's forces, which were distracted in French West Africa, offered little resistance, and the Blackshirt Division 23 March occupied Sidi Barrani on September 16. The Italians were now 60 miles inside the Egyptian border. Despite the superior Italian strength, the British attacked on December 9. General Richard O'Connor led two divisions, the 7th Armored and 4th Indian, in the attack, supported by the 7th Royal Tank Regiment. The Italians could not stop the British Matilda tanks, which quickly found a gap in the Italian defenses. Taking advantage of the rigid Italian tactics, poor leadership, and equipment deficiencies, they dashed through, surprising Graziani. The main British force raced for the coast at Sidi Barrani, while detachments slashed at the rear of the Italian units. The Italians did not have the flexibility to deviate from their formations. While individual soldiers fought bravely, within two days, nearly 40,000 Italians surrendered. The rest of Graziani's force retreated westward toward Libya.

The losses suffered by the Italian Army during the British winter offensive (Operation Compass) between November 1940 and February 1941 demonstrated that the Africa divisional organizations had significant weaknesses. The main problem was the lack of organic transportation within the Italian formations. The limited mobility of their units, adequate in Ethiopia, left them at the mercy of the fully motorized British forces. A second weakness was becoming apparent during this same period: the lack of firepower. However, in the initial assessment of Compass, the firepower issue was hidden by the mobility problem and the Supreme Command first efforts were to correct the latter shortcoming.

In May 1941, the General Staff assessed the requirements for the reconquest of Africa. Part of this assessment involved current unit organizations and availability of equipment. The infantry division type Africa was basically eliminated. In its place, the infantry divisions were divided into two types, motorized division type Africa and occupation division. This structure recognized that the Italian forces in Africa required a mobile striking force, but Italy lacked the resources to fully motorize all the divisions currently in Africa. Additionally, the armored division was redesigned, but this change affected all Italian armored divisions regardless of the theater, so is not Africa specific (this change reflected the availability of the M13/40 medium tanks and lessons learned). Only the armored division was authorized a Bersaglieri (high-mobility light infantry) regiment. The Bersaglieri units traditionally associated with the motorized division became corps assets.

The average Italian soldier began to have serious doubts as to his army's invincibility, and a lack of confidence in Italian leadership reached crisis level. The devastating British offensive of December 1940 had led to a series of severe reversals. Therefore, the Italian High Command requested German assistance. The Luftwaffe's *X Fliegerkorps* was ordered to Italy from Norway and arrived in Sicily in late December 1940. The Germans operated against Allied shipping and patrolled the sea lanes between Italy and Libya. However, by mid-February 1941, having not yet received the ground support he requested, Graziani's Italian forces were overrun and 115,000 men surrendered. In the wake of the Italian defeats, Hitler decided to send a German Army formation to Libya. The intervention was codenamed Operation Sunflower and included the 5th Light and 15th Panzer Divisions. Forward elements of the German force began to arrive in Tripoli on February 14, 1941. The *Deutsches Afrika Korps* was formed five days later. General Erwin Rommel commanded German forces in North Africa and, for the sake of diplomacy, was directed to serve under General Italo Gariboldi, who had succeeded the defeated Marshal Graziani as the Italian commander in North Africa. Immediately after his arrival at Tripoli, on February 12, 1941, Rommel began organizing the defense of Tripolitania, in western Libya, and making plans for offensive actions.

The Italian Ariete and Armored Division Trento arrived from Italy. The Ariete Division was composed of 6,949 men, 163 tanks, thirty-six field guns, and sixty-one anti-tank guns. Motorized infantry consisted of the 101st Division Trieste and the 102nd Division Trento. The semi-motorized infantry contingent included the 17th Division Pavia, 25th Division Bologna, and 27th Division Brescia. Like the motorized formations, these units had two regiments of infantry. The infantry divisions consisted of the 55th Savona and the 60th Sabratha. The Italians introduced the more modern M13/40 tanks grouped in motorized units and not thrown together like Graziani's tanks during his offensive. They also utilized their first company of armored cars.

To erase the poor performance of some obsolete artillery, the Italians introduced the use of self-propelled guns in close support and in anti-tank attacks by massing the artillery. The Ariete Division began to use the 90/53 anti-aircraft gun, which was capable of piercing 100 mm of armor at 1,000 yards. Rommel had at his disposal 100,000 Italian soldiers, 7,000 Italian trucks, 1,000 Italian guns, and fifteen Italian aircraft. Rommel's orders were to assume a defensive posture and hold the front line. Finding that the British defenses were thin, he quickly defeated the Allied forces at El Agheila on March 24. He then launched an offensive which, by April 15, had pushed the British back to Salurn, capturing all but Tobruk, which was encircled and besieged. During this drive, he also managed to capture two British generals, Richard O'Connor and Sir Philip Neame. Gariboldi tried to restrain Rommel, insisting that any further moves would be in direct violation of orders. Rommel ignored him, stating, "I decided to stay on the heels of the retreating enemy and make a bid to seize the whole of Cyrenaica at one stroke." Benghazi, Libya, fell on April 3, and El Meehili was taken the next day. By April 11, the Axis forces had bypassed Tobruk and reached Bardia, Sollum, and the Halfaya Pass. Rommel attacked Tobruk on April 4, but was repelled by the British. The Allies, under the command of British General Claude Auchinleck, launched Operation Crusader on November 18, 1941.

The years 1940 and 1941 saw the Italian military involved in combat operations in France, Greece, Albania, and North Africa. By early 1941, these campaigns had resulted in a significant loss of material that Italian industry was unable to rapidly replace. Simultaneously, the Italian senior leadership recognized that the pre-war organizations were in inadequate for modern maneuver warfare. In September 1941, the Upper Armed Forces Command Africa began examining options to increase the combat power of Italian formations in North Africa, yet at the same time reducing them in size so to be easier to equip and support. The losses suffered by the retreating Axis forces during Operation Crusader in November–December 1941 provided a window of opportunity to affect a reorganization of the divisions. The Italian Armed Forces Command on January 2, 1942 issued instructions for the reorganization of all Italian Divisions in North Africa as the Africa 42 series divisions.

The significant change in the organizations was the creation of combined arms platoons. Support weapons were decentralized to the platoon level, while the infantry element was reduced. The provision of automatic weapons created units that were smaller, yet reflected an increase in firepower. As a consequence of the losses in November–December 1941, the transition was planned for two phases.

The first phase was to reorganize the units using existing assets in Africa. Regiments would initially reorganize with only two battalions, and battalions would reorganize with only two companies. The second phase would bring the divisions up to the Africa type standard using reinforcements and replacements from Italy. The reality was none of the units were completed; losses both in transport from Italy and combat losses in Africa precluded the completion of the reorganization.

All the territory gained by Rommel was recaptured, with the exception of garrisons at Bardia and Sollum. Most significantly, the Axis siege of Tobruk was relieved. The front line was again set at El Agheila. Panzer Group *Afrika* was re-designated as Panzer Army Afrika on January 30, 1942. After pausing to replenish and reorganize his forces, General Rommel launched an attack against Gazala in late May 1942. Rommel personally led elements of Panzer Army *Afrika*, the *Afrika Korps*, the Italian XX Motorized Corps, and the German 90th Light *Afrika* Division in a flanking maneuver around the southern end of the British lines, trusting to the enemy's own minefields to protect his flank and rear. Under German leadership, the Italian X Corps pinned the Allied troops down with a frontal attack, and the Italian 101st Motorized Division Trieste attacked the fortified "box" at Bir Hakeim from the west while the Italian 132nd Armored Division Ariete, on the left flank of Rommel's sweep, attempted to seize it from the rear. The front line ran south from the coastal town of Gazala, west of Tobruk, to the oasis of Bir Hakeim. The British forces were surprised, but fought well, inflicting heavy casualties on the German forces and cornering them. Finding himself trapped between a minefield and the British defenses, Rommel was on the verge of surrender. On May 29, the Italian Division Trieste cleared a path through the center of the Gazala line. Rommel managed to break through the Cauldron area and overwhelm the British defenses.

The British counterattack was confused and useless, easily defeated by the Italian and German forces who then continued toward Tobruk. This campaign had seen the Armored Division Ariete fight as a single entity for the first time and had demonstrated that it could be a formidable force in the right circumstances. It had stopped the British 12th Armored Brigade in its tracks from defensive positions at Bir el Gubi. It had kept the 1st South African Brigade out of the fight for extended periods simply by its presence, and it held its own in the face of considerable harassment from various British armored formations throughout the fighting. It captured a vital position from rough New Zealand troops almost without firing a shot and helped its German allies to destroy the 2nd New Zealand Division. The Armored Division Ariete's performance had been impressive at many levels, and it is arguable that it made a more positive contribution to Axis success than the Germans at a number of points during the fighting. This was a significant change from the Italian Army of 1940. The *Afrika Korps* and the XX Italian Corps, with the assistance of the Luftwaffe, began to assault Tobruk on June 20. Throughout that day, 150 bombers flew 580 sorties. "They dived on the perimeter in one of the most spectacular attacks I have ever seen," wrote Major Friedrich von Mellenthin, Rommel's intelligence officer:

> A great cloud of dust and smoke rose from the sector under attack while our bombs crashed into the defenses … the entire German and Italian artillery joined in with a tremendous and well-coordinated fire.

As soon as the Italian engineers cleared a path through the mines that the Tobruk defenders had planted, German and Italian infantry engaged in hand-to-hand combat with the Allied troops. Tobruk fell to Rommel on June 21. Throughout July, Axis forces hammered at the British Eighth Army, which had abandoned its positions and retreated east to the El Alamein line. By this time, the combat power of Panzer Army *Afrika* comprised 66 percent Italian personnel, 57 percent Italian tanks, 57 percent Italian artillery, and 55 percent Italian aircraft. Even with impressive numbers, the differences between the German and Italian soldiers were becoming apparent. German Field Marshal Albert Kesselring, who rose to command of Axis forces in the Mediterranean, provided a post-war evaluation of operations in North Africa, concluding of the Italians:

> They seemed to have a garrison mentality, and, in fact, much of their training was done in garrison—a totally inappropriate practice for exposing troops to the hardships of the battlefield. Their training remained superficial, without having reached a satisfactory level. The Italian soldier was not a soldier from within. The Italian soldier cannot be compared to the German soldier. There was a lack of contact between the officers and the men. The officers enjoyed rations equivalent to their rank while the common soldier survived on minimal rations.

The differences between the German soldier and the Italian soldier were obvious to many. While the Germans conveyed discipline and order, the Italian soldier was seen to be happy-go-lucky and disorganized. Many Italian soldiers performed well, while others seemed to lose their enthusiasm for the war. On August 31, Rommel, impatient to break through the El Alamein–El Qattara line and move on the Suez Canal, launched an attack against the Alam Haifa Ridge. He committed the German 15th and 21st Panzer Divisions and the Italian Ariete, Littorio, and the Paratroopers Division Folgore. The Italian infantry advanced through the British minefields the entire day as a sandstorm raged. During the nights of August 31 and September 1, the Germans and Italians were the targets of heavy British bomber and fighter attacks. On September 2, the British pushed the Axis forces back. By September 6, owing to fuel shortages, Rommel decided to withdraw his forces. During this time, the German–Italian Armored formations were beginning to suffer severe supply shortages. Kesselring expressed disappointment with the Italian Navy and its effort to protect precious supply convoys in the Mediterranean. "Victory cannot be expected where action is governed by fear of losses," he lamented.

On October 23, 1942, the Second Battle of El Alamein began. Rommel's Panzer Army *Afrika* comprised the *Afrika Korps*, Panzer Army *Afrika* Troops, the Luftwaffe *Fliegerkorps*, Italian X Corps, Italian XX Motorized Corps, and Italian XXI Corps, which included eight Italian divisions, and the Italian 5th Squadron, *Regia Aeronautica*. The attack on German–Italian lines starred with over 800 heavy guns firing at the German and Italian positions. The infantry attacked as the shells pounded Rommel's lines. Many Italian units demonstrated bravery in the face of the Allied advance. One of those units was the 3rd Battalion, 61st Infantry Regiment, commanded by Captain Attilio Caimi. Uncertain of the situation in the darkness and with about 350 men equipped with six heavy machine guns, eighteen light machine guns, and four 81-mm mortars, the Sicilians maintained a curtain of indiscriminate shell and machine-gun fire along the western side of Miteirya Ridge, successfully delaying the efforts of

British sappers to clear Axis minefields. Units within the 102nd Division Trento performed quite differently under enemy fire.

At about 4 a.m. on October 24, the Allies had overwhelmed the remnants of Captain Manasseri's 2nd Battalion, 62nd Regiment. One company continued to resist for some time. Another was observed to be in full flight, screaming "Front kaput!" as they encountered American-built Sherman and Grant tanks. Several units of the 102nd Division Trento, including the anti-tank gunners of Captain Vigano's Sardegna Grenadiers and Captain Alberti's 51st Engineer Battalion, were reported to have fought well. The 102nd Division Trento artillery of Colonel Randi's 46th Artillery Regiment had also waged a brave fight against superior Allied artillery. However, when it came to withdrawal in the face of overwhelming odds, the Sicilians of the 62nd Infantry Regiment tended to become disorganized. The better trained and led German 382nd Grenadier Regiment, on the other hand, was able to stage short, orderly withdrawals, maintaining the integrity of its battalions in the face of heavy attacks. Opposite the 25th New Zealand Infantry Battalion and the South Africans of the Cape Town Highlanders, Captain Caimi's 3rd Battalion, 61st Regiment, continued to hold along Miteirya Ridge. With the loss of the 11th Company, 3rd Battalion, 61st Infantry Regiment, Captain Caimi's battalion had been reduced to about nineteen officers and 340 men equipped with six 47-mm anti-tank guns, seven 20-mm anti-tank rifles, six heavy machine guns, six light machine guns, and four 81-mm mortars. Second Lieutenant Eithel Torelli, who was described as "bold, merry, and refreshingly outspoken," was assigned to Captain Caimi's 12th Company. The lieutenant's attitude epitomized that of many of the Italian soldiers. He described the situation as follows:

> At three o'clock, it was our turn. The bombardment stopped when the sun rose, and the breeze cleared the smoke and dust. The enemy infantry were a few hundred yards distant. We were firing away with our automatic weapons all morning, but things got a bit hot for us when they began to find the range with their mortars. On the Rat stretch to the north there must have been about a hundred tanks. Our mortars got four of them and set them on fire. In the evening, we established communications among ourselves and exchanged news and opinions. I made the usual report to the captain, and we cracked a few old jokes; but it was obvious that we were both worried.

Throughout the night, the Italian 2nd and 2rd Battalions, 61st Infantry Regiment, had resolutely defended their positions against the heavy, but uncoordinated British attacks. In the process, the Italians had suffered more casualties. The 10th Company of 3rd Battalion, 61st Infantry Regiment, was overpowered, with 250 Italians captured. Describing the events of the morning of October 25, Second Lieutenant Torelli wrote:

Toward morning the fighting began again, shortly after sun-up we witnessed a terrible hand-to-hand struggle over on our left. The German 5th/382nd was completely annihilated. Their CO [commander], a lieutenant, was one of the last to fall; we could pick him out easily enough because of his great height. The enemy got to within 200 yards of our position, but our mortar fire was too much for them and they beat a retreat. At 0900, a solitary Stuka circled overhead, then dived on us, and let go its bombs. A short while after the incident enemy tanks infiltrated behind our positions and captured the remains of the 10th Company, the assault platoon and the H.Q. So our battalion was now reduced to the 12th Company and the remnants of the 9th. A tank came toward us with a man head and shoulders out of the turret brandishing a machine gun. Then it about-turned and made off. The boys turned the 47 mm completely around, 180 degrees, but allowed the tank to get away. This was returning cowardice for cowardice if you like; but there were a hundred or more tanks roundabout. Three of the men, whose dugout was in pretty shaky condition, asked if they could come in with me; so there were four of us. The enormous superiority of the enemy tanks was getting them down a bit.

The battalion commander, Captain Caimi, collected the scattered remnants of his Headquarters Company and counterattacked, reoccupying his battalion headquarters position. Rommel's *Afrika Korps* had suffered great losses, and he became convinced that the main thrust of Montgomery's attack would be near the Mediterranean. The British and New Zealand infantry attacked south, and Rommel was taken by surprise. Across from the 25th New Zealand Infantry Battalion and the South Africans of the Cape Town Highlanders, the Italian 3rd Battalion, 61st Regiment, continued to hold its ground along Miteirya Ridge, even after experiencing heavy losses. Rommel put tank against tank, but he was hopelessly outnumbered. On November 4, 1942, Rommel began his long retreat to Tunisia.

Epilogue

Many believe the Italian Army, as a whole, performed in a cowardly manner in North Africa. The reality is not so simple. The question remains as to whether the Italians were really cowards or actually victims of circumstance. The Italian Littorio and Ariete Divisions earned Allied admiration at Tobruk, Gazala, and El Alamein. The Italian Army played a significant role as part of the German *Afrika Korps* and made up a large portion of the Axis combat power in North Africa during 1941 and 1942.

The Italian officers and their men were unready, their tanks too weak, their artillery unable to fire beyond 5 miles. Italian troops had no field kitchens and were frequently begging food and drink from their German comrades. In *Rommel: A Narrative and Pictorial History*, Richard Law and Craig Luther wrote:

> They're useless except for defense, and even then they're useless if the British infantry attacks with fixed bayonets. The ordinary Italian soldiers are good, their officers are worthless. The Italian troops have failed once more exactly as during the last offensive. The reasons for this are as follows: the command is not equal to the mobile direction of battle in desert warfare.… The training of Italian units does not correspond to the demands of a modern war. For example, units brought up to replace lost battalions for a division fired for the first time near the front. Officers who had not served since the end of World War I were detailed as battalion commanders. The arms of Italian units do not permit the Italian soldier to withstand British attacks without German assistance. Apart from the well-known faults of Italian tanks—short range and feeble engines—the artillery, with its lack of mobility and inadequate range (6 kilometers—maximum 8 kilometers), is absolutely inferior to the British artillery, which is known to be good Also weak equipment with anti-tank weapons gives the Italian soldier a feeling of inferiority. Supply of the Italian

troops is not adequate. Troops have no field kitchen and quantities of food are small. For this reason, the Italian soldiers, who are usually extremely contented and unassuming, often come to their German comrades to beg something to eat and drink. The great difference in food allocation to officers and men has an adverse effect on morale of the troops. The Italian soldier is not equal to the bayonet attacks of the British infantry. He has not got the nerve to hold on when enemy tanks have broken through. Continual bombing attacks and artillery fire quickly wear down his will to resist. The Italian soldier can maintain defense only with German support, and then only if the German soldier bears the brunt of the fighting.[1]

While the average Italian soldier was not quite as enthusiastic about the cause as Mussolini was, once the reality of the task became clear, they performed well as part of the *Afrika Korps* and Panzer Army *Afrika*. In the end, Rommel suffered many of the same problems that Graziani did earlier. The lack of transport and supplies and an enemy that had air superiority and almost limitless supplies were too much to overcome. While the Italian Army was defeated easily in early 1941, the army commanded by Rommel was much more formidable and proved that with proper leadership and equipment the Italian soldier was up to the task. The early Italian defeats helped create the reputation that, to this day, defines the Italian Army's performance in North Africa. The grueling conditions of the desert, the lack of equipment, and the lack of preparation for the venture did nothing to instill the Italian soldier with duty to a distant dictator. The fact that tens of thousands of Italians chose, voluntarily, to join with the Allies later in the war and fight the Germans in the equally inhospitable terrain of their homeland is often overlooked. The fact that the average Italian soldier chose not to lay down his life in pursuit of Mussolini's dream of conquest is cause for re-examination of the question as to whether the Italian Army in North Africa was a cowardly lot or doomed by circumstance. During the North African campaign, the Italian losses included 22,341 dead or missing, with 250,000 to 350,000 captured.[2]

As we examine the performance of the Italian Army in North Africa, it becomes obvious that despite inadequate equipment and poor leadership, the Italian soldier fought bravely and, in many cases, to the last man. The Italians were praised by the Germans, the British, and the New Zealanders for the tenacity and bravery. The Italian soldier was certainly doomed by circumstances beyond his control.

Endnotes

Introduction

1. Walker, I. W., *Iron Hulls, Iron Hearts: Mussolini's Elite Armored Divisions in North Africa,* (Marlborough: Crowood, 2003), p. 22.
2. *Ibid.*
3. Heddlesten, J., "Graziani vs. Rommel," www.comandosupremo.com/Graziani2.html (Retrieved 21 September 2003).
4. *Ibid.*
5. Howe, G., *Northwest Africa: Seizing the Initiative in the West,* (Washington D.C: United States Army Center of Military History, 1993), p. 7.
6. *Ibid.*
7. *Ibid.*
8. Turnbow, W., "Italian Army: Conflict between theories of employment," www.comandosupremo.com/ItalianArmy.html (Retrieved 21 September 2003).
9. Toppe, A., *Desert Warfare: German Experiences in World War II*. Combined Arms Research Library. Command & General Staff College, www-cgsc.army.mil/ carl/ resources/csi/Toppe/toppe.asp# (1991) (Retrieved 20 June 2017).
10. *Ibid.*

Chapter 1

1. Garratt, G. T., *Mussolini's Roman Empire,* (London: Penguin Books, 1938), pp. 46-47.
2. Quirico, D., *White Squadron*, first edition, (Milan: Mondadori, 2003), p. 267.
3. Quirico, p. 271.
4. Shinn, D. H., Ofcansky, Thomas P., and Prouty, C., *Historical Dictionary of Ethiopia,* (Lanham: Scarecrow Press, 2004), p. 392.
5. Quirico, p. 272.
6. Barker, A. J., *Rape of Ethiopia, 1936,* (New York: Ballantine Books, 1971), p. 17.
7. Mockler, A., *Haile Sellassie's War,* (New York: Olive Branch Press, 2002), p. 46.
8. Nicolle, D., *The Italian Invasion of Abyssinia 1935–1936* (Westminster: Osprey, 1997), p. 48.
9. Quirico, pp. 268-271.
11. Shinn, p. 392.

12. *Ibid.*
13. *Ibid.*
14. Walsh, B., *GCSE Modern World History, Second Edition* (London: John Murray Publishers, 2001), p. 252.
15. Mockler, p. 50.

Chapter 2

1. Barker, A. J., *Rape of Ethiopia, 1936,* (New York: Ballantine Books, 1971), p. 29.
2. Barker, p. 57.
3. Barker, p. 29.
4. Barker, p. 20.
5. Del Boca, A., *Mussolini's Gas. Fascism and the Ethiopian War,* (Rome: Editori Riunita,1996), p. 167.
6. MacGregor, K., *Mussolini Unleashed, 1939–1941. Politics and Strategy in Fascist Italy* (Cambridge: Cambridge University Press, 1986), p. 33.
7. Mockler, A., *Haile Sellassie's War,* (New York: Olive Branch Press, 2002), p. 88.

Chapter 3

1. Schreiber, G., *Germany and the Second World War, vol. 3* (New York: Oxford University Press, 1995), p. 54.
2. *Ibid.*
3. Schreiber, pp. 54-56.
4. *Ibid.*
5. Schreiber, pp. 58-59.
6. *Ibid.*
7. *Ibid.*
8. Schreiber, p. 61.
9. Buchner, A., *The Handbook of the German Infantry 1939–1945,* (Eggolsheim: Dörfler Publishing, 2001), p. 200.
10. Nafziger, G. F., *Italian Order of Battle: An organizational history of the Italian Army in World War II* (3 vols) (Fort Leavenworth: Combined Arms Research Library, 2010).
11. Schreiber, pp. 61-65.
12. *Ibid.*

Chapter 4

1. Paoletti, C., *A Military History of Italy,* (Westport: Greenwood Publishing Group, 2008), p. 98.
2. Montanari, M., *El Alamein. Operations in North Africa III,* (Rome: Army Staff, Historical Office, 1993), p. 132.
3. Niehorster, L., "1940 Truck-Moveable Division, North African Type," www. niehorster. org/019_italy/40_organ/div_autotrans_40as.html (Retrieved 09 June 2106).
4. Wendal, M., "Italian Army," *Axis History,* www.axishistory.com/axis-nations/italy/army (Retrieved 3 May 2009).
5. "Regio Esercito–Divisione Pavia." www.regioesercito.it/reparti/fanteria/rediv17.htm (Retrieved 5 November 2016).
6. Ford, K., *Operation Crusader 1941: Rommel in Retreat,* (Oxford: Osprey Publishing, 2010), p. 40.
7. Kurowski, F., *Das Afrika Korps: Erwin Rommel and the Germans in Africa, 1941–43* (Mechanicsburg: Stackpole Books, 2010), p. 111.

8. Congdon, D., *Combat: The War with Germany, World War II,* (New York: Dell Publishing Company, 1963), p. 131.

9. Maughan, B., "Tobruk and El Alamein," *Australia in the War of 1939–1945, Series 1– Army. III ,1st ed.,* (Canberra: Australian War Memorial, 1966), p. 509.

10. Murphy, W. E., Fairbrother, M. C., ed., *The Relief of Tobruk. The Official History of New Zealand in the Second World War 1939–1945,* (Wellington: War History Branch, Department of Internal Affairs, 1961), p. 496.

11. Humble, R., *Crusader: Eighth Army's Forgotten Victory, November 1941–January 1942,* (South Yorkshire: Leo Cooper, 1987), p. 187.

12. Aldea, D., and Peluso, J., "The Bologna Division: 19 November–10 December, 1941," Comando Supremo: Italy at War. www.comandosupremo.com/bologna-division. html/ (Retrieved 10 July 2017).

13. Mitcham, S. W., *Rommel's Desert War: The Life and Death of the Afrika Korps,* (Mechanicsburg: Stackpole Books, 2007), p. 564.

14. Aldea, D., "First Battle of El Alamein," *Commando Supremo: Italy at War.* www. comandosupremo.com/1elalamein.html/2 (Retrieved 26 April 2011).

15. Barr, N., *Pendulum of War: The Three Battles of El Alamein,* (London: Pimlico, 2004), p. 131.

16. "25th Infantry Division Bologna," *Regio Esercito,* www.regioesercito.it/reparti/ fanteria/rediv25.htm (Retrieved 10 April 2106).

17. Dominioni, P. C., and Izzo, G., *Takfír: Chronicle of the Last Battle of Alamein,* (Milan: Ugo Mursia Editore, 1967), p. 18.

18. Johnston, M., *That Magnificent 9th: An Illustrated History of The 9th Australian Division,* (Crow's Nest: Allen and Unwin, 2002), p. 38.

19. Converse, A., *Armies of Empire: The 9th Australian and 50th British Divisions in Battle 1939-1945* (Cambridge: Cambridge University Press, 2011), p. 86.

20. Jones, E., and Wessely, S., *Shell Shock to PTSD: Military Psychiatry from 1900 to the Gulf War,* (New York: Psychology Press, 2005), p. 67.

21. Greene, J. and Massignani, A., *Rommel's North Africa Campaign: September 1940-November 1942,* (Conshohocken: Combined Books, 1994), p. 110.

22. Murphy, W. E., and Fairbrother, M. C., ed., *The Relief of Tobruk. The Official History of New Zealand in the Second World War 1939–1945,* (Wellington: War History Branch, Department of Internal Affairs, 1961), p. 93.

23. Toppe, Generalmajor A., *German Experiences in Desert Warfare During World War II,* volume II, (Washington: Historical Division, European Command: US Marine Corps, 1947), FMFRP 12-96-I., p. A-8-8.

24. Aldea.

25. Mitcham, p. 552.

26. Hammond, B., *El Alamein: The Battle That Turned the Tide of the Second World War,* (Oxford: Osprey Publishing, 2012), p. 27.

27. "German Attack at El Alamein: August 31-September 5, 1942," *Tactical and Technical Trends, No.17,* January 28, 1943.

28. "Aftermath Of War: The Eighth Army From Alamein To The Sangro." *The illustrated London News & Sketch Ltd., Volume 212, Issues 5672-5684, 1948,* p. 262.

29. Bungay, S., *Alamein,* (London: Aurum Press, 2013), p. 201.

30. Spirit, M., *Sid's War: The Story of an Argyll at War,* The war time memories of Private Sid Martindale (1st Battalion Argyll & Sutherland Highlanders, 2005).

31. Watson, B. A., *Exit Rommel: The Tunisian Campaign, 1942-43,* (Mechanicsburg: Stackpole, 2007), p. 27.

32. Zinder, "A Pint of Water per Man," *Time Magazine. No. 16 November 1942.* content.time.com/time/magazine/article/0,9171,932852,00.html (Retrieved 16 August 2017).

33. Ready, J. L., *The Forgotten Axis: Germany's Partners and Foreign Volunteers in World War II,* (Jefferson: McFarland & Company, 1987), p. 310.
34. Johnston, p. 38.
35. Paoletti, *A Military History of Italy* (2008), p. 170.
36. Fellgiebel, *The Bearers of the Knights Cross of the Iron Cross 1939-1945* (2000), p. 461.
37. Kriebel and Gudmundsson, *Inside the Afrika Korps: The Crusader Battles, 1941–1942* (1999), p. 300.
38. Johnston, p. 38.
39. Mitcham, p. 50.
40. Kippenberger, *Infantry Brigadier* (1949), p. 101.
41. Aldea.
42. Kurowski, *Das Afrika Korps: Erwin Rommel and the Germans in Africa, 1941–43* (2010), p. 125.
43. Sadkovich, "Of Myths ad Men: Rommel and the Italians in North Africa," (*The International History Review XIII,* 1991), p. 302.
44. Kurowski, p. 125.
45. Paoletti, p. 101.
46. Ford, p. 153.
47. Kurowski, p. 130.
48. Playfair; Butler, ed., "The Mediterranean and Middle East: The Early Successes Against Italy to May 1941," *History of the Second World War, United Kingdom Military Series. I* (1954), pp. 362-366.
49. Playfair, p. 371.
50. "The Text of the Day's Communiques on Fighting in Europe and Africa: British," *New York Times, 18 April 1941,* (Retrieved 14 March 2016).
51. Appendix Number 30: Summary Number 2, entry for 16 April, 2/43 Infantry Battalion War Diary, April 1941, (Campbell: Australian War Memorial).
52. Johnston, M., *Fighting the Enemy: Australian Soldiers and Their Adversaries in World War II* (Cambridge: Cambridge University Press, 2000), p. 13.
53. Associazione Bersaglieri della Regione. www.bersaglieri.net/ (Retrieved 16 August 2017).
54. *Ibid.*
55. *Ibid.*
56. Chant, C., *The Encyclopaedia of Codenames of World War II* (Abingdon: Routledge, 2013), p. 21.
57. Hastings, R. H. W. S., *The Rifle Brigade in the Second World War 1939–1945* (Aldershot: Gale & Polden, 1950), p. 70.
58. Gooch, J., ed., *Decisive Campaigns of the Second World War* (London: Frank Cass, 1990), p. 100.
59. *Ibid.*
60. Paoletti, p. 170.
61. *Ibid.*
62. Wendal.
63. Paoletti, p. 170.
64. Arena, N., *Folgore: History of Italian Military Parachuting* (Rome: National Editorial Center for Historical Sociological Humanistic Divulgations, 1966), pp. 50-54.
65. Arena, p. 55.
66. Arena, pp. 65-66.
67. Arena, p. 73.
68. Wendal.
69. Bennighof, "The Folgore at Alamein," *Avalanche Press,* June 2017, www.avalanchepress.com/FolgoreAtAlamein.php (Retrieved 16 August 2017).

70. *Ibid.*
71. Nafziger, G. F., *Blackshirt, Mountain, Assault & Landing Divisions, Corps Troops and the 1944 Liberation Army. The Italian Order of Battle in WWII: An Organizational History of the Divisions and Independent Brigades of the Italian Army, III volumes* (West Chester: G. Nafziger, 1996).
72. *Ibid.*
73. *Ibid.*
74. *Ibid.*
75. Jowett, P. S., *The Italian Army 1940–45 (1): Europe 1940-1943* (New York Osprey, 2000), p. 10.
76. *Ibid.*
77. "Infantry Division Africa Hunters," *Royal Army*, www.regioesercito.it/reparti/fanteria/redivafrica.htm (Retrieved 09 August 2016).
78. *Ibid.*
79. *Ibid.*
80. *Ibid.*
81. Orpen, N. D., *War in the Desert (South African Forces World War II, Volume III)*, (London: Purnell & Sons, 1971), p. 367.
82. Orpen, p. 187.
83. *Ibid.*
84. "61st Infantry Division Sirte," *Royal Army*. www.regioesercito.it/reparti/fanteria/rediv61.htm (Retrieved 16 August 2017).
85. "62nd Infantry Division Marmarica," *Royal Army*, www.regioesercito.it/reparti/fanteria/rediv62.htm (Retrieved 16 August 2017).
86. "63rd Infantry Division Cirene," *Royal Army*, www.regioesercito.it/reparti/fanteria/rediv63.htm (Retrieved 16 August 2017).
87. *Ibid.*
88. Wendal.
89. Bedeschi, *Fronte d'Africa* (1979), p. 100.
90. *Ibid.*
91. *Ibid.*
92. Paoletti, p. 183.
93. *Ibid.*
94. "16th Infantry Division Pistoia," *Royal Army*, www.regioesercito.it/ reparti/fanteria/rediv16.htm (Retrieved 16 August 2017).
95. *Ibid.*

Chapter 5

1. Playfair, B., ed., "The Mediterranean and Middle East: The Early Successes Against Italy to May 1941," *History of the Second World War* (1954), p. 266.
2. Macksey, M. K., Pitt, B., and Mason, D., eds. Beda Fomm, "The Classic Victory." *Ballantine's Illustrated History of the Violent Century, Battle Books. 22* (New York: Ballantine Books, 1971), pp. 106-121.
3. Hunt, Sir D., *A Don at War*, (London: Frank Cass, 1966), p. 51.
4. Christie, H. R., *Fallen Eagles: The Italian 10th Army in the Opening Campaign in the Western Desert, June 1940–December 1940*, (Fort Leavenworth: U. S. Army Command and General Staff College, 1999), pp. 32-48.
5. Walker, I. W., *Iron Hulls, Iron Hearts: Mussolini's Elite Armored Divisions in North Africa*, (Marlborough: Crowood, 2003), p. 61.
6. Playfair, p. 262.
7. Pitt, B., *The Crucible of War: Western Desert, 1941*, (J. Cape, 1980), p. 102.
8. Playfair, pp. 112-113.

9. Hunt, p. 21.
10. Mackenzie, C., *Eastern Epic: September 1939–March 1943 Defense,* (London: Chatto and Windus, 1951), pp. 26-27.
11. Playfair, p. 210.
12. Mackenzie, p. 27.
13. Playfair, p. 264.
14. Mead, R., *Churchill's Lions: A Biographical Guide to the Key British Generals of World War II,* (Stroud: Spellmount, 2007), p. 331.
15. Playfair, p. 265.
16. Playfair, p. 261.
17. Playfair, pp. 263, 265.
18. Macksey, p. 68.
19. Playfair, p. 281.
20. Playfair, pp. 265-267.
21. Playfair, p. 374.
22. Playfair, pp. 267-268.
23. *Ibid.*
24. *Ibid.*
25. *Ibid.*
26. Pitt, p. 114.
27. Playfair, p. 270.
28. Playfair, pp. 271-273.
29. Bierman, J., and Smith, C., *The Battle of Alamein: Turning Point, World War II,* (New York: Viking Adult, 2002), p. 46.
30. Richards, D., *Royal Air Force 1939–1945. Vol.1: The Fight at Odds 1939–1941!* (Her Majesty's Stationary Office, 1953), pp. 270-273.
31. Playfair, p. 273.
32. *Ibid.*
33. *Ibid.*
34. *Ibid.*
35. Bauer, E., and Young, P., ed., *The History of World War II,* (London: Orbis, 1979), p. 44.
36. *Ibid.*
37. *The First British Offensive in North Africa (October 1940–February 1941),* I. Annex 32 (1979), p. 234.
38. Playfair, p. 293.
39. Macksey, pp. 121-123.
40. Playfair, pp. 353.
41. Long, G., *To Benghazi: Australia in the War of 1939–1945,* 12th edition, (Canberra: Australian War Memorial, 1952), p. 242.
42. Macksey, p. 123.
43. Long, pp. 242-245.
44. Macksey, pp. 124-127.
45. Long, pp. 250-256.
46. Macksey, pp. 127-129.
47. Playfair, pp. 351-356.
48. *Ibid.*
49. Pitt, pp. 229-240.
50. Pitt, pp. 230-231.
51. Playfair, p. 297.
52. Pitt, p. 225.
53. Harding, "Appendix E, H.Q. Cyrenaica Command Intelligence Summary Number 6, (23 February 1941) WO 169/1258," *The National Archives* (Retrieved 5 June 2016).

54. French, D., *Raising Churchill's Army: The British Army and the War against Germany 1939-1945* (Oxford: Oxford University Press, 2000), pp. 215-216.
55. *Ibid.*
56. Terraine, J., *The Right of the Line*, Wordsworth ed., (London: Hodder and Stoughton, 1985), p. 318.
57. Playfair, pp. 2-3.
58. Playfair, pp. 359-362.
59. Christie, pp. 68-78.
60. Christie, p. 86.

Chapter 6

1. Carver, M., Spellmount ed., *Dilemmas of the Desert War: The Libyan Campaign 1940–1942*, (London: Batsford, 1986), p. 243.
2. Cooper, M., *The German Army 1933–1945: Its Political and Military Failure,* (New York: Stein & Day, 1978) pp. 354-355.
3. Wilmot, C., *Tobruk,* (Sydney: Halstead Press, 1944), p. 65.
4. Bauer, E., and Young, P., ed., *The History of World War II,* (London: Orbis, 1979), p. 121.
5. Jentz, T. L., *Tank Combat In North Africa: The Opening Rounds, Operations Sonnenblume, Brevity, Skorpion and Battleaxe, February 1941–June 1941,* (Rheinberg: Schiffer, 1998), pp. 24-38.
6. Jentz, p. 214.
7. Jentz, p. 37.
8. Jentz, p. 215.
9. Jentz, p. 36.
10. *Ibid.*
11. Cooper, p. 355.
12. *Ibid.*

Chapter 7

1. Taylor, A. J. P., and Mayer, S. L., ed., *A History of World War Two,* (London: Octopus Books, 1974), p. 86.
2. *Ibid.*
3. *Ibid.*
4. *Ibid.*
5. Clifford, A., *Three Against Rommel: The Campaigns of Wavell, Auchinleck and Alexander,* (London: George G. Harrap, 1943), p. 123.
6. Creveld, M., *Supplying War: Logistics from Wallenstein to Patton,* (Cambridge: Cambridge University Press, 1977), pp. 182-185.
7. Creveld, pp. 185-187.
8. Creveld, pp. 189-190.
9. *Ibid.*
10. Clifford, p. 127.
11. French, D., *Raising Churchill's Army: The British Army and the War against Germany 1939-1945* (Oxford: Oxford University Press, 2000), p. 219.
12. Toppe, Generalmajor A., *German Experiences in Desert Warfare During World War II*, volume II, (Washington: Historical Division, European Command: US Marine Corps, 1947), p. A-8-3.
13. Clifford, pp. 130-133.
14. Murphy, W. E., and Fairbrother, Monty C., ed., *The Relief of Tobruk. The Official History of New Zealand in the Second World War 1939-1945,* (Wellington: War History Branch, Department of Internal Affairs, 1961), pp. 88-90.

15. *Ibid.*
16. Clifford, p. 161.
17. Maughan, B., "Tobruk and El Alamein," *Australia in the War of 1939–1945, Series 1– Army III, 1st ed.,* (Canberra: Australian War Memorial, 1966), pp. 439-442.
18. Greene, J., and Massignani, A., *Rommel's North Africa Campaign: September 1940– November 1942,* (Conshohocken: Combined Books, 1994), pp. 116-122.
19. Koskodan, K. K., *No Greater Ally: The Untold Story of Poland's Forces in World War II,* (Oxford: Osprey, 2011), p. 100.
20. Murphy, pp. 91-93.
21. *Ibid.*
22. *Ibid.*
23. Toppe, p. A-8-6.
24. Murphy, p. 96.
25. Murphy, p. 98.
26. Murphy, pp. 103-105.
27. Clifford, pp. 142-144.
28. Murphy, p. 108.
29. *Ibid.*
30. Glass, "Sidi Rezegh: Reminiscences of the late Gunner Cyril Herbert Glass, 143458, 3rd Field Regiment (Transvaal Horse Artillery)," *Military History Journal, 2009, The South African Military History Society.*
31. *Ibid.*
32. Horn, K., *South African Prisoner-of-War Experience during and after World War II: 1939–c. 1950,* (unpublished), Faculty of Arts and Social Sciences (Stellenbosch: Stellenbosch University, 2012, p. 46. Bentz, G., "From El Wak to Sidi Rezegh: The Union Defense Force's First Experience of Battle in East and North Africa, 1940–1941," *Scientia Militaria: South African Journal of Military Studies, No. 40* (Stellenbosch Stellenbosch University, 2012), pp. 177-199.
33. Murphy, p. 119.
34. Murphy, pp. 124-127.
35. Murphy, p. 214.
36. "The Battle of the Omars," *U.S. Military Intelligence Service (15 April 1942). Information Bulletin No. 11* (1942), p. 41.
37. Murphy, pp. 136-137.
38. Murphy, p. 151.
39. Toppe, pp. A-8-7 to A-8-8
40. Murphy, p. 203.
41. Mitcham, *The Rise of the Wehrmacht, in 2 volumes* (2008), p. 550
42. Toppe, p. A-8-9
43. Millen, J., *Salute to Service: A History of the Royal New Zealand Corps of Transport and Its Predecessors, 1860–1996,* (Wellington: Victoria University Press, 1997), p. 216.
44. Murphy, p. 299.
45. Murphy, p. 304.
46. Murphy, pp. 315-332.
47. Murphy, p. 325.
48. Lyman, R., *The Longest Siege: Tobruk, The Battle That Saved North Africa,* (Basingstoke MacMillian, 2009), p. 269
49. *Ibid.*
50. Rommel, E., and Liddell-Hart, B., ed., *The Rommel Papers,* (Boston: De Capo Press, 1953), pp. 167-168.
51. Murphy, pp. 330-331.

52. Murphy, pp. 336-340.
53. Murphy, p. 342.
54. Murphy, p. 354.
55. Clifford, pp. 149-150.
56. Rommel, p. 121.
57. Murphy, pp. 286-297.
58. Murphy, p. 355.
59. Clifford, p. 157
60. *Ibid.*
61. Murphy, p. 367.
62. *Ibid.*
63. Greene, pp. 121-122.
64. *Ibid.*
65. Cox, P., *Desert War: The Battle of Sidi Rezegh,* (Wollombi: Exisle Publishing, 2015), pp. 156-7.
66. Murphy, p. 390.
67. *Ibid.*
68. Murphy, pp. 400-402.
69. Kippenberger, H., *Infantry Brigadier,* (Oxford: Oxford University Press, 1949), p. 101.
70. Mason, W. W., "The Second Libyan Campaign and After (November 1941–June 1942)," *The Official History of New Zealand in the Second World War 1939–1945,* (Wellington: Historical Publications Branch, 1954), p. 105.
71. Thomson, J., *Warrior Nation: New Zealanders at the Front, 1900–2000* (Bloomington: Hazard Press, 2000, p. 187.
72. Murphy, p. 406.
73. Murphy, p. 411.
74. Maughan, pp. 475-478.
75. Murphy, pp. 418-422.
76. Murphy, pp. 452.
77. Chant, C., *The Encyclopaedia of Codenames of World War II* (Abingdon: Routledge, 2013), p. 37.
78. Murphy, pp. 458-464.
79. *Ibid.*
80. Murphy, pp. 476-478.
81. Gooch, J., ed., *Decisive Campaigns of the Second World War* (London: Frank Cass, 1990), p. 100.
82. Murphy, pp. 479-480.
83. Ready, J. L., *The Forgotten Axis: Germany's Partners and Foreign Volunteers in World War II,* (Jefferson: McFarland & Company, 1987), p. 313.
84. Murphy, p. 479.
85. Murphy, p. 483.
86. Murphy, p. 484.
87. Murphy, p. 490.
88. Maughan, p. 509
89. Mitcham, S. W., *The Rise of the Wehrmacht, in 2 volumes* (Santa Barbara: Praeger, 2008), p. 552.
90. Koskodan, p. 102.
91. Mackenzie, *Eastern Epic* (1951), p. 166.
92. Murphy, p. 495.
93. Murphy, p. 496.
94. Murphy, p. 497.
95. Mackenzie, p. 167

96. Humble, R., *Crusader: Eighth Army's Forgotten Victory, November 1941-January 1942,* (South Yorkshire: Leo Cooper, 1987), p.187.
97. Mackenzie, p. 169
98. Murphy, pp. 499-500.
99. Murphy, p. 501.
100. Murphy, pp. 502-504.
101. Toppe, A-8-15.
102. "The British Capture of Bardia (December 1941–January 1942): A Successful Infantry-Tank Attack," *Military Intelligence Service, Information Bulletin No. 21* (1942), p. MID 461.
103. Clifford, pp. 219-21.
104. Greene, p. 127.
105. Cox, G., *A Tale of Two Battles: Crete & Sidi Rezegh* (London: William Kimber, 1987), p. 196f.
106. *Ibid.*

Chapter 8

1. Barr, N., *Pendulum of War: The Three Battles of El Alamein,* (London: Pimlico, 2004), p. 39.
2. Barr, p. 40.
3. Watson, B. A., *Exit Rommel: The Tunisian Campaign, 1942–43,* (Mechanicsburg: Stackpole, 2007), p. 22.
4. Barr, p. 184.
5. Mackenzie, C., *Eastern Epic: September 1939–March 1943 Defense,* (London: Chatto and Windus, 1951), p. 589.
6. Playfair, Major-General I. S. O., Butler, J. R. M., ed., "The Mediterranean and Middle East: The Early Successes Against Italy to May 1941," *History of the Second World War, United Kingdom Military Series I,* (Uckfield: Naval & Military Press, 1954), p. 279.
7. Playfair, pp. 281 and 283.
8. Playfair, pp. 284-285.
9. Playfair, p. 281.
10. Playfair, p. 285.
11. Hinsley, F. H., Thomas, E. E., Ransom, C. F. G., and Knight, R. C., *British Intelligence in the Second World War. Its Influence on Strategy and Operations,* Vol. II (London: Her Majesty's Stationary Office, 1979), p. 390.
12. Playfair, p. 290.
13. Scoullar, J. L., Kippenberger, H., ed., *The Battle for Egypt: The Summer of 1942. The Official History of New Zealand in the Second World War, 1939–1945* (Wellington: Historical Publications Branch, 1955), Chapters 10, 11, and 12.
14. Playfair, pp. 292-293.
15. Playfair, pp. 294-295.
16. Panzer Army Africa Battle Report, dated 29 June 1942 K.T.B. 812, pp. 1-2.
17. Latimer, *Alamein* (2002), p. 58.
18. Playfair, p. 332.
19. Playfair, pp. 333-334.
20. Barr, p. 69.
21. Playfair, p. 295.
22. Playfair, pp. 332-333.
23. Hinsley, p. 392.
24. Playfair, p. 331.
25. Playfair, p. 340.
26. Hinsley, pp. 392-393.
27. Barr, p. 81.

28. Mackenzie, p. 580.
29. Playfair, pp. 340-341.
30. Mackenzie, pp.581-582.
31. Playfair, p. 341.
32. Mackenzie, p. 582.
33. Playfair, pp. 342-343.
34. Barr, p. 88.
35. Playfair, p. 343.
36. Playfair, p. 335.
37. "No. 38177," *The London Gazette (Supplement), 13 January 1948*, p. 367.
38. Mitcham, S. W., *Rommel's Desert War: The Life and Death of the Afrika Korps*, (Mechanicsburg: Stackpole Books, 2007), p. 113.
39. *Ibid.*
40. Barr, p. 92.
41. Playfair, p. 344.
42. Clifford, A., *Three Against Rommel: The Campaigns of Wavell, Auchinleck and Alexander*, (London: George G. Harrap, 1943), p. 285.
43. Scoullar, p. 79.
44. Mackenzie, p. 583.
45. Playfair, p. 345.
46. Playfair, p. 346.
47. Johnston, M., and Stanley, P., *Alamein: The Australian Story*, (South Melbourne: Oxford University Press, 2002), p. 58.
48. Caccia Dominioni de Sillavengo, P., *Alamein 1933–1962: An Italian Story*, Translated by Chamberlin, Dennis, (Crows Nest: Allen & Unwin, 1966), pp. 70-71.
49. Bates, P., *Dance of War: The Story of the Battle of Egypt* (London: Leo Cooper 1992), pp. 139-141.
50. Scoullar, p. 205.
51. Stewart, A., *The Early Battles of Eighth Army: 'Crusader' to the Alamein Line 1941–1942*, (London: Leo Cooper, 2002), p. 125.
52. Johnston and Stanley, p. 65.
53. Scoullar, p. 220.
54. *Ibid.*
55. Caccio-Dominioni, p. 74.
56. Johnston and Stanley, p. 67.
57. Playfair, pp. 346-347.
58. Johnston and Stanley, p. 68.
59. *Ibid.*
60. Barr, p. 114.
61. Johnston and Stanley, p. 70.
62. *Ibid.*
63. Johnston and Stanley, pp. 73-76.
64. *Ibid.*
65. Maughan, B., "Tobruk and El Alamein," *Australia in the War of 1939–1945, Series 1– Army III, 1st ed.*, (Canberra: Australian War Memorial, 1966), pp. 565-566.
66. Johnston and Stanley, pp. 78-80.
67. Johnston and Stanley, p. 86.
68. Johnston and Stanley, p. 81.
69. Johnston and Stanley, p. 66.
70. Barr, pp. 112-114.
71. Playfair, p. 347.
72. Hinsley, p. 404.

73. Playfair, p. 348.
74. Playfair, p. 349.
75. Playfair, p. 351.
76. Playfair, p. 350.
77. Bharucha, P. C., and Prasad, B., "The North African Campaign, 1940–43," *OfficialHistory of the Indian Armed Forces in the Second World War, 1939–45,* (Delhi: Combined Inter-Services Historical Section, India & Pakistan, 1956), p. 422.
78. Barr, pp. 143-146.
79. Barr, pp. 118-142.
80. Scoullar, pp. 232-298.
81. Hinsley, p. 405.
82. Johnston and Stanley, pp. 83-85.
83. Maughan, pp. 572-574.
84. Stewart, p. 130.
85. *Ibid.*
86. Johnston, M., *Fighting the Enemy: Australian Soldiers and Their Adversaries in World War II,* (Cambridge: Cambridge University Press, 2000), p. 13.
87. Maughan, p. 575.
88. Playfair, p. 353.
89. Maughan p. 577.
90. Scoullar, p. 328.
91. Scoullar, pp. 319-337.
92. Scoullar, pp. 338-351.
93. Scoullar, pp. 352-363.
94. Playfair, p. 355.
95. Playfair, p. 356.
96. Playfair, p. 357.
97. Johnston and Stanley, pp. 88-93.
98. *Ibid.*
99. Johnston and Stanley, pp. 93-96.
100. *Ibid.*
101. Panzer Army Africa Battle Report, dated 29 June 1942 K.T.B. 812.
102. Playfair, p. 358.
103. Barr, p. 216.
104. *Ibid.*
105. Johnston and Stanley, pp. 102-106.
106. Barr, pp. 178-179.
107. Barr, pp. 179-181
108. Rommel, E., and Liddell-Hart, B., ed., *The Rommel Papers,* (Boston: De Capo Press, 1953), pp. 261-262.
109. Gannon, J., *Stealing Secrets, Telling Lies: How Spies and Codebreakers Helped Shape the Twentieth Century,* (Lincoln: Potomac Books, 2002), p. 81.
110. Hinsley, p. 407
111. Alanbrooke, A., Danchev, A., and Todman, D., eds., *War Diaries 1939–1945,* rev. ed., (London: Phoenix Press, 2002), p. 294.
112. Clifford 1943, p. 296.
113. Alanbrooke.

Chapter 9

1. Buffetaut, Y., "Operation Supercharge: Second Battle of El Alamein," *The Great Battles of the Second World War. Military Collectio*n, (Paris: Histoire et Collections, 1995), p. 95.

2. Playfair, I., and Butle., J. R. M., ed., "The Mediterranean and Middle East: The Early Successes Against Italy to May 1941," *History of the Second World War, United Kingdom Military Series I,* (Uckfield: Naval & Military Press, 1954), p. 30.

3. Playfair, p. 9-11.

4. Barr, N., *Pendulum of War: The Three Battles of El Alamein* (London: Pimlico, 2004), p. 304.

5. Playfair, p. 3.

6. Barr, p. 276.

7. Playfair, p. 10.

8. Playfair, p. 9.

9. *Ibid.*

10. Mason, "A 5-Minute History Of The Battle Of El Alamein," *Imperial War Museum.* www.iwm.org.uk/history/a-5-minute-history-of-the-battle-of-el-alamein (Retrieved 11 August 2017).

11. Bierman, J., and Smith, C., *The Battle of Alamein: Turning Point, World War II,* (New York: Viking Adult, 2002), p. 255.

12. Hinsley, F. H., Thomas, E. E., Ransom, C. F. G., and Knight, R. C., *British Intelligence in the Second World War. Its Influence on Strategy and Operations,* Vol. II, (London: Her Majesty's Stationary Office, 1979), p. 425.

13. Hinsley, p. 423.

14. Hinsley, p. 427.

15. Greene, J., and Massignani, A., *Rommel's North Africa Campaign: September 1940-November 1942,* (Conshohocken: Combined Books, 1994), p. 219.

16. Playfair, p. 34.

17. *Ibid.*

18. Hinsley, pp. 430-431.

19. Modelski, T., *The Polish Contribution to The Ultimate Allied Victory in The Second World War,* (Worthing: Caldra House Ltd., 1986), p. 221.

20. *Ibid.*

21. Barr, Niall, p. 269

22. *Ibid.*

23. Creveld, M., *Supplying War: Logistics from Wallenstein to Patton,* (Cambridge: Cambridge University Press, 1977), p. 196.

24. Playfair, p. 26.

25. Hinsley, pp. 432-433.

26. Playfair, pp. 27-28.

27. Jentz, *Panzertruppen 2: The Complete Guide to the Creation & Combat Employment of Germany's Tank Force 1943–1945* (Shiffler Publishing, 1996), p. 8.

28. Playfair, pp. 28-29.

29. *Ibid.*

30. Hinsley, p. 431.

31. *Ibid.*

32. *Ibid.*

33. Barr, p. 308.

34. Clifford, A., *Three Against Rommel: The Campaigns of Wavell, Auchinleck and Alexander,* (London: George G. Harrap, 1943), p. 307.

35. Hinsley, p. 438.

36. Bierman, J., and Smith, C., *War Without Hate: The Desert Campaign of 1940–1943,* (New York: Penguin Books, 2002), Chapters 22-24.

37. Bauer, E. Young, ed., *The History of World War II,* rev. ed., (London: Orbis 2000), pp. 366-368.

38. Bauer, p. 368.

39. Playfair, p. 42.
40. Playfair, p. 44.
41. Playfair, p. 50.
42. Young, P., *A Short History of World War II 1939–1945*, (1970 ed.) (London: Pan Books, 1966), p. 260.
43. Playfair, p. 46.
44. Playfair, p. 47.
45. Playfair, p. 48.
46. Clifford, p. 308.
47. Playfair, p. 49.
48. Greene and Massignani, p. 177.
49. Montanari, M., *El Alamein. Operations in North Africa III,* (Rome: Army Staff, Historical Office, 1993), pp. 753-754.
50. Young, p. 261.
51. Watson, B. A., *Exit Rommel: The Tunisian Campaign, 1942–43,* (Mechanicsburg: Stackpole, 2007), p. 23.
52. Playfair, pp. 50-51.
53. Strawson, J., *El Alamein: Desert Victory,* (London: J. M. Dent, 1981), p. 119.
54. Barr, p. 360.
55. Hinsley, p. 439.
56. Playfair, p. 51.
57. Vivian, C., *The Western Desert of Egypt: An Explorer's Handbook,* (Cairo: American University in Cairo Press, 2000), p. 278.
58. *Ibid.*
59. Halley, J. J., *The Squadrons of the Royal Air Force,* (Kent: Air Britain Historians Ltd., 1980), p. 297.
50. Playfair, p. 52.
61. Playfair, pp. 53-54.
62. Playfair, p. 54.
63. Playfair, p. 55.
64. Playfair, p. 56.
65. Lucas-Phillips, C., *Alamein,* (London: Heinemann, 1962), p. 296.
66. Playfair, pp. 56-57.
67. Playfair, p. 57.
68. Lucas-Phillips, p. 285.
69. Hinsley, p. 441.
70. Walker, I. W., *Iron Hulls, Iron Hearts: Mussolini's Elite Armored Divisions in North Africa,* (Marlborough: Crowood, 2003), p. 35.
71. Playfair, p. 58.
72. Johnston, M., "The Battle of El Alamein, 23 October 1942," *Remembering 1942* (Canberra: Australian War Memorial, 2002).
73. Playfair, p. 63.
74. Vivian, p. 279.
75. Playfair, p. 59.
76. Playfair, p. 61.
77. Playfair, pp. 61-62.
78. Barr, p. 380.
79. Watson, p. 26.
80. Playfair, map 10.
81. Playfair, pp. 64-65.
82. Hinsley, p. 445.
83. Playfair, p. 66.

84. Barr, p. 387.
85. Playfair, p.67
86. Barr, p. 386.
87. Walker, p. 395.
88. Watson, p. 24.
89. Barr, pp. 388-389.
90. Lucas-Phillips, p. 358.
91. Playfair, p. 70.
92. Playfair, p. 68.
93. Playfair, p. 69.
94. Playfair, p. 71.
95. Rommel, E., and Liddell-Hart, B., ed., *The Rommel Papers,* (Boston: De Capo Press, 1953), p. 319.
96. Rommel, p. 321.
97. Playfair, p. 73.
98. Playfair, p. 74.
99. Playfair, p. 75.
100. Playfair, p. 81.
101. Playfair, p 83.
102. Playfair, p. 84.
103. Rommel, p. 325.
104. Montanari, p. 815.
105. *Ibid.*
106. Montanari, p. 812.
107. Spirit, M., *Sid's War: The Story of an Argyll at War,* The war time memories of Private Sid Martindale (1st Battalion Argyll & Sutherland Highlanders, 2005).
108. Watson, p. 27.
109. Caccia Dominioni de Sillavengo, P., *Alamein 1933–1962: An Italian Story*, Translated by Chamberlin, Dennis, (Crow's Nest: Allen & Unwin, 1966), p. 130.
110. Zinder, "A Pint of Water per Man," *Time Magazine. No. 16 November 1942.* content.time.com/time/magazine/article/0,9171,932852,00.html (Retrieved 16 August 2017).
111. Rommel, p. 325.
112. Bierman and Smith, Chapter 27.
113. Bauer, p. 372.
114. Playfair, pp. 86-87.
115. Playfair, p. 87.
116. Playfair, p. 88.
117. Playfair, p. 89.
118. Playfair, p. 90.
119. Playfair, p. 91.
120. Playfair, p. 93.
121. Playfair, p. 94.
122. Playfair, p. 95.
123. Churchill, W., *The Hinge of Fate,* (The Yale Book of Quotations By Fred Shapiro, 2006), p. 154.
124. Playfair, p. 76.
125. Hamilton, N., "Montgomery, Bernard Law," *Oxford Dictionary of National Biography* (Oxford: Oxford University Press, 2004).
126. Barr, p. 404.
127. Rommel, p. 330.
128. Montanari, p. 838.

129. Giuseppe R., *Holes and crosses in the desert* (Verona: Aurora, 1969), p. 549.
130. Playfair, pp. 78-79.
131. Playfair, p. 78.
132. Playfair, pp. 404, 78.
133. Watson, p. 30.
134. Hinsley, pp. 452-453.
135. Clifford, p. 317.
136. Clifford, p. 318.
137. Watson, p. 39.
138. Watson, p. 42.
139. Clifford, p. 319.
140. Watson, p. 43.
141. Clifford, pp. 320, 322.
142. Clifford, pp. 325-327.
143. Watson, p. 44.

Chapter 10

1. Zabecki, D. T, *World War II in Europe: an encyclopaedia,* (New York: Garland Publishing, 1999), p. 1270.
2. Mackenzie, S.P., *The Second World War in Europe: Second Edition*, (Abingdon: Routledge, 2014), pp. 54-55.
3. Smith, J. E., *Eisenhower in War and Peace,* (New York: Random House, 2012), p. 213.
4. Watson, B. A., *Exit Rommel: The Tunisian Campaign, 1942–43,* (Mechanicsburg: Stackpole, 2007), p. 50.
5. *Ibid.*
6. Playfair, I., and Butler, J. R. M., ed., "The Mediterranean and Middle East: The Early Successes Against Italy to May 1941," *History of the Second World War, United Kingdom Military Series I,* (Uckfield: Naval & Military Press, 1954), pp. 126, 141-142.
7. Smith, pp. 88-89.
8. Smith, pp. 214-215.
9. Smith, p. 90.
10. Stirlinget, T., *Intelligence co-operation between Poland and Great Britain during World War II*, volume I, (London, Vallentine Mitchell, 2005).
11. Churchill, W. S., *The Second World War: Closing the Ring* (Boston Houghton Mifflin Company, 1951), p. 643.
12. Slowikowski, R., *In the Secret Service: The Lightning of the Torch* (London: The Windrush Press, 1988), p. 285.
13. Hague, A., *The Allied Convoy System 1939–1945,* (Annapolis: Naval Institute Press, 2000), pp. 179-180.
14. Mangold, P., *Britain and the Defeated French: From Occupation to Liberation, 1940-1944,* (London: I. B. Tauris, 2012), p. 159.
15. Brown, J. D., *Carrier Operations in World War II: The Royal Navy* (London: Ian Allan, 1968), p. 93.
16. *Ibid.*
17. Howe, G. F., *North West Africa: Seizing the Initiative in the West. The United States Army in World War II*, CMH Pub 6-1, (Washington: United States Army Center of Military History, 1957), pp. 97 and 102.
18. Rohwer, J. and Hummelchen, G., *Chronology of the War at Sea 1939–1945,* (Annapolis: Naval Institute Press, 1992), p. 175.
19. Playfair, pp. 146-147, map 19.
20. Playfair, p. 149.

21. *Ibid.*
22. Playfair, pp. 126, 140-141, map 18.
23. Eisenhower, D., *Crusade In Europe,* (New York: Doubleday, 1948), pp. 99-105, 107-110.
24. Gaujac, P., *The French Expeditionary Force in Italy: 1943–1944* (Paris: Histoire et collections, 2003), p. 31.
25. Watson, p. 60.
26. *Ibid.*

Chapter 11

1. Playfair; Butler, ed., *The Mediterranean and Middle East: British Fortunes reach their Lowest Ebb (September 1941 to September 1942). History of the Second World War United Kingdom Military Series*, Vol. III (Uckfield: Naval & Military Press, 2004), pp. 81-90.
2. Playfair, p. 83.
3. Playfair, p. 88.
4. Rommel, E., and Liddell-Hart, B., ed., *The Rommel Papers,* (Boston: De Capo Press, 1953), p. 602.
5. Stevens, "Bardia to Enfidaville," *The Official History of New Zealand in the Second World War 1939–1945* (1962) nzetc.victoria.ac.nz/tm/scholarly/tei-WH2Bard.html (Retrieved 17 August 2017).
6. *Ibid.*
7. Rommel, p. 604.
8. Rommel, p. 610.
9. Rommel, p. 611.
10. Hinsley, F. H., Thomas, E. E., Ransom, C. F. G., and Knight, R. C., *British Intelligence in the Second World War. Its Influence on Strategy and Operations*, Vol. II, (London: Her Majesty's Stationary Office, 1979), p. 455.
11. Playfair, p. 93.
12. Rommel, pp. 621, 626.
13. Hinsley, p. 456.
14. Playfair, p. 217.
15. Hinsley, pp. 455-457.
16. Playfair, pp. 200-221.
17. Hinsley, p. 457.
18. Hinsley, p. 458.
19. Rommel, p. 642.
20. Playfair, p. 224.
21. Rommel, p. 373.

Chapter 12

1. Mitcham, S., *Blitzkrieg No Longer: The German Wehrmacht in Battle, 1943,* (Mechanicsburg: Stackpole Books, 2010), p. 78.
2. Mitcham, pp. 56-84.
3. Churchill, W. S., *The Second World War: Closing the Ring* (Boston Houghton Mifflin Company, 1951), p. 697.
4. Playfair; Butler, ed., *The Mediterranean and Middle East: British Fortunes reach their Lowest Ebb (September 1941 to September 1942). History of the Second World War United Kingdom Military Series*, Vol. III (Uckfield: Naval & Military Press, 2004), p. 111.

5. Playfair, p. 114.

6. Playfair, pp. 151-152.

7. Playfair, p. 116.

8. Playfair, pp. 117-118.

9. Hinsley, pp. 472-473

10. Playfair, p. 239.

11. Hinsley, F. H., Thomas, E. E., Ransom, C. F. G., and Knight, R. C., *British Intelligence in the Second World War. Its Influence on Strategy and Operations*, Vol. II (London: Her Majesty's Stationary Office, 1979), p. 487.

12. Hinsley, p. 493.

13. Hinsley, pp. 495-496.

14. Playfair, p. 117.

15. Playfair, pp. 117-119.

16. Playfair, p. 171.

17. Anderson, C. R., "Tunisia 17 November 1942 to 13 May 1943," *WWII Campaigns*, CMH Pub 72-12, (Washington: United States Army Center of Military History, 1946) Appendix Number 30: Summary Number 2, entry for 16 April, 2/43 Infantry Battalion War Diary, April 1941 (Campbell: Australian War Memorial), p. 2.

18. Hinsley, p. 492.

19. Eisenhower, D., *Crusade In Europe* (New York: Doubleday, 1948), p. 90.

20. Playfair, p. 152.

21. Watson, B. A., *Exit Rommel: The Tunisian Campaign, 1942–43*, (Mechanicsburg: Stackpole, 2007), p. 60.

22. Anderson, pp. 4-6.

23. Anderson, p. 6.

24. Ford, K., *Battleaxe Division*, (Stroud: Sutton, 1999), p. 17.

25. Ford, pp. 19-22.

26. Ford, p. 23.

27. Ford, pp. 23-25.

28. Ford, p.25.

29. Ford, p.28.

30. Ford, p. 40.

31. Ford, pp. 37-38.

32. Watson, pp. 62-63.

33. Ford, p. 50.

34. Ford, pp. 53-54.

Epilogue

1. Law, R. D., and Luther, C. W. H., *Rommel, A Narrative and Pictorial History* (San Jose: R. James Bender Publishing, 1980), p. 179.

2. Westphal, S., *Fatal Decisions*, 1st Edition, (Marylebone: Michael Joseph, 1956), p. 256.

X Italian Corps: As of 22 August 1942

(Created by George Nafziger. First published in English online at the U.S. Army Combined Arms Research Library) (The database is open source)

Order of Battle

17th Infantry Division Pavia
  27th Infantry Regiment
    1st Infantry Battalion
      Four Companies (with twelve 47/32 anti-tank guns, twelve 20-mm anti-tank rifles, twelve heavy machine guns, and twenty-four light machine guns)
    2nd Infantry Battalion
      Four Companies (with twelve 47/32 anti-tank, twelve 20-mm anti-tank rifles, twelve heave machine guns, and twenty-four light machine guns)
    3rd Infantry Battalion
      Four Companies (with twelve 47/32 anti-tank guns, twelve 20-mm anti-tank rifles, twelve heavy machine guns, and twenty-four light machine guns)
      1 Mortar Company with nine 81-mm mortars
  28th Infantry Regiment
    1st Infantry Battalion
      Four Companies (with three 47/32 anti-tank guns, five 20-mm anti-tank rifles, six heavy machine guns, and twelve light machine guns)
    2nd Infantry Battalion
      Four Companies (with ten 47/32 anti-tank guns, five 20-mm anti-tank rifles, twelve heavy machine guns, and twenty-two light machine guns)
    3rd Infantry Battalion
      Four Companies (with twelve 47/32 anti-tank guns, twelve 20-mm anti-tank rifles, twelve heavy machine guns, and twenty-four light machine guns)
      1 Mortar Company (with six 81-mm mortars)*
  26th Motorized Rubicone Artillery Regiment
    1st Motorized Artillery Battalion
      1st Motorized Artillery Battery (with four 100/17 howitzers or 105/28 field guns)*
      2nd Motorized Artillery Battery (with four 100/17 howitzers or 105/28 field guns)*
      3rd Motorized Artillery Battery (with four 100/17 howitzers or 105/28 field guns)*
    2nd Motorized Artillery Battalion
      1st Motorized Artillery Battery (with four 75/27 Model 06 Field guns)
      2nd Motorized Artillery Battery (with four 75/27 Model 06 Field guns)
      3rd Motorized Artillery Battery (with four 75/27 Model 06 Field guns)

3rd Motorized Artillery Battalion (supporting the Division Folgore)
    1st Motorized Artillery Battery (with four 75/27 Model 06 Field guns)
    2nd Motorized Artillery Battery (with four 75/27 Model 06 Field guns)
    3rd Motorized Artillery Battery (with four 75/27 Model 06 Field guns)
4th Motorized Artillery Battalion (supporting the Division Folgore)
    1st Motorized Artillery Battery (with four 75/27 Model 06 Field guns)
    2nd Motorized Artillery Battery (with four 75/27 Model 06 Field guns)
    3rd Motorized Artillery Battery (with four 75/27 Model 06 Field guns)
5th Motorized Anti-aircraft Artillery Battalion
    1st Motorized Anti-aircraft Artillery Battery (with four 88/55 anti-aircraft/anti-tank guns)
    2nd Motorized Anti-aircraft Artillery Battery (with four 88/55 anti-aircraft/anti-tank guns)
    3rd Motorized Anti-aircraft Artillery Battery (with four 88/55 anti-aircraft/anti-tank guns)
    77th Motorized Anti-aircraft Artillery Battery (with six 20-mm guns)
    432nd Motorized Anti-aircraft Artillery Battery (with eight 20-mm guns)
18th Semi-Motorized Mixed Engineer Battalion
    46th Semi-Motorized Engineer Company
    17th Semi-Motorized Engineer Communications Company
    21st Semi-Motorized Medical Company
    3rd Motorized Administration Company

NOTE: The 17th Infantry Division Pavia was authorized 7,000 men. As of August 22, 1942, it only had seventy-four officers and 1,003 enlisted men assigned.

27th Infantry Division Brescia
  19th Infantry Regiment
    1st Infantry Battalion
      Four Companies (with eleven 47/32 anti-tank guns, seven 20-mm anti-tank rifles, eleven heavy machine guns, and twenty-four light machine guns)
    2nd Infantry Battalion
      Four Companies (with eleven 47/32 anti-tank guns, seven 20-mm anti-tank rifles, thirteen heavy machine guns, and twenty-five light machine guns)
    3rd Infantry Battalion*
      Four Companies (with twelve 47/32 anti-tank guns, twelve 20-mm anti-tank rifles, twelve heavy machine guns, and twenty-four light machine guns)
      1 Mortar Company (with nine 81-mm mortars)
  20th Infantry Regiment
    1st Infantry Battalion
      Four Companies (with eight 47/32 anti-tank guns, ten 20-mm anti-tank, twelve heavy machine guns and twenty-four light machine guns)
    2nd Infantry Battalion
      Four Companies (with twelve 47/32 anti-tank guns, seven 20-mm anti-tank rifles, twelve heavy machine guns, and nineteen light machine guns)
    3rd Infantry Battalion
      Four Companies (with no 47/32 anti-tank guns, three 20-mm anti-tank rifles, seven heavy machine guns, and twenty light machine guns)
      1 Mortar Company (with nine 81-mm mortars)
  1st Artillery Regiment Celere
    1st Motorized Artillery Battalion
      1st Motorized Artillery Battery (with four 100/17 model 14 howitzers)
      2nd Motorized Artillery Battery (with four 100/17 model 14 howitzers)
      3rd Motorized Artillery Battery (with four 100/17 model 14 howitzers)

2nd Motorized Artillery Battalion*
　1st Motorized Artillery Battery (with four 100/17 model 14 howitzers)
　2nd Motorized Artillery Battery (with four 100/17 model 14 howitzers)
　3rd Motorized Artillery Battery (with four 100/17 model 14 howitzers)
3rd Motorized Artillery Battalion (in support of the Division Folgore)
　1st Motorized Artillery Battery (with four 75/27 model 06 field guns)
　2nd Motorized Artillery Battery (with four 75/27 model 06 field guns)
　3rd Motorized Artillery Battery (with four 75/27 model 06 field guns)
4th Motorized Artillery Battalion
　1st Motorized Artillery Battery (with four 75/27 model 06 field guns)
　2nd Motorized Artillery Battery (with four 75/27 model 06 field guns)
　3rd Motorized Artillery Battery (with four 75/27 model 06 field guns)
5th Motorized Anti-aircraft Artillery Battalion
　1st Motorized Artillery Battery (with four 88/55 anti-aircraft/anti-tank guns)
　2nd Motorized Artillery Battery (with four 88/55 anti-aircraft/anti-tank guns)
　3rd Motorized Artillery Battery (with four 88/55 anti-aircraft/anti-tank guns)
　4th Anti-aircraft Artillery Battery (with eight 20-mm anti-aircraft guns)
　404th Anti-aircraft Artillery Battery (with eight 20-mm anti-aircraft guns)
26th Semi-Motorized Mixed Engineer Battalion
　52nd Semi-Motorized Engineer Company
　27th Semi-Motorized Communications Company
　34th Semi-Motorized Medical Company
　34th Motorized Administration Company

NOTE: The 27th Infantry Division Brescia was authorized 7,000 men. As of August 22, 1942, they only had 214 officers, 3,880 enlisted men assigned.

185th Parachute Infantry Division Folgore
　185th Parachute Infantry Regiment
　186th Parachute Infantry Regiment
　　5th Parachute Infantry Battalion (with three 47/32 anti-tank guns, six 20-mm Solothurn anti-tank rifles, ten heavy machine guns, and sixty light machine guns)
　　　13th, 14th and 15th Parachute Infantry Companies*
　　6th Parachute Infantry Battalion
　　　Three Companies (with three 47/32 anti-tank guns, six 20-mm Solothurn anti-tank rifles, ten heavy machine guns, and sixty light machine guns)
　　　186th Anti-tank Company
　　　　Two Platoons of four 47/32 anti-tank guns each
　187th Parachute Infantry Regiment
　　Headquarters Detachment
　　2nd Parachute Infantry Battalion
　　　Three Companies (with three 47/32 anti-tank guns, six 20-mm Solothurn anti-tank rifles, ten heavy machine guns and sixty light machine guns)
　　4th Parachute Infantry Battalion
　　　Three Companies (with three 47/32 anti-tank guns, six 20-mm Solothurn anti-tank rifles, ten heavy machine guns, and sixty light machine guns)
　　9th Parachute Infantry Battalion
　　　Three Companies (with three 47/32 anti-tank guns, six 20-mm Solothurn anti-tank rifles, ten heavy machine guns, and sixty light machine guns)
　　10th Parachute Infantry Battalion
　　　Three Companies (with three 47/32 anti-tank guns, six 20-mm Solothurn anti-tank rifles, ten heavy machine guns, and sixty light machine guns)

187th Anti-tank Company

Two platoons of four 47/32 anti-tank guns each

Ruspoli Group

7th Parachute Infantry Battalion

Three Companies (with three 47/32 anti-tank guns, six 20-mm Solothurn anti-tank rifles, ten heavy machine guns, and sixty light machine guns)

8th Parachute Combat Engineer Battalion

Battalion Headquarters

22nd Parachute Combat Engineer Company

3 Combat Engineer Platoons

1 Labor Platoon

Motor Transportation Park

23rd Parachute Combat Engineer Company

Headquarters Section

3 Combat Engineer Platoons

1 Labor Platoon

Motor Transportation Park

24th Parachute Combat Engineer Company

Headquarters Section

3 Combat Engineer Platoons

1 Labor Platoon

Motor Transportation Park

185th Parachute Artillery Regiment

5th Parachute Artillery Battalion

1st Parachute Artillery Battery (with four 47/32 infantry/anti-tank guns)

2nd Parachute Artillery Battery (with four 47/32 infantry/anti-tank guns)

2nd Parachute Artillery Battalion

3rd Parachute Artillery Battery (with four 47/32 infantry/anti-tank guns)

4th Parachute Artillery Battery

3rd Parachute Artillery Battalion

5th Parachute Artillery Battery (with four 47/32 infantry/anti-tank guns)

6th Parachute Artillery Battery (with four 47/32 infantry/anti-tank guns)

4th Motorized Artillery Battalion (in support of the Division Folgore)

1st Motorized Artillery Battery (with four 75/27 model 06 field guns)

2nd Motorized Artillery Battery (with four 75/27 model 06 field guns)

3rd Motorized Artillery Battery (with four 75/27 model 06 field guns)

121st Motorized Artillery Battalion (attached from 101st Division Trieste)

1st Motorized Artillery Battery (with four 100/17 howitzers)

2nd Motorized Artillery Battery (with four 100/17 howitzers)

3rd Motorized Artillery Battery (with four 100/17 howitzers)

146th Motorized Anti-aircraft Artillery Battery with five 20-mm guns (in support of 1st Battalion, 21st Artillery Regiment)

3rd Motorized Artillery Battalion, 260th Motorized Rubicone Artillery Regiment (in support of the Division Folgore)

1st Motorized Artillery Battery (with four 75/27 model 06 field guns)

2nd Motorized Artillery Battery (with four 75/27 model 06 field guns)

3rd Motorized Artillery Battery with four 75/27 model 06 field guns

4th Motorized Artillery Battalion, 206th Motorized Rubicone Artillery Regiment (in support of the Division Folgore)

1st Motorized Artillery Battery (with four 75/27 model 06 field guns)

2nd Motorized Artillery Battery (with four 75/27 model 06 field guns)

3rd Motorized Artillery Battery (with four 75/27 model 06 field guns)

41th Motorized AA Artillery Battery (attached from 101st Division Trieste, with five 20-mm guns

103rd Motorized Artillery Battalion

1st Motorized Artillery Battery (with four 100/17 howitzers and two heavy machine guns)

2nd Motorized Artillery Battery (with four 100/17 howitzers and two heavy machine guns)

3rd Motorized Artillery Battery (with four 100/17 howitzers and two heavy machine guns)

20th Mortar Company (with twelve 81-mm mortars)

185th Parachute Engineer Company

185th Signals Company

185th Mixed Carabinieri (Police) Section

260th Field Post Office

20th Supply Section

185th Transportation Detachment

185th Medical Detachment

Corps Troops Assigned to the Division

9th Motorized Bersaglieri (Sharpshooters) Regiment

27th Motorized Bersaglieri Battalion

Three Companies (with eight 47/32-mm anti-tank guns, two anti-tank rifles, two heavy machine guns, and fifteen light machine guns)

30th Motorized Bersaglieri Battalion**

Three Companies (with nine 47/32-mm anti-tank guns, nine anti-tank rifles, nine heavy machine guns, and eighteen light machine guns)

1 Tank Battalion**

Three Companies (with fifty-two medium tanks)

16th Motorized Artillery Regiment

49th Motorized Artillery Battalion

1st Motorized Battery (with four 105/28 field guns)

2nd Motorized Battery (with four 105/28 field guns)

3rd Motorized Battery (with four 105/28 field guns)

47thMotorized Artillery Battalion

4th Motorized Battery (with four 149/28 field guns)

2nd Motorized Battery (with three 149/28 field guns)

31st Combat Engineer Battalion

1st Company

7th Company

8th Company

10th Engineer Regiment

10th Motorized Engineer Mechanics Battalion

1st Motorized Engineer Mechanics Company

2nd Motorized Engineer Mechanics Company

15th Defense Engineers Company

10th Motorized Engineer Communications Battalion

89th Motorized Telephone Company

124th Motorized Radio Company

One supply battalion

One 60-cubic meter water transport column

One 50-cubic meter POL (Petroleum, Oils, and Lubricants) transport column

One 30-ton motorized transport column

One motorized ambulance platoon

One motorized administration company

* Not on hand by August 22, 1942

XX Italian Motorized Corps: As of August 22, 1942

(Created by George Nafziger. First published in English online at the U.S. Army Combined Arms Research Library) (The database is open source)

Order of Battle

132nd Armored Division Ariete
  132nd Armored Regiment
      Command Section
      Signals Platoon
        Service Squad
      Radio Platoon
      Three Reserve Tank Platoons (with nine M14s, nine heavy trucks, nine trailers each)
     Transport detachment (with two command cars, five light trucks, three heavy trucks, one ambulance, one trailer, six motorcycles with sidecars)
    9th Armored Battalion (with fifty-two M14 tanks in three companies)
      Command Company (with four M14 tanks, including two with radios)
        Command Platoon (with two M14 tanks and two M14s with radios)
          Staff Squad (with four motorcycles)
          Service Squad
      Transportation Detachment (with two cars, three all-terrain trucks, five heavy trucks, one trailer, one tank truck, six motorcycles, four motorcycles with sidecars)
        Maintenance Platoon with two Maintenance Squads
        Recovery Platoon (with three recovery squads each with one heavy truck, one repair truck, one special carriage)
      Three tank companies (with sixteen M14 tanks, four motorcycles, two motorcycles with sidecars, a car, one all-terrain truck, three heavy trucks, one light truck, three tank platoons)
    10th Armored Battalion
      Command Company (with four4 M14 tanks, including two with radios)
        Command Platoon (with two M4 machine guns and two M14 tanks with radios)
          Staff Squad with four motorcycles
          Service Squad
      Transportation Detachment (with two cars, three all-terrain trucks, five heavy trucks, one trailer, one tank truck, six motorcycles, four motorcycles with sidecars)
        Maintenance Platoon (with two Maintenance Squads)
        Recovery Platoon (with three Recovery Squads each with one heavy truck, one repair truck, one special carriage)

Three Tank Companies (with sixteen M14 tanks, four motorcycles, two motorcycles with sidecars, a car, one all-terrain truck, three heavy trucks, one light truck, three Tank Platoons)

13th Armored Battalion
  Command Company (with four M14 tanks, including two with radios)
    Command Platoon (with two M14 tanks and two with radios)
      Staff Squad with four motorcycles
      Service Squad
  Transportation Detachment (with two cars, three all-terrain trucks, five heavy trucks, one trailer, one tank truck, six motorcycles, four motorcycles with sidecars)
    Maintenance Platoon (with two Maintenance Squads)
    Recovery Platoon (with three recovery squads each with one heavy truck, one repair truck, one special carriage)
  Three Tank Companies (with sixteen M14 tanks each)
    Command Platoon (with one M14 tank, four motorcycles, two motorcycles with sidecars, a car, one all-terrain truck, three heavy trucks and one light truck)
    Three Tank Platoons (with five M14 tanks each)
  One 20-mm Anti-aircraft Company with eight guns
  One Maintenance Company

8th Motorized Bersaglieri Regiment
  Command Company
    Command Platoon (with a Clerical Squad and an Information Squad)
    Communications Platoon (with One Radio Squad, four light trucks, one Telephone/Lineman Squad, one Observer/Signal Squad, one Motorcycle Courier Squad with nine motorcycles)
    Service Platoon with one car, two light trucks, two heavy trucks
  5th Motorized Bersaglieri Battalion (with twelve model 37 anti-tank guns, four 20-mm anti-tank rifles, twelve heavy machine guns, and thirteen light machine guns)
    Command Platoon (with one Command Squad, one Signals Squad with four motorcycles, one Service Squad, six light trucks)
    Three Infantry Companies each (with one Command Platoon with three heavy trucks, one Rifle Platoon with three Squads, one Machine Gun Platoon with three Squads with one machine gun each)
    20-mm Anti-tank Platoon (with three Squads each with one 20-mm anti-tank rifle, 47/32 Anti-tank Platoon, three Squads each with one 47/32 anti-tank gun)
  12th Motorized Bersaglieri Battalion (with twelve model 37 anti-tank guns, four 20-mm anti-tank, twelve heavy machine guns and eleven light machine guns)
    Command Platoon (with one Command Squad, one Signals Squad with four motorcycles, one Service Squad with six light trucks)
    Three Infantry Companies each (with one Command Platoon with three heavy trucks, one Rifle
    Platoon with three Squads, one Machine Gun Platoon with one Squad with one machine gun each)
    20-mm Anti-tank Platoon (with three Squads each with one 20-mm anti-tank rifle, 47/32 Anti-tank Platoon, three Squads each with one 47/32 anti-tank gun each)
  13th Motorized Anti-tank Bersaglieri Battalion
    Command Platoon (with one Command Squad, one Signals Squad with four motorcycles, one Service Squad and six light trucks)
    Three Anti-tank Companies each (with eight 47/32 model 37 anti-tank guns, eleven medium trucks, seven motorcycles one with side car, three light trucks, four Gun Platoons each with one motorcycle, two Gun Squads each with one 47/32 anti-tank gun and one light truck)

132nd Armored Artillery Regiment
>   Regimental Staff Battery
>>   One Staff Platoon (with one Observation Section, one Calibration Section, one Signals Section, one Reserve Section, three Observer Platoons each with one Observation Section, one Signals Section)
>   1st Motorized Artillery Battalion
>>   1st Motorized Artillery Battery (with three 75/27 field guns)
>>   2nd Motorized Artillery Battery (with two 75/27 field guns)
>>   3rd Motorized Artillery Battery (with four 75/27 field guns)
>   2nd Motorized Artillery Battalion
>>   1st Motorized Artillery Battery (with three 75/27 field guns)
>>   2nd Motorized Artillery Battery (with three 75/27 field guns)
>>   3rd Motorized Artillery Battery (with three 75/27 field guns)
>   3rd Motorized Artillery Battalion
>>   1st Motorized Artillery Battery (with six 105/28 field guns)
>>   2nd Motorized Artillery Battery (with six 105/28 field guns)
>>   3rd Motorized Artillery Battery with four 105/28 field guns
>>>   One 20-mm Anti-aircraft Platoon
>   501st Motorized Anti-aircraft Artillery Battalion (sometimes identified as the 4/132nd Artillery Regiment with twelve 90/53 guns, in three batteries of four guns, and two batteries of eight 20-mm anti-aircraft guns (one battery detached to XX Corps Troops))
>>   1st Motorized Battery (with four 90/53 anti-aircraft/anti-tank guns)
>>   2nd Motorized Battery (with four 90/53 anti-aircraft/anti-tank guns)
>>   3rd Motorized Battery (with eight 20mm anti-aircraft guns)
>>   4th Motorized Battery (with eight 20mm anti-aircraft guns)
>   551st Self-Propelled Artillery Battalion (sometimes identified as the 5/132nd Artillery Regiment) (with ten 75/18 Semovente assault guns in two batteries of four and two with the battalion headquarters)
>>   Headquarters Battery (with two 75/18 Semovente assault guns)
>>   1st Battery with (four 75/18 Semovente assault guns)
>>   2nd Battery with (four 75/18 Semovente assault guns)
>   552nd Self-Propelled Artillery Battalion (sometimes identified as the 6/132nd Artillery Regiment) (with ten 75/18 Semovente assault guns in two batteries of four and two with the Battalion Headquarters)
>>   Headquarters Battery (with two 75/18 Semovente assault guns)
>>   5th Battery (with three 75/18 Semovente assault guns)
>>   2nd Battery (with three 75/18 Semovente assault guns)
>   15th Motorized Artillery Battalion (attached from XX Corps)
>>   5th Motorized Battery (with four 105/28 field guns)
>>   2nd Motorized Battery (with four 105/28 field guns)
>>   3rd Motorized Battery (with four 105/28 field guns)
>   31st Motorized Anti-aircraft Artillery Battalion (with twelve 88/55 anti-aircraft/anti-tank guns [German] guns, in three batteries of four guns)
>>   5th Motorized Artillery Battery (with four 88/55 anti-aircraft/anti-tank guns)
>>   2nd Motorized Artillery Battery (with four 88/55 anti-aircraft/anti-tank guns)
>>   3rd Motorized Artillery Battery (with four 88/55 anti-aircraft/anti-tank guns)
>   3rd Recon Battalion of Nizza Cavalleria Regiment (with twelve Autoblinda 41 armored cars)
>>   Command Company
>>>   Armored Car Couriers with one armored car
>>>   Staff Squad with four motorcycles
>>>   Service Squad

Transportation Detachment (with two command cars, four light trucks, two heavy trucks, two recovery trucks, and two motorcycles)

Reserve Armored Car Platoon

Maintenance Squad (with one heavy truck and one workshop truck)

Armored Car Section (with four reserve Armored cars)

4th Armored Car Company

Command Platoon (with one armored car, Service Squad with ten motorcycles, one Command car, two light trucks, and one heavy truck)

4 Armored Car Platoons each (with four armored cars)

5th Armored Car Company (with twelve Autoblinda 41 Armored cars)

Command Platoon (with one armored car, Service Squad with authorized ten motorcycles, one command car, two light trucks and one heavy truck)

4 Armored Car Platoons each with four armored cars

32nd Motorized Mixed Engineer Battalion

132nd Motorized Engineer Company

132nd Motorized Signal Company

42nd Supply Regiment

1st Battalion (with three heavy machine guns)

Four 30-ton motorized transport columns

2nd Battalion (with two heavy machine guns)

Two 30-ton motorized transport columns

Two 50-cubic-meter motorized POL (Petroleum, Oils, and Lubricants) columns

132nd Motorized Medical Company

132nd Motorized Administration Platoon

1 motorized vehicle Maintenance Company

NOTE: The 132nd Armored Division Ariete was authorized 8,600 men. As of August 22, 1942, it only had 196 officers and 4,676 enlisted men assigned.

133rd Armored Division Littorio

133rd Armored Regiment (with Command Company and Reserve Tanks with thirty-three M14 tanks, including six radio tanks)

Command Company (with a Signals Platoon, Service Squad, field office radio, Radio Platoon with six radio central medium tanks, Radio Squad, Courier and Batman Squad, three Reserve Tank Platoons, each with nine M14 tanks, nine heavy trucks, nine trailers, Transport Detachment with two command cars, five light trucks, three heavy trucks, one ambulance, one trailer, and six motorcycles with sidecars)

4th Armored Battalion

Command Company (with four M14 tanks, including two with radios)

Command Platoon (with two M14 tanks, including two with radios)

Staff Squad (with four motorcycles)

Service Squad

Transportation Detachment (with two cars, three all-terrain trucks, five heavy trucks, one trailer, one tank truck, six motorcycles, and four motorcycles with sidecars)

Maintenance Platoon (with two Maintenance Squads)

Recovery Platoon (with three Recovery Squads each with one heavy truck, one repair truck, and one special carriage)

Three Tank Companies each (with sixteen M14 tanks)

Command Platoon (with one M14 tank, four motorcycles, two motorcycles with sidecars, a car, one all-terrain truck, three heavy trucks, and one light truck)

Three Tank Platoons each (with five M14 tanks)

7th Armored Battalion (with three companies, thirty-four M14 tanks)

Command Company (with four M14 tanks, including two with radios)
> Command Platoon (with two M14 tanks, including two with radios)
>> Staff Squad (with four motorcycles)
>> Service Squad
> Transportation Detachment (with two cars, three all-terrain trucks, five heavy trucks, one trailer, one tank truck, six motorcycles, and four motorcycles with sidecars)
>> Maintenance Platoon (with two maintenance squads)
>> Recovery Platoon (with three Recovery Squads each with one heavy truck, one repair truck, and one special carriage)
> Three Tank Companies (with sixteen M14 tanks)
>> Command Platoon each (with one M14 tank, four motorcycles, two motorcycles with sidecars, a car, one all-terrain truck, three heavy trucks, and one light truck)
>> Three Tank Platoons each (with five M14 tanks)

51st Armored Battalion
> Command Company (with four M14 tanks, including two with radios)
>> Command Platoon (with two M14 tanks, including two with radios)
>>> Staff Squad (with four motorcycles)
>>> Service Squad
>> Transportation Detachment (with two cars, three all-terrain trucks, five heavy trucks, one trailer, one tank truck, six motorcycles, and four motorcycles with sidecars)
>>> Maintenance Platoon (with two Maintenance Squads)
>>> Recovery Platoon (with three Recovery Squads each with one heavy truck, one repair truck, and one special carriage)
>> Three Tank Companies (with sixteen M4 tanks)
>>> Command Platoon (with one M14 tank, four motorcycles, two motorcycles with sidecars, a car, one all-terrain truck, three heavy trucks, and one light truck)
>>> Three Tank Platoons each (with five M14 tanks)

3rd Armored Recon Battalion of Lancicrie
> Command Company (with two L6 tanks, including two with radios)
>> Command Platoon (with two L6 tanks, including two with radios)
>>> Staff Squad (with four motorcycles)
>>> Service Squad (with one car, one light truck and three heavy trucks)
>>> Maintenance Squad (with one car and two heavy trucks)
> 2 Light Tank Companies each (with twenty-seven L6 tanks)
>> Command Platoon each (with two L6 tanks, one with radio, eight motorcycles, two with sidecar, one command car, five heavy trucks, three light trucks, and one recovery truck)
>> Four Tank Platoons each (with five L6 tanks)
>> Reserve Tank Platoon each (with four L6 tanks and two trains each with one heavy truck, one trailer and one ramp)
> One 20-mm Anti-aircraft Company (with eight guns)
> 1 Maintenance Company*

12th Motorized Regiment Bersaglieri
> Command Company
>> Command Platoon (with a Clerical Squad and an Information Squad)
>> Communications Platoon (with one Radio Squad with three light trucks, one telephone/lineman squad with one light truck, one Observer/Signal Squad, one Motorcycle Courier Squad (with nine motorcycles)
>> Service Platoon (with one car, two light trucks, two heavy trucks)
> 23rd Motorized Battalion Bersaglieri (with three motorized infantry companies with twelve model 37 anti-tank guns, two 20-mm anti-tank rifles, seven heavy machine guns and eight light machine guns)

Command Platoon (with one command squad, one signals squad with four motorcycles and one service squad with six light trucks)

Three Infantry Companies each (with one Command Platoon with three heavy trucks, 1 Rifle Platoon (3 Squads), 1 Machine Gun Platoon (3 Squads with one machine gun each), one 20-mm Anti-tank Platoon (three Squads each with one 20-mm anti-tank rifle), one 47/32 Anti-tank Platoon (three Squads each with one 47/32 anti-tank gun)

36th Motorized Bersaglieri Battalion (with three motorized infantry companies with six 47/32 Model-37 anti-tank guns, five 20-mm anti-tank rifles, six heavy machine guns and seven light machine guns)

Command Platoon (with one Command Squad, one Signals Squad with four motorcycles and one Service Squad with six light trucks)

Three Infantry Companies each (with one Command Platoon with three heavy trucks, one Rifle Platoon (three squads), one Machine Gun Platoon (three Squads with one machine gun each), one 20-mm Anti-tank Platoon (three Squads each with one 20mm anti-tank rifle, and one 47/32 Anti-tank Platoon (three squads each with one 47/32 anti-tank gun)

21st Motorized Anti-tank Battalion Bersaglieri

Command Platoon (with one Command Squad, one Signals Squad with four motorcycles, one Service Squad with six light trucks)

Three Anti-tank Companies each (with eight 47/32 model 37 anti-tank guns, eleven medium trucks, seven motorcycles, one Command Squad with three motorcycles, one with side car, three light trucks, four Gun Platoons (each with one motorcycle, two gun squads each with one 47/32 anti-tank gun and one light truck))

3rd Celere Artillery Regiment

Regimental Staff Battery

One Staff Platoon (with one Observation Section, one Calibration Section, one Signals Section, and one Reserve Section)

Three Observer Platoons each (with one Observation Section and one Signals Section)

3rd Artillery Battalion Celere

1st Artillery Battery Celere (with four 75/27 field guns)

2nd Artillery Battery Celere (with four 75/27 field guns)

3rd Artillery Battery Celere (with four 75/27 field guns)

32nd Motorized Artillery Battalion

1st Battery (with four 100/17 howitzers)

2nd Battery (with four 100/17 howitzers)

3rd Battery (with four 100/17 howitzers)*

29th Motorized Anti-aircraft Artillery Battalion

1st Motorized Anti-aircraft Battery (with six 88/55-mm anti-aircraft/anti-tank guns)

2nd Motorized Anti-aircraft Battery (with six 88/55-mm anti-aircraft/anti-tank guns)

5th Motorized Anti-aircraft Battery/133rd Artillery Regiment (with six 20-mm anti-aircraft guns)

554th Self-propelled Artillery Battalion (sometimes identified as the 5/3rd Artillery Regiment Celere or 554th Self-Propelled Artillery Battalion)

Headquarters Battery (with two 75/18 Semovente assault guns)*

1st Battery (with four 75/18 Semovente assault guns)

2nd Battery (with four 75/18 Semovente assault)

556th Self-propelled Artillery Battalion (sometimes identified as the 6/3rd Artillery Regiment Celere or 556th Self-Propelled Artillery Battalion)

Headquarters Battery (with two 75/18 Semovente assault guns)

1st Battery (with four 75/18 Semovente assault guns)

2nd Battery (with four 75/18 Semovente assault guns)

406th Anti-aircraft Battery with 20-mm anti-aircraft guns

33rd Motorized Mixed Engineer Battalion*
  1 Motorized Engineer Company
  1 Motorized Communications Company
  1 Motorized Medical Company
  1 Motorized Maintenance Company
    1 Administration Platoon
      1 Motorized Supply Section
1st Motorized Supply Battalion (with four 30-ton motorized transport columns)*
2nd Motorized Supply Battalion (with two 30-ton motorized transport columns and two 50-cubic-meter motorized POL (Petroleum, Oils, and Lubricants) columns)*
101st Motorized Infantry Division Trieste
    One Motorized Division Staff Company (with two 20mm anti-aircraft guns, two heavy machine guns, and two light machine guns)
  65th Motorized Infantry Regiment
    1st Motorized Infantry Battalion (with two companies with six 47/32 anti-tank guns, six anti-tank rifles, six heavy machine guns, and twelve light machine guns)
    2nd Motorized Infantry Battalion (with two companies with six 47/32 anti-tank guns, six anti-tank rifles, six heavy machine guns, and twelve light machine guns)
    Motorized Mortar Company (with nine 81-mm mortars)*
  66th Motorized Infantry Regiment
    1st Motorized Infantry Battalion (with two companies with five 47/32 anti-tank guns, six anti-tank rifles, six heavy machine guns, and twelve light machine guns)
    2nd Motorized Infantry Battalion (with two companies with six 47/32 anti-tank guns, six anti-tank rifles, six heavy machine guns, and twelve light machine guns)
    Motorized Mortar Company (with nine 81-mm mortars)*
  11th Armored Battalion
    Command Company (with four M14 tanks, including two with radios)
      Command Platoon (with two M14 tanks, including two with radios)
        Staff Squad (with four motorcycles)
        Service Squad
    Transportation Detachment (with two cars, three all-terrain trucks, five heavy trucks, one trailer, one tank truck, six motorcycles, and four motorcycles with sidecars)
      Maintenance Platoon (with two maintenance squads)
      Recovery Platoon (with three recovery squads each with one heavy truck, one repair truck, and one special carriage)
    Three Tank Companies each (with sixteen M14 tanks)
      Command Platoon each (with one M14 tank, four motorcycles, two motorcycles with sidecars, one all-terrain truck, three heavy trucks, and one light truck)
      3 tank platoons each (with five M14 tanks)
21st Motorized Po Artillery Regiment
    1 Headquarters Company
    1 Motorized Artillery Battalion (detached to 185th Division Folgore, with twelve 100/17 howitzers, and six heavy machine guns)
      1st Motorized Artillery Battery (with four 100/17 howitzers)
      2nd Motorized Artillery Battery (with four 100/17 howitzers)
      3rd Motorized Artillery Battery (with four 100/17 howitzers)
    2nd Motorized Artillery Battalion
      1st Motorized Artillery Battery (with four 100/17 howitzers)
      2nd Motorized Artillery Battery (with four 100/17 howitzers)
      3rd Motorized Artillery Battery (with four 100/17 howitzers)
    3rd Motorized Artillery Battalion
      1st Motorized Artillery Battery (with three 75/27 field guns)

2nd Motorized Artillery Battery (with three 75/27 field guns)

3rd Motorized Artillery Battery (with three 75/27 field guns)

4th Motorized Artillery Battalion

1st Motorized Artillery Battery (with three 75/27 field guns)

2nd Motorized Artillery Battery (with three 75/27 field guns)

3rd Motorized Artillery Battery (with three 75/27 field guns)

5th Motorized Anti-aircraft Artillery Battalion*

1st Motorized Anti-aircraft Artillery Battery (with four 75/50 anti-aircraft guns)

2nd Motorized Anti-aircraft Artillery Battery (with four 75/50 anti-aircraft guns)

3rd Motorized Anti-aircraft Artillery Battery (with four 75/50 anti-aircraft guns)

146th Motorized Anti-aircraft Artillery Battery with five 20-mm guns (in support of 1st Battalion/21st Artillery Regiment)

411th Motorized Anti-aircraft Artillery Battery (detached to the Division Folgore, with five 20-mm guns)

7th Armored Car Battalion Bersaglieri (with six Autoblinda 41 armored cars)

Command Company

    Armored Car Couriers (with one armored car)

    Staff Squad (with four motorcycles)

    Service Squad

Transportation Detachment (with two command cars, four light trucks, two heavy trucks, two recovery trucks, and two motorcycles)

    Reserve Armored Car Platoon

        Maintenance Squad with one heavy truck and one workshop truck

        Armored Car Section with four reserve Armored cars

1 Armored Car Company (with six Autoblinda 41 armored cars)

    Command Platoon with one armored car, Service Squad (with authorized ten motorcycles, one command car, two light trucks, and one heavy truck)

    Four Armored Car Platoons each (with four armored cars)*

52nd Motorized Mixed Engineer Battalion

28th Motorized Engineer Company

91st Motorized Communications Company

90th Medical Company

Supply Regiment (with fourteen 30-ton motorized supply columns in three Battalions plus one 50-cubic-meter POL (Petroleum, Oils, and Lubricants) column)

    176th Administration Platoon

    One Motorized Cavalry Reconnaissance Platoon*

    One Motorized Field Post Office*

One Motorized Bersaglieri Regiment (with two Motorized Infantry Battalions of three Companies, two Motorcycles Companies of the 2nd Bersaglieri Regiment with three 47/32 anti-tank guns, three 20-mm anti-tank guns, three heavy machine guns, and six light machine guns)

One Tank Battalion with three Companies (with fifty-two medium tanks)

One Motorized Artillery Regiment

15th Motorized Artillery Battalion (detached to the Ariete Division)

1st Motorized Artillery Battery (with four 105/28 field guns)

2nd Motorized Artillery Battery (with four 105/28 field guns)

3rd Motorized Artillery Battery (with four 105/28 field guns)

2nd Motorized Artillery Battalion

1st Motorized Artillery Battery (with four 105/28 field guns)

2nd Motorized Artillery Battery (with four 105/28 field guns)

3rd Motorized Artillery Battery (with four 105/28 field guns)

3rd Motorized Artillery Battalion
    1st Motorized Artillery Battery (with four 105/28 field guns)
    2nd Motorized Artillery Battery (with four 105/28 field guns)
    3rd Motorized Artillery Battery with four 105/28 field guns
    1st Anti-aircraft Battery/132nd Artillery Regiment (attached from the Ariete
Division, with eight 20-mm Anti-aircraft guns)
    24th Motorized Engineer Battalion
    1st Motorized Engineer Company
    2nd Motorized Engineer Company
    1st Motorized Engineer Communications Battalion
    One Motorized Telephone Company
    One Motorized Radio Company
    One Supply Battalion
    One 60-cubic-meter Water Transport Column
    One 50-cubic-meter POL (Petroleum, Oils, and Lubricants) Transport Column
    One 30-ton Motorized Transport Column
      One Motorized Ambulance Platoon
    One Motorized Administration Company

* Not on hand by 22 August 1942

NOTE: The 101st Motorized Infantry Division Trieste was authorized 5,932 men. As of August 22, 1942, it only had 181 officers and 3,392 enlisted men assigned.

XXI Italian Corps Order of Battle: As of August 22, 1942

(Created by George Nafziger. First published in English online at the U.S. Army Combined Arms Research Library) (The database is open source)

Order of Battle

25th Infantry Division Bologna
  39th Infantry Regiment
    1st Battalion (with four Companies with twelve 47/32 anti-tank guns, twelve 20-mm anti-tank rifles, twelve heavy machine guns, and twenty-four light machine guns)
    2nd Battalion (with twelve 47/32 anti-tank guns, twelve 20-mm anti-tank rifles, twelve heavy machine guns, and twenty-four light machine guns)
    3rd Battalion (with twelve 47/32 anti-tank guns, twelve 20-mm anti-tank rifles, twelve heavy machine guns, twenty-four light machine guns, and one Mortar Company with nine 81-mm mortars)
  40th Infantry Regiment
    1st Battalion (with twelve 47/32 anti-tank guns, eleven 20-mm anti-tank rifles, thirteen heavy machine guns, and twenty-eight light machine guns)
    2nd Battalion (with twelve 47/32 anti-tank guns, ten 20-mm anti-tank rifles, fifteen heavy machine guns, and twenty-eight light machine guns)
    3rd Battalion (with twelve 47/32 anti-tank guns, twelve 20-mm anti-tank rifles, twelve heavy machine guns, twenty-four light machine guns, and one mortar company)
  205th Motorized Artillery Regiment
    1st Motorized Artillery Battalion
      1st Motorized Artillery Battery (with four 100/17 model 14 howitzers)
      2nd Motorized Artillery Battery (with four 100/17 model 14 howitzers)
      3rd Motorized Artillery Battery (with four 100/17 model 14 howitzers)
    2nd Motorized Artillery Battalion
      1st Motorized Artillery Battery (with four 100/17 model 14 howitzers)
      2nd Motorized Artillery Battery (with four 100/17 model 14 howitzers)
      3rd Motorized Artillery Battery (with four 100/17 model 14 howitzers)
    3rd Motorized Artillery Battalion
      1st Motorized Artillery Battery (with four 75/27 field guns)
      2nd Motorized Artillery Battery (with four 75/27 field guns)
      3rd Motorized Artillery Battery (with four 75/27 field guns)

4th Motorized Artillery Battalion
   1st Motorized Artillery Battery (with four 75/27 field guns)
   2nd Motorized Artillery Battery (with four 75/27 field guns)
   3rd Motorized Artillery Battery (with four 75/27 field guns)
5th Motorized Anti-aircraft Artillery Battalion
   1st Motorized Anti-aircraft Artillery Battery (with four 88/55 anti-aircraft/anti-tank guns)
   2nd Motorized Anti-aircraft Artillery Battery (with four 88/55 anti-aircraft/anti-tank guns)
   3rd Motorized Anti-aircraft Artillery Battery (with four 88/55 anti-aircraft/anti-tank guns)
   4th Motorized 20-mm Anti-aircraft Artillery Battery
   437th Motorized 20-mm Anti-aircraft Artillery Battery
25th Semi-motorized Mixed Engineer Battalion
   62nd Combat Engineer Company (under control of the German Panzer Army)
   63rd Semi-motorized Engineer Company
   25th Semi-motorized Communications Company
   24th Semi-motorized Medical Company
   171st Motorized Administration Company

NOTE: The 25th Infantry Division Bologna was authorized 7,000 men. As of August 22, 1942, it only had 206 officers and 3,794 enlisted men assigned.

102nd Motorized Division Trento
  61st Infantry Regiment
    1st Battalion (with four Companies with eight 47/32-mm anti-tank guns, nine 20-mm anti-tank rifles, twelve heavy machine guns, and twenty-six light machine guns)
    2nd Battalion with four Companies (with seven 20-mm anti-tank rifles, twelve heavy machine guns, and twenty-six light machine guns)
    3rd Battalion with four Companies (with six 47/32-mm anti-tank guns, nine 20-mm anti-tank rifles, eight heavy machine guns, and twenty-four light machine guns)
    One Mortar Company (with twelve 81-mm mortars)
  62nd Infantry Regiment (from Sicily)
    1st Battalion (with four Companies with seven 47/32-mm anti-tank guns, ten 20-mm anti-tank rifles, eleven heavy machine guns, and twenty-seven light machine guns)
    2nd Battalion (with four Companies with ten 47/32-mm anti-tank guns, eight 20-mm anti-tank rifles, eleven heavy machine guns, and twenty-four light machine guns)
    3rd Battalion (with four Companies with eight 47/32-mm anti-tank guns, nine 20-mm anti-tank rifles, eight heavy machine guns, and twenty-four light machine guns)
    One Mortar Company (with thirteen 81-mm mortars)
  46th Motorized Artillery Regiment
    1st Motorized Artillery Battalion
      1st Motorized Artillery Battery (with four 100/17 model 14 howitzers)
      2nd Motorized Artillery Battery (with four 100/17 model 14 howitzers)
      3rd Motorized Artillery Battery
    2nd Motorized Artillery Battalion
      1st Motorized Artillery Battery (with four 100/17 model 14 howitzers)
      2nd Motorized Artillery Battery (with four 100/17 model 14 howitzers)
      3rd Motorized Artillery Battery (with four 100/17 model 14 howitzers)
    3rd Motorized Artillery Battalion
      1st Motorized Artillery Battery (with four 75/27 model 06 field guns)
      2nd Motorized Artillery Battery (with four 75/27 model 06 field guns)
      3rd Motorized Artillery Battery (with four 75/27 model 06 field guns)

4th Motorized Artillery Battalion
    1st Motorized Artillery Battery (with four 75/27 model 06 field guns)
    2nd Motorized Artillery Battery (with four 75/27 model 06 field guns)
    3rd Motorized Artillery Battery (with four 75/27 model 06 field guns)
5th Motorized Anti-aircraft Artillery Battalion
    1st Motorized Artillery Battery (with four 88/55 anti-aircraft/anti-tank guns)
    2nd Motorized Artillery Battery (with four 88/55 anti-aircraft/anti-tank guns)
    3rd Motorized Artillery Battery (with four 88/55 anti-aircraft/anti-tank guns)
254th Artillery Battalion (attached from XXI Corps, sometimes identified as the 354th Artillery Battalion)
    1st Artillery Battery (with four 77/28 field guns)
    2nd Artillery Battery (with four 77/28 field guns)
    3rd Artillery Battery (with four 77/28 field guns)
355th Artillery Battalion (attached from XXI Corps, sometimes identified as the 357th Artillery Battalion)
    1st Artillery Battery (with four 77/28 field guns)
    2nd Artillery Battery (with four 77/28 field guns)
    3rd Artillery Battery (with four 77/28 field guns)
    412th Motorized Anti-aircraft Artillery Battery with two 20-mm anti-aircraft guns
    414th Motorized Anti-aircraft Artillery Battery with two 20-mm anti-aircraft guns
51st Semi-Motorized Mixed Engineer Battalion
    15th Semi-motorized Engineer Company
    96th Semi-motorized Communications Company
4th Anti-tank Battalion
    51st Semi-motorized Medical Company
    51st Motorized Administration Company
7th Motorized Bersaglieri Regiment
    10th Motorized Bersaglieri Battalion (with four companies with eight 47/32 anti-tank guns, three 20-mm anti-tank rifles, eight heavy machine guns, and nineteen light machine guns)
    11th Motorized Bersaglieri Battalion (with one company with two 47/32 anti-tank guns, two 20-mm anti-tank rifles, two heavy machine guns, and six light machine guns)
    16th Tank Battalion (with three Companies with fifty-two medium tanks)
8th Motorized Artillery Regiment
    52nd Motorized Artillery Battalion
        1st Motorized Artillery Battery (with two 152/37 guns)
        2nd Motorized Artillery Battery
    33rd Motorized Artillery Battalion
        1st Motorized Artillery Battery (with three 149/40 guns)
        2nd Motorized Artillery Battery (with three 149/40 guns)
        3rd Motorized Artillery Battery (with three 149/40 guns)
    31st Motorized Artillery Battalion
        1st Motorized Artillery Battery (with three Krupp 149/28 field guns)
        2nd Motorized Artillery Battery (with three Krupp 149/28 field guns)
        3rd Motorized Artillery Battery (with four 149/28 field guns)
    254th Artillery Battalion (detached to the Trento Division, sometimes identified as the 354th Artillery Battalion) (authorized twelve 77/28 guns in three batteries of four guns)
        1st Artillery Battery (with four 77/28 field guns)
        2nd Artillery Battery (with four 77/28 field guns)
        3rd Artillery Battery (with four 77/28 field guns)
    355th Artillery Battalion (detached to the Trento Division, sometimes identified as the 357th Artillery Battalion)

1st Artillery Battery (with four 77/28 field guns)
2nd Artillery Battery (with four 77/28 field guns)
3rd Artillery Battery (with four 77/28 field guns)
9th Anti-aircraft Artillery Battery
27th Motorized Engineer Mechanics Battalion
1st Motorized Engineer Mechanics Company
2nd Motorized Engineer Mechanics Company
65th Motorized Engineer Communications Battalion
127th Motorized Telephone Company
113th Motorized Radio Company
One Supply Battalion
One 60-Cubic Meter Water Transport Column
One 50-Cubic Meter POL (Petroleum, Oils, and Lubricants) Transport Column
One 30-Ton Motorized Transport Column
One Motorized Ambulance Platoon
One Motorized Administration Company

NOTE: The 102nd Motorized Division Trento was authorized 7,000 men. As of August 22, 1942, it only had 252 officers and 4,362 enlisted men assigned.

XXII Corps:
As of August 22, 1942

(Created by George Nafziger. First published in English online at the U.S. Army Combined Arms Research Library) (The database is open source)

Order of Battle

4th Blackshirt Division 3 January
   250th Blackshirt Legion
      150th G. Carli Blackshirt Battalion
      154th D. Mastronuzzi Blackshirt Battalion
      156th Lucania Blackshirt Battalion
   270th Blackshirt Legion
      170th Agrigentum Blackshirt Battalion
      172nd Enna Blackshirt Battalion
      174th Segesta Blackshirt Battalion
        4th Blackshirt Anti-tank Company
      204th Blackshirt Heavy Machine Gun Battalion
   204th Artillery Regiment
      204th Mixed Engineer Battalion
            204th Medical Section
            204th Logistics Section
            Transport Section (1,600 pack mules)
            Mixed Trucks Section (eighty light and medium trucks)
64th Infantry Division Catanzaro
  141th Infantry Regiment Catanzaro
  142th Infantry Regiment Catanzaro
  203rd Artillery Regiment
    64th Machinegun Battalion
    64th Mixed Engineer Battalion
      64th anti-tank Company
    20th Armor Battalion
    63th Armor Battalion (transferred from 63rd Infantry Division Cirene on December 9, 1940)

XXIII Corps:
As of August 22, 1942

(Created by George Nafziger. First published in English online at the U.S. Army Combined Arms Research Library) (The database is open source)

Order of Battle

1st Blackshirt Division 23 March
   19th Blackshirt Legion
      114th G. Veroli Blackshirt Battalion
      118th Volsca Blackshirt Battalion
      119th N. Ricciotti Blackshirt Battalion
   233rd Blackshirt Legion
      129th Adriatica Blackshirt Battalion
      133rd Lupi di Matese Blackshirt Battalion
      148th Tavogliere Blackshirt Battalion
      41st Light Tank Battalion (with CV3/33 and CV3/35 tanks)
         1st Blackshirt Anti-tank Company
      201st Machine Gun Battalion
   201st Artillery Regiment
   201st Mixed Engineer Battalion
1st Libyan Division Sibelle
   1st Libyan Infantry Regiment
   2nd Libyan Infantry Regiment
      1st Libyan Artillery Battalion
      2nd Libyan Artillery Battalion
         Anti-Tank Company
      1st Libyan Engineer Battalion
2nd Libyan Division Pescatore
      9th light Tank Battalion (with L3 light tanks reinforcing the 2nd Libyan Division Pescatore)
   3rd Libyan Infantry Regiment
      2nd Battalion
      6th Battalion
      7th Battalion
   4th Libyan Infantry Regiment
      3rd Battalion
      15th Battalion

16th Battalion
2nd Colonial Artillery Regiment
2nd Colonial Engineer Battalion
62nd Infantry Division Marmarica
 63rd Light Tank Battalion (with L3 light tanks reinforcing the 62nd Division Marmarica)
115th Infantry Regiment
116th Infantry Regiment
44th Motorized Artillery Regiment
  1st Motorized Anti-aircraft Battery (with eight 20-mm guns)
  2nd Motorized Anti-aircraft Battery (with eight 20-mm guns)
 3rd Artillery Battalion (with twelve 75/27 Model 11 guns)
 4th Artillery Battalion (with twelve 75/27 Model 11 guns)
 5th Artillery Battalion (with twelve 100/17 Model 14 guns)
 62nd Engineer Battalion
 62nd Machine Gun Battalion
 Training Battalion
 Tankette Battalion
  Motorcycle Company
  62nd Anti-tank Gun Company (with 47/32 anti-tank guns)
 2nd Medium Tank Battalion
63rd Infantry Division Cirene
 62nd Light Tank Battalion with L3 light tanks (reinforcing the 63rd Division Cirene)
157th Infantry Regiment
158th Infantry Regiment
45th Artillery Regiment
 63rd Armor Battalion (transferred to 64th Infantry Division Catanzaro 9 December 1940)
 20th Light Tank Battalion (with L3 tanks)
 61st Motorized Libyan Infantry Battalion

Italian Army Vehicles and Weapons Used in North Africa

(Source: Italian Army Archives)

Vehicles

M11/39 Medium Tank
Originally designated as the Fiat-Ansaldo 8T, the M11/39 was developed for infantry support in 1937. Engine—125-hp Fiat SPA* 8T V-8 engine; weight—12 tons; speed—32 kph; range—210 km; length—4.85 meters; width—2.15 meters; height—2.10 meters; crew—three; armor—thin and only designed to protect against 20-mm fire; armament—37-mm Vickers-Terni L40 with eighty-four rounds; two Breda Model 88 machine guns.

M14/41 Medium Tank
The M14/41 tank was essentially the M13/40 fitted with a more powerful diesel engine that was equipped with air filters designed to cope with the harsh conditions of the desert. Production amounted to just over 1,100 of these vehicles. Engine—192-hp SPA 15 TB M42 eight-cylinder gasoline engine; weight—15,500 kg; speed—40 kph; range—220 km; length—5.04 meters; width—2.23 meters; height—2.39 meters; crew—four; armor—4 mm to 45 mm; armament—one 47-mm, 40-caliber gun and four 8-mm machine guns (one co-axial, one on the roof, and one twin in the front hull).

L6/40 Light Tank
The L6/40 was developed from a series of 4.92-ton tracked vehicles from Fiat-Ansaldo, mainly for the export market. The first prototypes were completed in 1936 with one armed with twin 8-mm Breda machine guns and another armed with a 37-mm cannon. The Italian Army ordered 283 of the L6/40s, which were delivered in 1941 and 1942. Many of the tanks were finished as Semovante L6/47 self-propelled anti-tank guns. Engine—70-hp SPA 180 four-cylinder inline engine; weight—6,800 kg; speed—42 kph; range—200 km; length—3.78 meters; width—1.92 meters; height—2.03 meters; crew—two; armor—6 mm to 30 mm; armament—one Breda 35 20-mm cannon and one Breda 8-mm co-axial machine gun.

L3/33 Light Tank

The CV-33 or L3/33 was a tankette originally built in 1933 and used by the Italian Army before and during World War II. It was based on the imported British Carden-Loyd tankette. Many CV-33s were retrofitted to meet the specifications of the CV-35in 1935. In 1938, the CV-33 was renamed the L3/33 while the CV-35s became known as L3/35s. The original CV-33 carried a two-man crew protected by 12 mm of welded armor and was armed with a single 6.5-mm machine gun. Engine—43-hp Fiat SPA CV3 water-cooled engine; weight—2.7 tons; speed—42 kph; range—110 km; length—3.03 meters; width—1.4 meters; height—1.2 meters; crew—two; armor—six 12 mm; armament—one 6.5-mm machine gun.

Autoblinda 41 Armored Car

The Autoblinda 41 armored car had their origins in a requirement for a high-performance car for use by the Italian colonial police in the new Italian colonies in Africa. For its time, the Autoblinda 41 was an advanced design and possessed good performance, marred only by recurring steering troubles that never were entirely eliminated. Engine—one 80-hp SPA 1 six-cylinder, water-cooled inline gasoline engine; weight—7,500 kg; speed—78.8 kph; off road speed—38.6 kph; crew—four; armament— one 20-mm Breda model 35 cannon, one hull-mounted 8-mm Breda model 38 machine gun, and one 8-mm Breda model 38 machine gun at hull rear.

AS/37 Light Truck

The AS/37 Light Truck was developed from 1937 on the frame of the TL 37 artillery tractor and was especially conceived to be employed in the North African desert. Engine—52-hp SPA petrol four-cylinder; weight—3.77 kg; speed—50 kph; range—870 km; length—4.67 meters; width—2.02 meters; height—2.65 meters; crew—four.

Lancia 3Ro Heavy Truck

The Lancia 3Ro 4 × 2 heavy truck evolved from the earlier Lancia Ro by receiving a stronger five-cylinder engine to replace two- and three-cylinder engines, pneumatic tires, and an improved transmission. Engine—93-hp five-cylinder diesel; weight—5,610 kg; speed—45 kph; length—7.08 meters; width—2.350 meters; height—3 meters; crew—one.

* Note: SPA is an abbreviation for the *Società Piemontese Automobili* Company.

Major Weapons

47/32** Model 37 Anti-tank Gun

The little Böhler 47-mm anti-tank gun was first produced in 1935 and is sometimes known as the Model 35. It was first produced in Austria, but its use soon spread outside Austria and licenses to produce the gun were taken up by Italy. The gun could fire both armor piercing and high-explosive projectiles. Caliber—47 mm; length—1.68 meters; travelling weight—315 kg; elevation—minus 15 degrees to 56 degrees; traverse—62 degrees; maximum range—7,000 meters; armor penetration—43 mm at 500 meters; ammunition—powder charge grenade, piercing projectile, anti-tank projectile, blank projectile, and exercitation grenade.

88/55 Anti-aircraft/Anti-tank Gun

The 88/55 is in fact the German 88-mm Flak 18. The guns delivered by the Germans were used by the Italian Army in North Africa. The ammunition employed by the

Italians was of three types: anti-aircraft S/30 round, piercing L/3.9 rounds, and high-explosive L/4.5 rounds for fire against ground targets. Contrary to the Germans, the Italians primarily used the gun as an anti-aircraft weapon and seldom as an anti-tank weapon, although this gun had very appreciable capacities of penetration. Caliber—88 mm; length—4.93 meters; firing weight—5,500 kg; elevation—minus 3 degrees to 85 degrees; traverse—360 degrees; maximum range—14,800 meters; maximum ceiling—10,600 meters; armor penetration—105 mm at 1,000 meters.

90/53 Self-propelled Anti-tank Gun

The 90/53 was an Italian designed cannon used both in an anti-aircraft role and as an anti-tank gun during World War II. It was one of the most successful anti-aircraft guns to see service during the conflict. The first prototype was completed on March 5, 1942, and after some tests, a first order was placed for thirty vehicles plus fifteen command ones, which were to be delivered no later than the end of April. Caliber—90 mm; length—5.2 meters; height—2.14 meters; armor—8 mm to 30 mm; engine—145-hp SPA 15T diesel powered; max speed—35 kph; maximum range—200 km; weight—17 tons.

20/65 Model 35 (Brenda) Anti-aircraft Gun

One of the two standard Italian 20-mm anti-aircraft guns was the 20/65 model 35 (Breda) that was first manufactured in 1934. The Breda was designed as a dual-purpose weapon for use against ground and air targets and was taken into service by the Italian Army in 1935. The 20-mm Breda was a very effective weapon and was much used by the Italian Army. Caliber—20 mm; length—1.3 meters; firing weight—307.3 kg; maximum ceiling—2,500 meters; elevation—minus 10 degrees to 80 degrees; traverse—360 degrees; cyclic rate of fire—200 to 220 rounds per minute.

20/77 (Scotti) Anti-aircraft Gun

The 20/77 (Scotti), first designed in 1932 and produced by the Swiss Oerlikon company, used a sixty-round drum that was eventually discarded in favor of twelve-round trays for the ammunition. Compared to the Breda, the Scotti was a far simpler weapon. Caliber—20 mm; length—1.54 meters; firing weight—227.5 kg; maximum ceiling—2,135 meters; elevation—minus 10 degrees to 85 degrees; traverse—360 degrees; cyclic rate of fire—250 rounds per minute.

37/54 (Brenda) Model 39 Anti-aircraft Gun

The 37/54 (Breda) was a 37-mm automatic anti-aircraft gun produced by the Breda company in Italy. It was used by both the navy and the army during World War II, with the former using it as the standard light anti-aircraft weapon on its battleships and cruisers. Caliber—37 mm; length—3.28 meters; firing weight—277 kg; elevation—minus 10 degrees to 90 degrees (single mount), minus 10 degrees to 80 degrees (twin mount); traverse—360 degrees; maximum range—7,800 meters.

75/46 Anti-aircraft Gun

The 75/46 was an anti-aircraft gun produced by Italy and used by Italy, Germany, and the Allies during World War II. Caliber—75 mm; length—7.4 meters; barrel length—3.45 meters; travelling weight—4,405 kg; elevation—minus 2 degrees to 90 degrees; traverse—360 degrees; maximum range—8,300 meters.

75/50 Model 37 Anti-aircraft Gun

The 7.5-cm anti-aircraft Gun Model 37 was a Czech anti-aircraft gun used in World War II. Those weapons captured after the German occupation of Czechoslovakia in March 1939 were taken into Wehrmacht service as the 7.5-cm Flak M37. The Germans sold many of them to Italy where they were designated as the 75/49 or 75/50 guns. Caliber—75 mm; length—3.65 meters; firing weight—2,800 kg; elevation—0 degrees to 85 degrees; traverse—360 degrees; maximum range—6,000 meters; maximum ceiling—9,200 meters.

75/27 Model 11 Field Gun

The 75/27 model 11 was a French-designed field gun produced in Italy prior to World War I. The gun was designed with two notable features. It was the first artillery piece to introduce the split trail, as well as the last to utilize its novel dual-recoil system. Caliber—75 mm; length—2.3 meters; firing weight—1,015 kg; elevation—minus 15 degrees to 65 degrees; traverse—52 degrees; rate of fire—four to six rounds per minute; maximum range—10,240 meters.

105/28 Cannon

Originally designed by France as the L13 S. With Italy, they became the 105/28 and remained one of the Italian guns until 1943. Caliber—105 mm; length—2.987 meters; firing weight—2,300 kg; elevation—minus 0 degrees to 37 degrees; traverse—6 degrees; maximum range—12,000 meters.

77/28 Model 5 Gun

The 8-cm Field Canon M5 was a field gun used by Austria-Hungary during World War I. Guns captured by Italy were used as the 77/28 model 5 gun. Caliber—76.5 mm; length—2.285 meters; firing weight—1,065 kg; elevation—minus 7 degrees to 18 degrees; traverse—7 degrees; range—7,000 meters.

152/37 Gun

The 15-cm Auto Cannon M15/16 was a heavy field gun used by Austria-Hungary in World War I. Guns turned over to Italy as reparations after World War I were taken into Italian service as the 152/37 gun. Caliber—152.4 mm; length—6 meters; firing weight—11,900 kg; elevation—minus 6 degrees to 45 degrees; traverse—6 degrees; maximum range—21,840 meters.

149/40 Gun

The 149/40 gun was a heavy gun, which served with Italy during World War II. It was intended to replace the obsolete 149/35A, but the small numbers produced prevented that. Caliber—149.1 mm; length—6.036 meters; firing weight—11,340 kg; elevation—minus 60 degrees to 45 degrees; traverse—60 degrees; maximum range—23,700 meters.

149/28 Field Howitzer

The 15-cm heavy field howitzer, model 18, nicknamed "Evergreen," was the basic German division-level heavy howitzer during World War II. The gun originated with a contest between Rheinmetall and Krupp, both of whom entered several designs that were all considered unsatisfactory for one reason or another. In the end, the army decided the solution was to combine the best features of both designs, using the Rheinmetall gun on a Krupp carriage. Italy designated it 149/28. Caliber—149 mm; length—7.849 meters; firing weight—5,512 kg; elevation—minus 0 degrees to 45 degrees; traverse—60 degrees; maximum range—13,325 meters.

100/17 Field Howitzer Model 14

The 10cm M14 field howitzer was a dual-purpose field and mountain gun used by Austria-Hungary during World War I. Between the wars, it was used by Austria, Italy, and Poland. It served as the standard Italian medium howitzer as the 100/17 model 14.

Caliber—100 mm; length—1.93 meters; firing weight—1,350 kg; elevation—minus 8 degrees to 50 degrees; traverse—6 degrees; maximum range—8,400 meters.

75/18 Semovente Howitzer Model 34

In 1934, the Italian firm of Ansaldo produced a new mountain howitzer design, the 75/18 model 34. The gun was also used as the main armament of the Semovente 75/18 self-propelled gun where, due to its high-explosive anti-tank warhead ammunition, it also had a good anti-tank capability. Caliber—75 mm; length—1.557 meters; firing weight—1,050 kg; elevation—minus 10 degrees to 45 degrees; traverse—50 degrees; maximum range—9,564 meters.

65/17 Model 13 Gun

The 65-mm gun was first accepted into service with Italian mountain troops in 1913, and it served with them throughout World War I. Replacements arrived in the 1920s and the gun was transferred to the regular infantry. It was well liked by the infantry due to its minimal weight and high reliability in adverse conditions. Despite its light caliber, it served through World War II with the Italian forces as a close support weapon. It was effective also mounted on truck, in North Africa, as anti-tank artillery. Caliber—65 mm; length—1.1 meters; firing weight—560 kg; elevation—minus 10 degrees to 20 degrees; traverse—8 degrees; maximum range—6,200 meters.

75/34 Model SF Gun

The 75/34 model SF is directly derived from howitzer 75/34 model 1937, designed by the Artillery Armory Construction of Naples. The original 75/34 instead, thanks to its excellent anti-tank performance, was installed on tanks. Caliber—75 mm; length—2.5 meters; firing weight—560 kg; elevation—minus 10 degrees to 20 degrees; traverse—8 degrees; maximum range—6,200 meters.

** Note on weapon designations: The designation 90/53, for example, meant that the gun had a 90-mm caliber and a barrel 53-caliber-lengths long.

Small Arms

Beretta Model 1934

It was the standard infantry pistol during World War II, chambered for the so-called "9-mm Corto", a shortened version of the 9-mm Parabellum caliber. This semi-automatic gun was able to hold seven rounds in the magazines.

Beretta Model 1935

This version was chambered for the 7.65 mm and issued to the *Regia Marina* (Navy) and the militia in limited numbers.

Bodeo Revolver Model 1889

This revolver, used even during World War I, was based on the French Chamelot-Delvigne Model 1874. It was chambered for the 10.35-mm caliber (six rounds).

Glisenti Model 1910

A 9-mm semi-automatic handgun produced by MBT (Metallurgica Bresciana Tampini) and issued to the Italian troops in World War I after field tests showed that it performance was superior to the Colt M1911 and the German Luger P08.

Carcano Model 1891

The standard rifle of the Italian Army; just like in most cases (except the U.S.), it was the same bolt-action that fought in World War I with little modifications. With 750,529 pieces as of 1939, it was by far the most common Italian weapon during World War II.

Automatic Weapons

Beretta MAB 38

The official submachine gun during World War II and considered one of the most successful weapons of the conflict. It was originally intended to be used only by the air force, but was later extended to the entire army. The 9-mm magazine was available with ten, twenty, thirty, and forty rounds.

FNAB Model 1943

This submachine gun was based on captured Soviet PPSh-41 and chambered for the 9-mm caliber.

TZ-45

Just like the FNAB, this weapon was produced during the last part of the conflict and issued to RSI conflict, but it was a really cheap and simple weapon (made with metal stampings).

Breda Model 1930

It was the standard light machine gun of the Italian Army (one Model 30 issued to every squad). It was chambered for the 7.35-mm caliber.

FIAT Model 1914/35

It was an updated version of the Model 1935, the standard heavy-machine gun of World War I. The new model was air cooled (while the earlier version was water cooled) and was fed with 300 8-mm round belts in order to cancel the bad feeding system that affected the Model 1930.

Breda Model 1937

This heavy machine gun was more sophisticated than the FIAT (it was capable of both semi and full auto fire). It suffered from the same feeding problems of the Model 1930, which also slowed down its rate of fire and it was a fairly heavy weapon. The 1937 was considered a heavy machine gun, while the 8-mm Brenda or 7.92-mm Mauser cartridge was used by the German forces as standard ammunition.

Italian Tropical Uniform

(Source: Commando Supremo)

Tropical Uniform

> The tropical M40 uniform was made in the same cut as the M40 g-v uniform (bluish green-grey), using khaki cotton fabric instead of wool. Rank, insignia, mostrini (colar patch), etc., were the same. A tropical helmet (casco) was generally issued instead of the steel helmet. The casco was light-weight, comfortable to wear, and gave protected the wearer from the heat, but did not offer any ballistic protection. A tricolor, in the Italian national colors with a brass fregio (decoration), was worn on the front of the casco.

Bersaglieri (motorized infantry)

> Red fez with a blue cord and tassel instead of a bustina (forage cap). Leather leggings instead of puttees (leather legging). Dress uniform included a low crowned, black, waxed-leather hat with plume.

Paracadutisti (Paratroopers)

> M41 g-v uniform (collarless tunic, long pants), g-v beret with fregio, tall parachutist jump boots.

Corazzato (Armored)

> Black leather coat.

Blackshirt (Camicia Nera)

> Blackshirt instead of the g-v, black fez with black cord and tassel. Black puttees.

In the Field

> The M40 overcoat was made from the same g-v wool as the uniform. There was a dismounted and mounted version, distinguished mainly by the size of the collar and cut of the coat skirts. The dismounted version had a smaller, angular collar and straight skirts. The mounted had a large, rounded collar and the skirts flared from the waist. Both were single-breasted with two large slit hip pockets, closed by a straight flap. No button was provided to secure the flap. There were two small slit breast pockets without flaps, closed by a small button. These pockets were unusual, as the pocket opening was vertical, not horizontal. The attached shoulder straps were of the same material and fixed with one small button. The large straight cuffs could be rolled down over the hands for

protection. A small button on the back of the sleeve secured the cuffs when not being used in this manner. No mostrini was worn on the collar, only large size aluminum stars.

The M1929 Tenda Telo (tent cloth) served both as a poncho and could be assembled with other telos into a tent. The telo was a square cloth made from cotton duck material, printed with a camouflage pattern on one side. The telo has an array of buttons and button holes for connecting multiple telos, and the necessary poles and ropes. No other rain gear was provided to the soldier.

In all, the Italian service uniform was both distinctive and striking. The very functional bustina and the open-collar belted tunic made for a very modern appearance. This was counterbalanced by the old style pants and puttees. This combination gave the Italian soldier a unique appearance from other armies during the war.

Bibliography

"16th Infantry Division Pistoia," *Royal Army* www.regioesercito.it/reparti/fanteria/rediv 16.htm

"25th Infantry Division Bologna" *Regio Esercito* www.regioesercito.it/reparti/fanteria/rediv25.htm.

"61st Infantry Division Sirte," *Royal Army* www.regioesercito.it/reparti/fanteria/rediv61. htm

"63rd Infantry Division Cirene," *Royal Army* www.regioesercito.it/reparti/fanteria/rediv 63.htm

"Aftermath Of War: The Eighth Army From Alamein To The Sangro" *The illustrated London News & Sketch Ltd., Volume 212, Issues 5672–5684, 1948*

"German Attack at El Alamein: August 31-September 5, 1942" *Tactical and Technical Trends, No.17,* January 28, 1943

"Infantry Division Africa Hunters," *Royal Army* www. regioesercito.it/reparti/fanteria/redivafrica.htm

"No. 38177," *The London Gazette* (Supplement), 13 January 1948

"Regio Esercito—Divisione Pavia" www.regioesercito.it/reparti/fanteria/rediv17.htm

"The Battle of the Omars," *U.S. Military Intelligence Service (15 April 1942)*

"The British Capture of Bardia (December 1941–January 1942): A Successful Infantry-Tank Attack," *Military Intelligence Service, Information Bulletin No. 21* (Washington: War Department, 1942)

"The Text of the Day's Communiques on Fighting in Europe and Africa: British," *New York Times,* 18 April 1941

3rd Field Regiment (Transvaal Horse Artillery)," *Military History Journal, 2009, The South African Military History Society*

Alanbrooke, A., Danchev, A., and Todman, D., eds., *War Diaries 1939–1945,* rev. ed., (London: Phoenix Press, 2002)

Aldea, D., "First Battle of El Alamein" *Commando Supremo: Italy at War* www. comandosupremo.com/1elalamein.html/2

Aldea, D., and Peluso, J., "The Bologna Division: 19 November–10 December, 1941" *Comando Supremo: Italy at War.* www.comandosupremo.com/bologna-division.html/6

Anderson, C. R., "Tunisia 17 November 1942 to 13 May 1943," *WWII Campaigns,* CMH Pub 72-12 (Washington: United States Army Center of Military History, 1946) Appendix Number 30: Summary Number 2, entry for 16 April, 2/43 Infantry Battalion War Diary, April 1941 (Campbell: Australian War Memorial)

Arena, N., *Folgore: History of Italian Military Parachuting* (Rome: National Editorial Center for Historical Sociological Humanistic Divulgations, 1966)

Associazione Bersaglieri della Regione www.bersaglieri.net/

Barker, A. J., *Rape of Ethiopia, 1936* (New York: Ballantine Books, 1971)

Barr, N., *Pendulum of War: The Three Battles of El Alamein* (London: Pimlico, 2004)

Bates, P., *Dance of War: The Story of the Battle of Egypt* (London: Leo Cooper 1992)

Bauer, E., and Young, P., ed., *The History of World War II* (London: Orbis, 1979); *The History of World War II*, rev. ed. (London: Orbis 2000)

Bedeschi, G., *Fronte d'Africa* (Milan: Mursia, 1979)

Bennighof, M., "The Folgore at Alamein," *Avalanche Press, June 2017* www.avalanchepress. com/FolgoreAtAlamein.php

Bentz, G., "From El Wak to Sidi Rezegh: The Union Defense Force's First Experience of Battle in East and North Africa, 1940–1941," *Scientia Militaria: South African Journal of Military Studies, No. 40* (Stellenbosch Stellenbosch University, 2012)

Bharucha, P. C., and Prasad, B., "The North African Campaign, 1940–43," *Official History of the Indian Armed Forces in the Second World War, 1939–45* (Delhi: Combined Inter-Services Historical Section, India & Pakistan, 1956)

Bierman, J., and Smith, C., *The Battle of Alamein: Turning Point, World War II* (New York: Viking Adult, 2002); *War Without Hate: The Desert Campaign of 1940–1943* (New York: Penguin Books, 2002)

Brown, J. D., *Carrier Operations in World War II: The Royal Navy* (London: Ian Allan, 1968)

Buchner, A., *The Handbook of the German Infantry 1939–1945*, (Eggolsheim: Dörfler Publishing, 2001)

Buffetaut, Y., "Operation Supercharge: Second Battle of El Alamein," *The Great Battles of the Second World War. Military Collection* (Paris: Histoire et Collections, 1995)

Bungay, S., *Alamein* (London: Aurum Press, 2013)

Caccia Dominioni de Sillavengo, Paolo, *Alamein 1933–1962: An Italian Story*, Translated by Chamberlin, Dennis (Crow's Nest: Allen & Unwin, 1966)

Carver, M., Spellmount ed., *Dilemmas of the Desert War: The Libyan Campaign 1940–1942* (London: Batsford, 1986)

Chant, C., *The Encyclopaedia of Codenames of World War II* (Abingdon: Routledge, 2013)

Christie, H. R., *Fallen Eagles: The Italian 10th Army in the Opening Campaign in the Western Desert, June 1940–December 1940* (Fort Leavenworth: U. S. Army Command and General Staff College, 1999)

Churchill, W. S., *The Second World War: Closing the Ring* (Boston Houghton Mifflin Company, 1951); *The Hinge of Fate* (The Yale Book of Quotations By Fred Shapiro, 2006)

Clifford, A., *Three Against Rommel: The Campaigns of Wavell, Auchinleck and Alexander* (London: George G. Harrap, 1943)

Congdon, D., *Combat: The War with Germany, World War II* (New York: Dell Publishing Company, 1963)

Converse, A., *Armies of Empire: The 9th Australian and 50th British Divisions in Battle 1939–1945* (Cambridge: Cambridge University Press, 2011)

Cooper, M., *The German Army 1933–1945: Its Political and Military Failure* (New York: Stein & Day, 1978)

Cox, G., *A Tale of Two Battles: Crete & Sidi Rezegh* (London: William Kimber, 1987)

Cox, P., *Desert War: The Battle of Sidi Rezegh* (Wollombi: Exisle Publishing, 2015)

Creveld, M. van, *Supplying War: Logistics from Wallenstein to Patton* (Cambridge: Cambridge University Press, 1977)

Del Boca, A., *Mussolini's Gas. Fascism and the Ethiopian War* (Rome: Editori Riunita, 1996)

Dominioni, P. C., and Izzo, G., *Takfir: Chronicle of the Last Battle of Alamein* (Milan: Ugo Mursia Editore, 1967)

Eisenhower, D.. *Crusade In Europe* (New York: Doubleday, 1948)

Fellgiebel, W.-P., *The Bearers of the Knights Cross of the Iron Cross 1939–1945* (Friedberg: Podzun-Pallas, 2000)

Ford, K., *Battleaxe Division* (Stroud: Sutton, 1999); *Operation Crusader 1941: Rommel in Retreat* (Oxford: Osprey Publishing, 2010)

French, D., *Raising Churchill's Army: The British Army and the War against Germany 1939–1945* (Oxford: Oxford University Press, 2000)

Gannon, J., *Stealing Secrets, Telling Lies: How Spies and Codebreakers Helped Shape the Twentieth Century* (Lincoln: Potomac Books, 2002)

Garratt, G. T., *Mussolini's Roman Empire* (London: Penguin Books, 1938)

Gaujac, P., *The French Expeditionary Force in Italy: 1943–1944* (Paris: Histoire et collections, 2003)

Glass, C., "Sidi Rezegh: Reminiscences of the late Gunner Cyril Herbert Glass, 143458,

Gooch, J., ed., *Decisive Campaigns of the Second World War* (London: Frank Cass, 1990)

Greene, J., and Massignani, A., *Rommel's North Africa Campaign: September 1940-November 1942* (Conshohocken: Combined Books, 1994)

Hague, A., *The Allied Convoy System 1939–1945* (Annapolis: Naval Institute Press, 2000)

Halley, J. J., *The Squadrons of the Royal Air Force* (Kent: Air Britain Historians Ltd., 1980)

Hamilton, N., "Montgomery, Bernard Law," *Oxford Dictionary of National Biography* (Oxford: Oxford University Press, 2004)

Hammond, B., *El Alamein: The Battle That Turned the Tide of the Second World War* (Oxford: Osprey Publishing, 2012)

Harding, J., "Appendix E, H.Q. Cyrenaica Command Intelligence Summary Number 6, (23 February 1941) WO 169/1258." *The National Archives*

Hastings, R. H. W. S., *The Rifle Brigade in the Second World War 1939–1945* (Aldershot: Gale & Polden, 1950)

Heddlesten, J., "Graziani vs. Rommel" www.comandosupremo.com/Graziani2.html

Hinsley, F. H., Thomas, E. E., Ransom, C. F. G., and Knight, R. C., *British Intelligence in the Second World War. Its Influence on Strategy and Operations*, Vol. II (London: Her Majesty's Stationary Office, 1979)

Horn, K., *South African Prisoner-of-War Experience during and after World War II: 1939–c. 1950*, (unpublished), Faculty of Arts and Social Sciences (Stellenbosch: Stellenbosch University, 2012)

Howe, G. F., *North West Africa: Seizing the Initiative in the West. The United States Army in World War II*, CMH Pub 6-1 (Washington: United States Army Center of Military History, 1957)

Howe, G., *Northwest Africa: Seizing the Initiative in the West* (Washington D.C: United States Army Center of Military History, 1993)

Humble, R., *Crusader: Eighth Army's Forgotten Victory, November 1941-January 1942* (South Yorkshire: Leo Cooper, 1987)

Hunt, Sir D., *A Don at War* (London: Frank Cass, 1966)

Information Bulletin No. 11 (Washington: U.S. War Department, 1942)

Jentz, T. L., *Panzertruppen 2: The Complete Guide to the Creation & Combat Employment of Germany's Tank Force 1943–1945* (Shiffler Publishing, 1996); *Tank Combat In North Africa: The Opening Rounds, Operations Sonnenblume, Brevity, Skorpion and Battleaxe, February 1941-June 1941*(Rheinberg: Schiffer, 1998)

Johnston, M., "The Battle of El Alamein, 23 October 1942," *Remembering 1942* (Canberra: Australian War Memorial, 2002); *Fighting the Enemy: Australian Soldiers and Their Adversaries in World War II* (Cambridge: Cambridge University Press, 2000); *That Magnificent 9th: An Illustrated History of The 9th Australian Division* (Crow's Nest: Allen and Unwin, 2002)

Johnston, M., and Stanley, P., *Alamein: The Australian Story* (South Melbourne: Oxford University Press, 2002)

Jones, E., and Wessely, S., *Shell Shock to PTSD: Military Psychiatry from 1900 to the Gulf War* (New York: Psychology Press, 2005)

Jowett, P. S., *The Italian Army 1940–45 (1): Europe 1940–1943* (New York Osprey, 2000)

Kippenberger, H., *Infantry Brigadier* (Oxford: Oxford University Press, 1949)

Koskodan, K. K., *No Greater Ally: The Untold Story of Poland's Forces in World War II* (Oxford: Osprey, 2011)

Kriebel, R., and Gudmundsson, B., *Inside the Afrika Korps: The Crusader Battles, 1941–1942* (London: Greenhill Books, 1999)

Kurowski, F., *Das Afrika Korps: Erwin Rommel and the Germans in Africa, 1941–43* (Mechanicsburg: Stackpole Books, 2010)

Latimer, J., *Alamein* (London: John Murray, 2002)

Law, R. D., and Luther, C. W. H., *Rommel, A Narrative and Pictorial History* (San Jose: R. James Bender Publishing, 1980)

Long, G., *To Benghazi: Australia in the War of 1939–1945*, 12th edition (Canberra: Australian War Memorial, 1952)

Lucas-Phillips, C., *Alamein* (London: Heinemann, 1962)

Lyman, R., *The Longest Siege: Tobruk, The Battle That Saved North Africa* (Basingstoke MacMillian, 2009)

MacGregor, K., *Mussolini Unleashed, 1939–1941. Politics and Strategy in Fascist Italy* (Cambridge: Cambridge University Press, 1986)

Mackenzie, C., *Eastern Epic: September 1939–March 1943 Defense* (London: Chatto and Windus, 1951)

Mackenzie, S. P., *The Second World War in Europe: Second Edition*, (Abingdon: Routledge, 2014)

Macksey, Major K., Pitt, B., and Mason, D., eds. Beda Fomm, "The Classic Victory." *Ballantine's Illustrated History of the Violent Century, Battle Books. 22* (New York: Ballantine Books, 1971)

Mangold, P., *Britain and the Defeated French: From Occupation to Liberation, 1940–1944* (London: I. B. Tauris, 2012)

Mason, A., "A 5-Minute History Of The Battle Of El Alamein," *Imperial War Museum* www.iwm.org.uk/history/a-5-minute-history-of-the-battle-of-el-alamein

Mason, Captain W. W., "The Second Libyan Campaign and After (November 1941–June 1942)," *The Official History of New Zealand in the Second World War 1939–1945* (Wellington: Historical Publications Branch, 1954)

Maughan, B., "Tobruk and El Alamein," *Australia in the War of 1939–1945, Series 1–Army III, 1st ed.* (Canberra: Australian War Memorial, 1966)

Mead, R., *Churchill's Lions: A Biographical Guide to the Key British Generals of World War II* (Stroud: Spellmount, 2007)

Millen, J., *Salute to Service: A History of the Royal New Zealand Corps of Transport and Its Predecessors, 1860–1996* (Wellington: Victoria University Press, 1997)

Mitcham, S. W., *Rommel's Desert War: The Life and Death of the Afrika Korps* (Mechanicsburg: Stackpole Books, 2007); *The Rise of the Wehrmacht*, in 2 volumes (Santa Barbara: Praeger, 2008); *Blitzkrieg No Longer: The German Wehrmacht in Battle, 1943* (Mechanicsburg: Stackpole Books, 2010)

Mockler, A., *Haile Sellassie's War* (New York: Olive Branch Press, 2002)

Modelski, T., *The Polish Contribution to The Ultimate Allied Victory in The Second World War* (Worthing: Caldra House Ltd., 1986)

Montanari, M., *El Alamein. Operations in North Africa III* (Rome: Army Staff, Historical Office, 1993)

Murphy, W. E., andf Fairbrother, Monty C., ed., *The Relief of Tobruk. The Official History of New Zealand in the Second World War 1939–1945* (Wellington: War History Branch, Department of Internal Affairs, 1961)

Nafziger, G. F., *Blackshirt, Mountain, Assault & Landing Divisions, Corps Troops and the 1944 Liberation Army. The Italian Order of Battle in WWII: An Organizational History of the Divisions and Independent Brigades of the Italian Army, III volumes* (West Chester: G. Nafziger, 1996); *Italian Order of Battle: An Organizational History of the Italian Army in World War II* (3 vol) (Fort Leavenworth: Combined Arms Research Library, 2010)

Nicolle, D., *The Italian Invasion of Abyssinia 1935–1936* (Westminster: Osprey, 1997)

Niehorster, L., "1940 Truck-Moveable Division, North African Type" www.niehorster. org/ 019_italy/40_organ/div_autotrans_40as.html

Orpen, N. D., *War in the Desert (South African Forces World War II, Volume III)* (London: Purnell & Sons, 1971)

Panzer Army Africa Battle Report, dated 29 June 1942 K.T.B. 812

Paoletti, C., *A Military History of Italy* (Westport: Greenwood Publishing Group, 2008)

Pitt, B., *The Crucible of War: Western Desert, 1941* (J. Cape, 1980)

Playfair, B., ed., *The Mediterranean and Middle East: British Fortunes reach their Lowest Ebb (September 1941 to September 1942). History of the Second World War United Kingdom Military Series*, Vol. III (Uckfield: Naval & Military Press, 2004)

Playfair, Major-General I. S. O., and Butler, J. R. M., ed., "The Mediterranean and Middle East: The Early Successes Against Italy to May 1941," *History of the Second World War, United Kingdom Military Series I* (Uckfield: Naval & Military Press, 1954)

Quirico, D., *White Squadron*, first edition (Milan: Mondadori, 2003)

Ready, J. L., *The Forgotten Axis: Germany's Partners and Foreign Volunteers in World War II* (Jefferson: McFarland & Company, 1987)

Richards, D., *Royal Air Force 1939–1945. Vol.1: The Fight at Odds 1939–1941!* (Her Majesty's Stationary Office, 1953)

Rizzo, G., *Holes and crosses in the desert* (Verona: Aurora, 1969)

Rohwer, J. and Hummelchen, G., *Chronology of the War at Sea 1939–1945* (Annapolis: Naval Institute Press, 1992)

Rommel, E., and Liddell-Hart, B., ed., *The Rommel Papers* (Boston: De Capo Press, 1953)

Sadkovich, J. J., "Of Myths ad Men: Rommel and the Italians in North Africa" (*The International History Review XIII*, 1991)

Schreiber, G., *Germany and the Second World War, vol. 3* (New York: Oxford University Press, 1995)

Scoullar, J. L., and Kippenberger, H., ed., *The Battle for Egypt: The Summer of 1942. The Official History of New Zealand in the Second World War, 1939–1945* (Wellington: Historical Publications Branch, 1955)

Shinn, D. H., Ofcansky, Thomas P., and Prouty, Chris, *Historical Dictionary of Ethiopia* (Lanham: Scarecrow Press, 2004)

Slowikowski, R., *In the Secret Service: The Lightning of the Torch* (London: The Windrush Press, 1988)

Smith, J. E., *Eisenhower in War and Peace* (New York: Random House, 2012)

Spirit, M., *Sid's War: The Story of an Argyll at War*, The war time memories of Private Sid Martindale (1st Battalion Argyll & Sutherland Highlanders, 2005)

Stevens, W. G., "Bardia to Enfidaville," *The Official History of New Zealand in the Second World War 1939–1945* (Wellington: War History Branch, Department of Internal Affairs, 1962) nzetc.victoria.ac.nz/tm/scholarly/tei-WH2Bard.html

Stewart, A., *The Early Battles of Eighth Army: 'Crusader' to the Alamein Line 1941-1942* (London: Leo Cooper, 2002)

Stirlinget, T., *Intelligence co-operation between Poland and Great Britain during World War II*, volume I (London, Vallentine Mitchell, 2005)

Strawson, J., *El Alamein: Desert Victory* (London: J. M. Dent, 1981)

Taylor, A. J. P., and Mayer, S. L., ed., *A History of World War Two* (London: Octopus Books, 1974)

Terraine, J., *The Right of the Line*, Wordsworth ed. (London: Hodder and Stoughton, 1985)

The First British Offensive in North Africa (October 1940–February 1941), I, Annex 32 (Rome: Esercito, 1979)

Thomson, J., *Warrior Nation: New Zealanders at the Front, 1900–2000* (Bloomington: Hazard Press, 2000)

Toppe, Generalmajor A., *German Experiences in Desert Warfare During World War II*, volume II, (Washington: Historical Division, European Command: US Marine Corps, 1947)

Turnbow, W., "Italian Army: Conflict between theories of employment" www.comando supremo.com/ItalianArmy.html

Vivian, C., *The Western Desert of Egypt: An Explorer's Handbook* (Cairo: American University in Cairo Press, 2000)

Walker, I. W., *Iron Hulls, Iron Hearts: Mussolini's Elite Armored Divisions in North Africa* (Marlborough: Crowood, 2003)

Walsh, B., *GCSE Modern World History, Second Edition* (London: John Murray Publishers, 2001)

Watson, B. A., *Exit Rommel: The Tunisian Campaign, 1942–43* (Mechanicsburg: Stackpole, 2007)

Wendal, M., "Italian Army," *Axis History* www.axishistory.com/axis-nations/italy/ army.

Westphal, S., *Fatal Decisions*, 1st Edition, (Marylebone: Michael Joseph, 1956)

Wilmot, C., *Tobruk* (Sydney: Halstead Press, 1944)

Young, P., *A Short History of World War II 1939–1945*, (1970 ed.) (London: Pan Books, 1966)

Zabecki, D. T., *World War II in Europe: an encyclopaedia* (New York: Garland Publishing, 1999)

Zinder, H., "A Pint of Water per Man" *Time Magazine. No. 16 November 1942* content. time. com/time/magazine/article/0,9171,932852,00.html

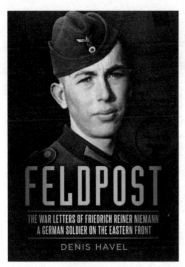

ISBN 978-1-62545-015-9
£25.00 $40.00   HB   234 × 156 mm
Feldpost: The War Letters of Friedrich Reiner Niemann
documents the frontline experiences of a German soldier
from the 6th Infantry Division from 1941- 1945. Niemann
describes the fighting at Rzhev, Russia, 1942-1943, and his
survival of the destruction of his division in 1944. His is a
rare view of the conflict on the Eastern front.

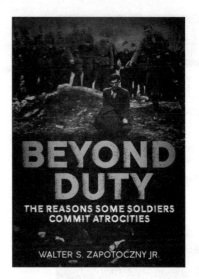

ISBN 978-1-62545-112-5
£25.00 $40.00   HB   234 × 156 mm
This book examines reasons for the horrific cruelty
of members of the Japanese in Nanking, China in
1937; the German Einsatzgruppen in Russia, from
1941–1943; the Russian Army in Dresden, Germany
in 1945; the Americans at Nogunri, Korea in 1950;
the Americans at My Lai, Vietnam in 1968; and the
Americans at the Abu Ghraib prison in Iraq in 2004.

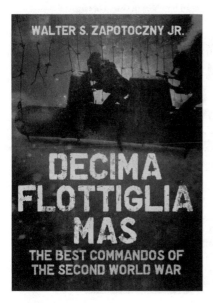

ISBN 978-1-62545-113-2
£20.00 $32.95   HB   234 × 156 mm
During the first years of the Second World War, Italian
commandos demonstrated how effective a weapon the
frogman could be. Concealed by the water, the Decima
Flottiglia MAS mined Allied ships as they were moored
in their own harbours, severely reducing British naval
power in the Mediterranean. This is the story of their
determination and bravery.

ISBN 978-1-78155-119-6
£16.99 $26.95   PB   248 × 172 mm
Luftwaffe aerial reconnaissance photographed all of
Great Britain. In June 1945 a British intelligence unit
stumbled upon 16 tonnes of pictures, dumped in a
barn in the Bavarian forest. The original Luftwaffe
archive was destroyed at the end of the war, and this
discovery was an incomplete German Intelligence
copy. This book reproduces 220 images.

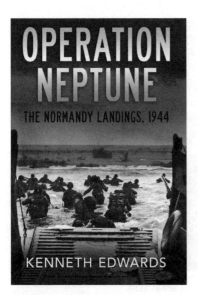

ISBN 978-1-78155-127-1

£16.99 $25.95 PB 234 × 156 mm

'Operation Neptune' was the codename for the naval component of the invasion of France. The complete invasion codename was 'Overlord', and 'Neptune' was therefore phase one. This book was written one year after the invasion by an officer who was closely involved, provides the detail behind the conception, planning and execution of 'Neptune'.

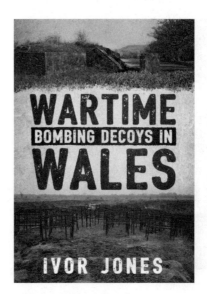

ISBN 978-1-78155-233-9

£18.99 $34.95 PB 248 × 172 mm

This book describes the night-time decoys which saved Cardiff, and much of Wales, from German WWII attack. By distorting what the bombers could see from the air, the Ministry of Home Security was successful in averting thousands of bombs from residential areas of the country. False 'lights' were created to mislead bombers in search of targets.

ISBN 978-1-78155-325-1

£16.99 $29.95 PB 234 × 156 mm

Early in 1945 the British Liberation Army, who had battled their way from the Normandy beaches to the borders of Germany, embarked on Operation Eclipse. This was the 'end-game' of the Second World War, the unique military campaign to invade and conquer Hitler's Third Reich. A thrilling race with Stalin's Red Army ensued to reach the Baltic.

ISBN 978-1-78155-329-9

£14.99 $24.95 PB 234 × 156 mm

Action begins immediately after D-Day with the euphoria surrounding the belief that the war would soon be won, however it was not to be as easy Monty hoped. The book covers the difficult next few months as the Allies slogged through France and Belgium fighting stern and skilled Nazi resistance. The centrepiece of which is Operation Market garden.

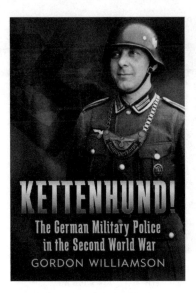

ISBN 978-1-78155-332-9
£30.00 $50.00   HB   248 × 172 mm
Military Police are among those who are least liked
by soldiers despite the essential duties they carry
out, often being first in and last out in war theatre.
German opinions were often those of fear as much as
dislike—so great were the powers they held. Many
wore a distinctive metal neck gorget, leading to their
nickname 'Kettenhund'—Chain Dogs.

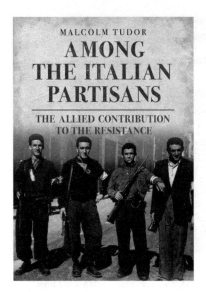

ISBN 978-1-78155-339-8
£20.00 $34.95   HB   234 × 156 mm
The remarkable story of the foreigners who
volunteered to join the guerrilla war against Germans
and Fascists in World War II Italy. The fighters
included Britons, Australians, Canadians, New
Zealanders, South Africans, Americans, Russians and
Yugoslavs. Most were escaped prisoners of war. The
book is a celebration of brave men and great events.

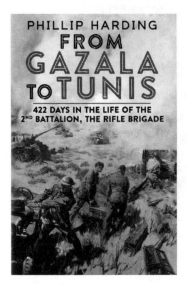

ISBN 978-1-78155-355-8
£25.00 $40.00   HB   234 × 156 mm
This details 422 Days in the Life of the 2nd Battalion,
The Rifle Brigade and their battles of Gazala and
successful end of the North African campaign.
This includes the battles of Gazala, conflict around
the Cauldron, the loss of Tobruk before the forced
withdrawal with the rest of the Eighth Army, along the
Coast, finally digging in at Alamein.

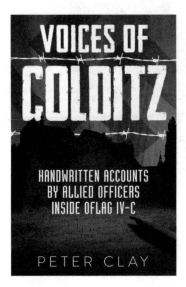

ISBN 978-1-78155-386-2
£25.00 $40.00   HB   248 × 172 mm
After 70 years in a drawer a battered log book reveals
its secrets through over a 100 hand-written stories. In
1942, two officers in Colditz passed a blank hard-cover
book among their fellow officers, so that as many as
possible could write their own accounts, to be printed
after the war ended. Fascinating stories and a few
sketches are the result.

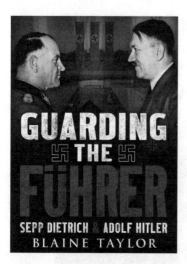

ISBN 978-1-78155-387-9
£18.99 $32.95   PB   248 × 172 mm
This is the exciting saga of Sepp Dietrich and his
SS, as well as of German government security
leader Johann Rattenhuber and his Reich Security
Service, the RSD. Here we see the measures
used to protect Hitler in public, his cars, planes,
trains, homes, military headquarters scattered
across conquered Europe, and during personal
appearances.

ISBN 978-1-78155-393-0
£25.00 $39.95   HB   234 × 156 mm
Few Eastern Front biographies can match Hans
Sturm in his rise from an infantry regiment
private, thrown into the bloody maelstrom of the
Eastern Front, to becoming a glorified war hero
whose role brought him into direct regular contact
with Prominenten of the Third Reich. This young
man's fearless heroism earned him the highest
military awards.

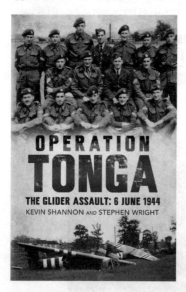

ISBN 978-1-78155-397-8
£20.00 $32.95   HB   234 × 156 mm
Operation Tonga is an account of the Glider Pilot
Regiment's role in the first stage of the airborne
assault in the Normandy landings, 6 June 1944. The
story is told through the eyes of those who were
there—glider pilots, paratroopers, pathfinders, tug
crews and passengers—and covers the operation
from training through to evacuations after D-Day.

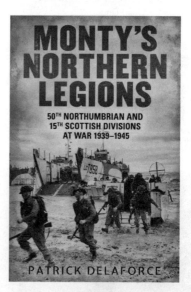

ISBN 978-1-78155-399-2
£16.99 $24.95   PB   234 × 156 mm
7th Armoured, 51st Highland & 50th
Northumbrian Divisions helped Monty win at El
Alamein and at Normandy after D-Day. This is the
story of distinguished formations which played
significant roles in the defeat of Hitler. They
fought their way through to the Low Countries
and were one of two assault divisions entrusted
with crossing the Rhine.

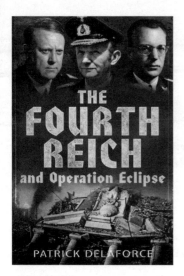

ISBN 978-1-78155-400-5
£16.99 $28.95   PB   234 × 156 mm
This examines the final weeks of WWII, after the Yalta Conference, when the question became how to prevent Hitler from implementing a scorched earth policy. Operation Eclipse, begun in March1945 led to the capture of Kiel and prevented the Russians from occupying Denmark. The events immediately after Hitler's suicide are also covered in summary.

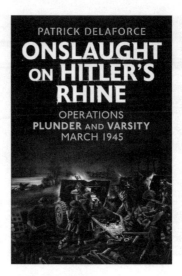

ISBN 978-1-78155-441-8
£20.00 $34.95   HB   234 × 156 mm
Operation Plunder was the crossing of the River Rhine at Rees, Wesel, and south of the Lippe River by the British 2nd Army, under Lieutenant-General Miles Dempsey. The American and Canadian forces south and north of Plunder were part of Field Marshal Bernard Montgomery's army. This was part of a set of Rhine crossings and the race to the Baltic.

ISBN 978-1-78155-448-7
£20.00 $34.95   PB   234 × 156 mm
Ciano was foreign minister of Italy 1936-43 and Mussolini's son-in-law. The diary gives accounts of meetings with the Duce and key figures including Hitler and Ribbentrop. Ciano was dismissed as minister in 1943 after being party to a plot to depose Mussolini and end the war. He was executed by firing squad in January 1944 on the orders of Hitler.

ISBN 978-1-78155-451-7
£16.99 $28.95   PB   234 × 156 mm
It isn't done with Mirrors—the Nazi state's total mobilization of resources to gather information. How they built their international information gathering apparatus—an organization where no nugget of news was too small to be taken note off. This was Total Espionage. Riess, an ex-Berlin journalist had all of the contacts to know what was going on.

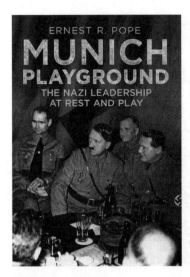

ISBN 978-1-78155-454-8
£18.99 $32.95   PB   234 × 156 mm
Twenty-six-year-old American Ernest Pope made
many friends in Munich with citizens and officials
alike. He heard jokes from Munichers that could
get them thrown in a concentration camp and he
poked fun at Nazis whenever he dared. *Munich
Playground* is a 'must read' for anyone who wishes
to understand what Hitler's Third Reich was really
like.

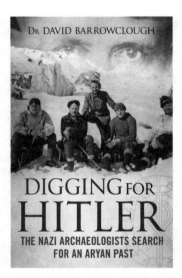

ISBN 978-1-78155-500-2
£25.00 $40.00   HB   234 × 156 mm
In the build up to the Second World War the
Nazis established a band of archaeologists, the
SS-Ahnenerbe, under the command of Heinrich
Himmler, to prove the superiority of the Aryan race,
and the unique right of the German people to rule
Europe. This book tells the story of their expeditions,
part 'science,' part espionage, and part fantasy, from
the mountains of Tibet to the lost world of Atlantis.

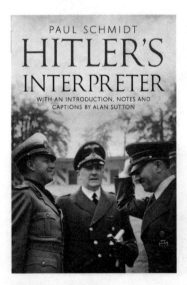

ISBN 978-1-78155-516-3
£18.99 $32.95   PB   234 × 156 mm
As interpreter for Adolf Hitler during the key pre-war
moments, such as the Munich Agreement, the British
Declaration of War and the surrender of France,
Schmidt was well placed to record his impressions
of events from 1935 to 1945. His memoires provide
an important contribution to our knowledge of
important meetings before and during the War.

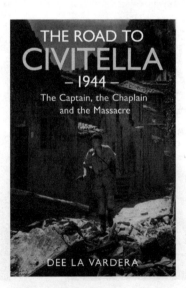

ISBN 978-1-78155-531-6
£20.00 $34.95   HB   234 × 156 mm
How a friendship forged in war between a Welsh
captain and an Irish chaplain with the Eighth Army
in Italy led to their adoption of a hilltop village
destroyed during a massacre by a German army in
retreat. The small Tuscan village still remembers
the acts of kindness by the British officers,
dedicating a street to their Good Samaritans.

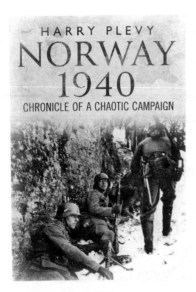

ISBN 978-1-78155-581-1
£25.00 $40.00   HB   234 × 156 mm
Germany used coordinated land, sea and air power to invade Norway. Britain and France thought, wrongly, that reactive use of sea power and unsupported ill-prepared infantry would suffice to eject the invader. The book comprehensively traces the progress of the Norwegian Campaign with much use of participant accounts, many previously unpublished.

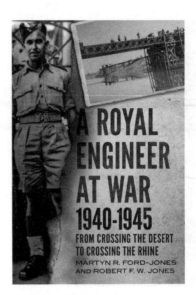

ISBN 978-1-78155-595-8
£25.00 $35.00   HB   234 × 156 mm
Based on the diaries of Royal Engineer Robert Jones, the narrative follows him across the North African desert, describes the bombing of Tripoli Harbour, the invasion of Sicily and the landing on the Normandy beaches on D-Day + 2. The story follows the advance through Belgium and Holland, to the battle that became known as the Rhine Crossing.

ISBN 978-1-78155-598-9
£25.00 $35.00   HB   234 × 156 mm
The story of Gestapo officer Horst Kopkow, who was responsible for coordinating the tracking down of all British and Soviet parachute agents in Europe. He was directly implicated in the concentration camp murders of several hundred agents. Despite this, Kopkow was a consultant with Britain's Secret Intelligence Service for 20 years after the war.

ISBN 978-1-78155-602-3
£20.00 $30.00   HB   234 × 156 mm
In early 1944, the Allies attempted to break through the German defences in Central Italy in a series of separate assaults, aiming to reach and conquer Rome. The assaults, on the rocky hill of Monte Cassino, ended up as one of the longest and deadliest engagements ever fought on European soil.

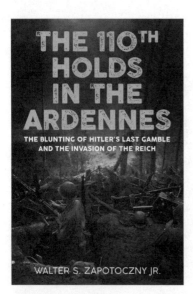

ISBN 978-1-78155-605-4
£25.00 $35.00   HB   234 × 156 mm
The story of 110th Regimental Combat Team during
the Battle of the Bulge is one of heroism in the face
of overwhelming odds. Fighting elements of three
Germany divisions, the 110th fought like they were
defending their own homes. Without their brave stand
against the German offensive, the 101st Airborne may
not have reached Bastogne in time.

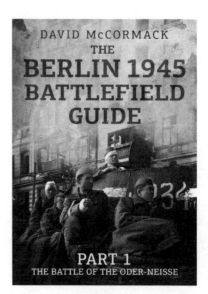

ISBN 978-1-78155-607-8
£16.99 $24.95   PB   235 × 165 mm
This highly detailed, yet accessible battlefield guide
takes the reader on a fascinating journey across
the Oder front battlefield as it is today. Eye witness
accounts and the author's intimate knowledge of the
terrain combine to provide the essential guide for
anyone seeking to further understand the Wehrmacht's
last desperate defensive battles before Berlin.

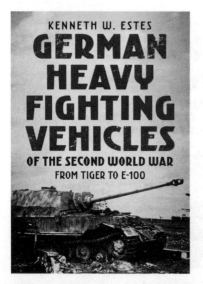

ISBN 978-1-78155-646-7
£18.99 $28.95   PB   248 × 172 mm
The German army faced a gun-armour race and placed
a premium on technological quality and superiority over
mass production. The army and Adolf Hitler pushed
for larger and more powerful tanks than had ever been
built. The heaviest tanks and assault guns developed
and fielded by Germany continue to capture interest
confirmed by current restorations.

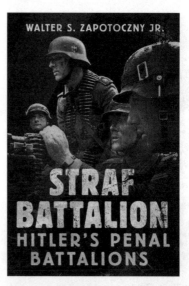

ISBN 978-1-78155-647-4
£25.00 $36.95   HB   234 × 156 mm
Hitler's penal battalions were designed to change
attitudes of prisoners towards national policy while
instilling a sense of duty honour and purpose. These
goals were to be achieved through harsh discipline
and punishments, indoctrination programs and leave
restrictions. Troops surviving their missions were
eventually transferred to regular units.